MID-ATLANTIC
GARDENER'S HANDBOOK

Quarto is the authority on a wide range of topics.

Quarto educates, entertains and enriches the lives of our readers—enthusiasts and lovers of hands-on living.

www.quartoknows.com

First published in 2016 by Cool Springs Press, an imprint of Quarto Publishing Group USA Inc., 400 First Avenue North, Suite 400, Minneapolis, MN 55401 USA. Telephone: (612) 344-8100 Fax: (612) 344-8692

quartoknows.com
Visit our blogs at quartoknows.com

Cool Springs Press titles are also available at discounts in bulk quantity for industrial or sales-promotional use. For details contact the Special Sales Manager at Quarto Publishing Group USA Inc., 400 First Avenue North, Suite 400, Minneapolis, MN 55401 USA.

10 9 8 7 6 5 4 3 2 1

ISBN: 978-1-59186-648-0

Library of Congress Cataloging-in-Publication Data

Elzer-Peters, Katie, author.
  Mid-Atlantic gardener's handbook : your complete guide : select, plan, plant, maintain, problem-solve - Delaware, Maryland, New Jersey, New York, Pennsylvania, Virginia, West Virginia, Washington D.C. / Katie Elzer-Peters.
      pages cm
  Includes bibliographical references and index.
  ISBN 978-1-59186-648-0 (sc)
  1. Gardening--Middle Atlantic States. I. Title.
  SB453.2.A12E48 2016
  635.90974--dc23
                    2015031141

Acquiring Editor: Billie Brownell
Project Manager: Alyssa Bluhm
Art Director: Cindy Laun
Layout: Kim Winscher

Printed in China

MID-ATLANTIC
GARDENER'S HANDBOOK

YOUR COMPLETE GUIDE:
SELECT • PLAN • PLANT • MAINTAIN • PROBLEM-SOLVE

DELAWARE, MARYLAND, NEW JERSEY,
NEW YORK, PENNSYLVANIA, VIRGINIA,
WEST VIRGINIA, WASHINGTON D.C.

KATIE ELZER-PETERS

COOL
SPRINGS
PRESS
Home and Garden Experts™
MINNEAPOLIS, MINNESOTA

DEDICATION

For Shelley Dawson Hendershot

ACKNOWLEDGMENTS

This book is dedicated to my friend Shelley, who taught me to love irises and always knows when I need a little "You can do it!" cheer. She was my partner in crime when we worked on our master's degrees at the University of Delaware through the Longwood Graduate Program. We worked a little, played a lot, and didn't appreciate it nearly enough while we were there.

I couldn't have written this book without all of the knowledge and opportunities afforded me by the Longwood Graduate Program and the professors and the staff members with whom I worked. I'm grateful for them and for all of the horticultural professionals who have mentored me over the years.

Big thank yous are in order for my husband, Joe, who had to live without me for months while I wrote this. My friends who listened patiently—you know who you are. Thank you to the staff of Epic Food Co. who let me camp out for hours and hours while I drained their unsweetened iced tea canister dry. I am grateful to Billie Brownell for her never-ending patience and for helping me improve my writing. I couldn't do this without you.

A book involves a huge amount of work by people other than the authors, including copy editors, designers, indexers, project managers, and more. Thank you so much to everyone who helped turn my words into this beautiful book.

And I want to thank you—whomever you are—who purchased this book and are embarking on new gardening adventures. Whether you're just starting or are experienced and looking for new ideas, I hope you find some good tidbits and enjoy your time in the sun.

Katie

CONTENTS

FEATURED PLANTS

ANNUALS

BULBS

PERENNIALS & ORNAMENTAL GRASSES

GROUNDCOVERS

USDA PLANT HARDINESS ZONES MID-ATLANTIC STATES

DELAWARE, MARYLAND, NEW JERSEY, NEW YORK, PENNSYLVANIA, VIRGINIA, WEST VIRGINIA, WASHINGTON D.C.

The USDA Plant Hardiness Zone Map indicates the average minimum cold temperatures for regions. The map was reissued in 2012 based on more recent historical data and reflects a warming trend affecting gardeners.

All plant labels and catalogs list hardiness zones to aid in plant selection—particularly trees, shrubs, vegetables, and perennial herbs. A plant is considered "hardy" to a zone if it can withstand the average minimum temperature in that area. If your area is too cold for a plant to live through winter, you can still grow it as an annual.

Look at the hardiness zone map and see which zone corresponds to your area. Remember both the zone number and the temperature range—they will come in handy when selecting plants.

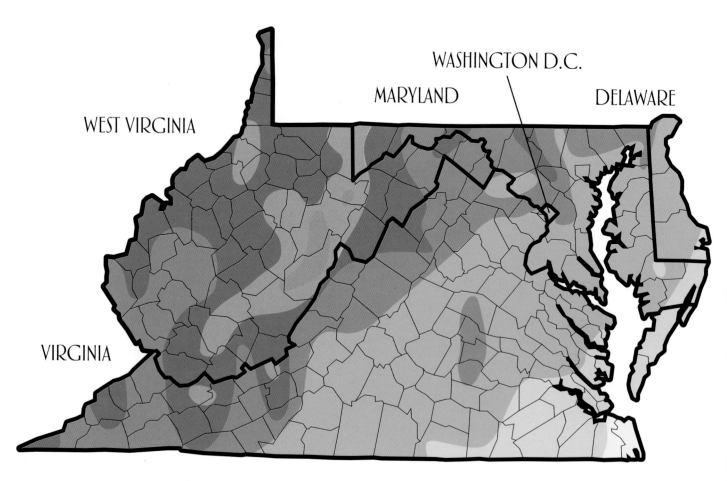

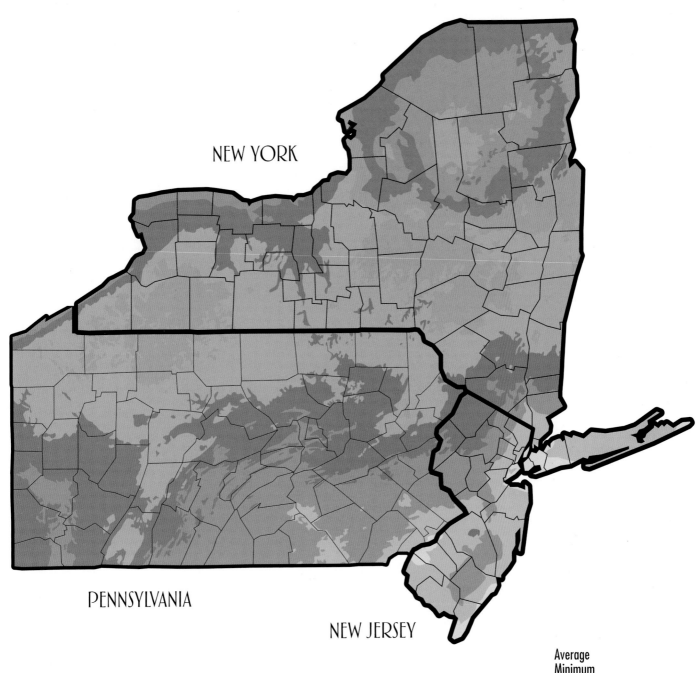

NEW YORK

PENNSYLVANIA

NEW JERSEY

Zone	Average Minimum Temperature
3b	-30 to -35
4a	-25 to -30
4b	-20 to -25
5a	-15 to -20
5b	-10 to -15
6a	-5 to -10
6b	0 to -5
7a	5 to 0
7b	10 to 5
8a	15 to 10

WELCOME TO GARDENING

in the Mid-Atlantic

Gardening with my mom and dad—growing sunflowers or rows of green beans, planting petunias, or leaning over to breathe the fragrance of lilies (I called them "bubblegum flowers," because that's what they smelled like to me)—are truly my earliest memories. I don't remember anything before a time when I gardened. And those memories don't stop there. I have made a lot of friends this way; gardeners are a sharing and caring bunch.

I studied horticulture in college, and I made gardening my life's work—first managing botanical gardens and now managing my own gardens and writing about gardening. I've tried to put what I know about creating a beautiful garden and landscape into this book, but I can tell you that experience is the best teacher. Use this book as a jumping-off point to get yourself pointed in the right direction—selecting the right plants for different areas of your garden and giving them the best care. Take notes. Get the book dirty. Stash plant labels and worksheets in it. Bring it with you when you shop for plants to use as a reference.

HOW TO GET THE MOST OUT OF THIS BOOK

Here's a bit of housekeeping to help you find the information you need in this book.

Introduction: This section covers more general gardening information that is applicable to all plant types described in the book. You might know all this—and you might not.

Chapters: Each chapter focuses on specific types of plants, such as trees, shrubs, perennials, edibles, and annuals. The chapter introductions cover that information *most applicable* to the plants described in the chapter.

Plant profiles: This "meat and potatoes" section gives information you need to grow specific plants. Individual planting, watering, fertilizing, pruning, or other maintenance needs are outlined in the plant profiles. I've used three sun icons to indicate light requirements. A fully colored sun indicates full sun is needed. A partially colored sun indicates partial sun/shade—preferably morning sun. A dark icon

indicates the plant prefers shade. Some plants fall into more than one sunlight category. When describing water needs, I use the terms "High," "Medium," and "Low." High means the plant needs frequent supplemental water or can grow in wet soil. Medium means water when the soil is dry or the plant is showing signs of water stress. Most plants fall into this category. Low means a plant must grow in fast-draining, almost dry soil. There are a few plants that have medium water needs but are drought tolerant when established. That is noted in the profiles, but those plants will not get a "dry" description for water needs.

Month-by-Month: These sections at the end of each chapter give you a year's overview of the most important gardening tasks for each plant during each month. These sections have been written to take into account variations in timing due to temperatures within the Mid-Atlantic region.

GARDENING IN THE MID-ATLANTIC: AN OVERVIEW

Gardeners in the Mid-Atlantic experience hot, humid summers and cool to cold winters within USDA Hardiness Zones 5b to 8a. Northern New York, northern Pennsylvania, and mountainous areas of Virginia and West Virginia are the coldest. The coastal plains of Virginia, Delaware, and Maryland along the Chesapeake Bay and Atlantic Ocean are the warmest. Cold weather isn't the only factor influencing gardening, though. Soil types, humidity, summer heat, and geographical features also influence plant growth. These gardening conditions, from soil to weather, are directly related to where you live, and there are huge variations in growing conditions throughout the Mid-Atlantic.

TEMPERATURE AND CLIMATE

All areas of the Mid-Atlantic have fairly defined cool seasons and warm seasons for growing. In some locations, you can garden during the entire fall, winter, and early spring (cool season) and grow completely different plants during the summer to early fall (warm season). Other locations have cool seasons in the spring and fall and a short warm season during the summer. Here are some climate challenges affecting the different areas of the Mid-Atlantic.

COASTAL PLAIN
Ice storms in the winter can damage trees and shrubs. Salt spray from the bay or ocean can damage plant leaves and soil. Periods of warm weather during the winter can impact dormancy of fruit trees.

MOUNTAINS
Many of the mountainous areas are shady. Availability of full-day sunlight can be a challenge in some gardens. The growing season in the highest elevations and coldest areas is also shorter than any other area. It is important for gardeners in the mountains to carefully read plant labels and to grow varieties well suited to their number of frost-free days.

INTERIOR FOOTHILLS
Hot, humid summers can be beneficial for fungal and bacterial diseases (and thus a problem for the gardener). Winters are cool—colder in the northern areas (Pennsylvania) of this region than in southern areas (Virginia).

ALLEGHENY AND PITTSBURGH PLATEAU
These areas can experience heavy winter snows and lake-effect snow.

For specific growing information related to your city, consult with your local garden club or Cooperative Extension office.

SOILS IN THE MID-ATLANTIC
In addition to cold weather, the other big variation in the Mid-Atlantic is in soil types. Soil is composed of three types of particles: sand, silt, and clay. Sand is the coarsest particle in soil and clay is the finest particle. The mixture of these three types of particles is what gives soil its structure and texture. That, in turn, affects the water-holding and nutrient-holding capacity of the soil and its suitability as-is for growing plants.

Soils in the Mid-Atlantic vary widely. In some areas, you'll stick a shovel in the ground and find nothing but coarse sand. Other areas are plagued with sticky, slow-to-drain clay that dries to be hard as a rock during a drought. But many areas of the Mid-Atlantic are blessed with loose, well-drained, nutrient-rich, loamy soils.

The pH of the soil can range from acidic (low) to alkaline (high). The only way to know what you're dealing with is to get a soil test. Because soil characteristics have a major impact on plant growth and health, it is worth learning about the specific type of soil you're working with in your garden and work to improve it prior to making any large changes to the landscape.

Have you heard the phrase, "Plant a five-dollar plant in a twenty-five-dollar hole"? Characteristics of the soil make it easy or difficult for plant roots to grow, spread, and reach more water, nutrients, and oxygen. Another phrase you see often in gardening literature is, "Feed the soil, not the plants." Time spent getting the soil where it needs to be in order to support healthy plant growth is time saved trying to fix problems later. The best way to improve the structure and nutrient availability in garden soil is to add compost, either as a mulch or by incorporating it into the soil.

COMPOSTING
You can buy compost if you're short on time. However, you can and should also make your own. Composting is a great way to cut down on the amount of trash you throw away. It's also a shame to have to buy something you can make yourself from food scraps, leaves, and yard debris that you have to pay someone else to take away!

There are two types of materials to add to compost piles: green materials, which are high in nitrogen, and brown materials, which are high in carbon. While there isn't a precise ratio of green to brown materials required in compost piles, if you add equal amounts of each over time, you'll get usable compost faster.

A compost pile with grass clippings and shredded newspaper.

GREEN MATERIALS
- Grass clippings
- Weeds
- Green leaves
- Kitchen scraps
- Eggshells

BROWN MATERIALS
- Shredded newspapers
- Dried leaves
- Sawdust
- Wood chips
- Paper bags
- Paper towels
- Twigs
- Tea bags
- Wheat straw
- Coffee grounds

You can compost almost any natural material, but if you're composting at home, don't put any animal products other than eggshells in the compost pile. No meat, cheese, dairy, or lasagna leftovers.

BUILDING THE PILE
Build a compost pile by layering green materials and brown materials, like you'd make lasagna. Start with chopped-up dried leaves (you can run over them with the lawn mower). Then add grass clippings or kitchen scraps, and keep layering. The smaller the pieces you add to the pile, the faster they will decompose.

Continuously add material to the compost pile—shredded newspapers, the stems of broccoli, last summer's dead annual flowers that you pulled up, even the Halloween pumpkin.

Keep the pile cooking (a healthy pile will heat up) by using a pitchfork or garden fork to turn the pile and mix it up. Why spend so much time on the soil before going into any other aspect of gardening? Because without good soil, you can't have a healthy garden. Even if all you're doing is planting a gigantic bed of sedum cultivars, you should still spend time on the soil! The soil affects every other aspect of gardening more than anything else.

CARING FOR THE GARDEN

These are some general garden care instructions that are important to get right, regardless of the plant type you're growing. Most are elaborated upon in individual chapters.

WATERING
Watering is probably the most important technique to master. If plants receive too much water, not enough water, or inconsistent water, they become stressed and can be afflicted by pests, diseases, and physiological problems.

Toolbox: 50-foot non-kink hose, soaker hose, sprinkler, watering wand, water breaker, watering can.

WATERING SEEDLINGS
Seeds and seedlings need to stay continually moist while sprouting. They don't have reserves to fall back on. If you plant seeds in the garden, check them at least twice a day to make sure they are staying moist.

WATERING BY HAND
Hand-watering is a good thing to do if you want to relax at the end of the day or spend some time outside before going to work. Water by holding the hose nozzle at the base of each plant and counting to five.

WATERING WITH IRRIGATION

Using irrigation or soaker hoses isn't a "fix it and forget it" option. You still have to monitor the plants to see if they need water, and turn on the irrigation or set the timer. It's better to water all plants as deeply as possible and as infrequently as possible without stressing them. Don't let the irrigation run for five minutes, five times a day. Set it up to give the plants enough water to soak the top inch of soil. When that's dry, water again.

PRUNING AND DEADHEADING

Pruning timing and techniques differ depending on what you're pruning, but the reasons for pruning are the same across all plant types:

- Stimulate new growth
- Control size
- Train or shape
- Delay flowering
- Remove dead or diseased plant parts
- Renew the plant

Do not be afraid to prune! Plants will grow back, even if you cut too much off. Hopefully you won't, though, if you follow instructions.

Toolbox: Bypass hand pruners, bypass loppers, pruning saw, scissors, snips

Deadheading is the process of removing flowers after they fade. This encourages the plant to continue blooming, cleans up the plant, and/or encourages the plant to put energy into producing a healthy root system instead of seeds. Perennials, annuals, and shrubs (including roses) most commonly need deadheading.

MULCHING

Mulching the garden will save you time watering and weeding. It will also create a buffer around trees and shrubs, lessening the chance that you will injure them during lawn maintenance. It is amazing the difference that a 3-inch-thick layer of mulch will make. When mulching around your plants, avoid mounding the mulch up around the stems of the plants, which can cause the plants to rot.

I prefer to mulch in the spring, but mulch anytime you are planting.

Toolbox: Pitchfork; hard rake; shrub rake; large, lightweight shovel

Mulching materials:
- Shredded hardwood bark
- Ground and sifted compost
- Shredded leaves
- Gravel

CONTROLLING WEEDS

Weeding is a constant battle, but by staying on top of it continuously, you can lessen the problems you have with weeds over time. Why should we bother to remove weeds? Weeds are unsightly, for one thing, but they also take sunlight, nutrients, and water from the plants you want to grow. It's worth it to remove them.

Toolbox: Garden fork, soil knife, hoe, rubber gloves, spray bottle

There are a few ways to deal with weeds:
- Use a pre-emergent herbicide to prevent weed seeds from sprouting. (This does not work on perennial weeds.)
- Hand-pull or dig weeds with large taproots (such as dandelions).
- Turn over the soil or rake under small weeds. (This works best for annual weeds.)
- Use herbicide to kill the weeds.

WEED TYPES

The following weed types are not official distinctions but rather categories of weeds you'll have to deal with. Here are the characteristics of certain types of weeds and how you deal with them.

ANNUAL

Annual weeds complete their life cycle during one season by growing, flowering, and setting seeds. The main objective in preventing annual weeds from spreading is to prevent them from flowering. You can mow or cut these weeds frequently, pull them out, or use herbicide to kill them. Pre-emergent herbicide works well on annual weeds.

Perennial and Biennial Clumping

Perennial clumping weeds come back every year. Biennial weeds grow a large plant with a taproot one year and then flower and set seeds the next year. Both types will eventually flower and set seeds, which will establish new clumps. These types of weeds respond well to hand-digging, because they do not have runners or stems that can break off and start new plants.

Perennial Spreading

Perennial spreading weeds are the most difficult to control. These weeds are most easily eradicated with systemic herbicides, which are weedkillers that are absorbed by the plant and kill the plant from the inside.

FERTILIZING

Some plants need regular applications of fertilizer, particularly if the soil is not nutrient rich. Other plants actually do not respond well to being fed. Perennials, in particular, tend to generate soft, weak growth that is highly susceptible to pests if they are fertilized. Annuals, vegetables, and turfgrass are the "hungriest" plants that require regular feeding. Trees, shrubs, and vines might need fertilizing if they have nutrient deficiencies.

NUTRIENT DEFICIENCIES

If your plant leaves are turning weird colors (purple, yellow), they might have nutrient deficiencies. If you see nutrient-deficiency problems in your plants, test the soil pH. If the pH is too high or too low, it won't matter if you fertilize—the plants won't be able to get the nutrients from the soil. Nutrient deficiencies cause highly predictable results, and it's usually possible to diagnose whether a nutrient deficiency is a problem by looking at the plant (below).

This diagram shows the symptoms caused by the most common nutrient deficiencies.

If your plant has a deficiency, or it is time for a routine feeding, head to the garden center or home-improvement store to pick up a fertilizer that's right for the plant that needs to be fed. Before you go, measure the area you need to feed

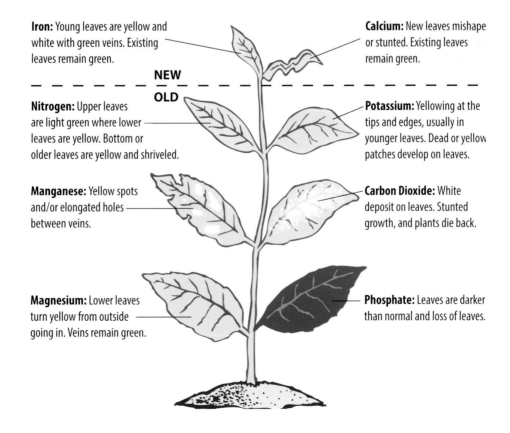

Iron: Young leaves are yellow and white with green veins. Existing leaves remain green.

NEW
OLD

Nitrogen: Upper leaves are light green where lower leaves are yellow. Bottom or older leaves are yellow and shriveled.

Manganese: Yellow spots and/or elongated holes between veins.

Magnesium: Lower leaves turn yellow from outside going in. Veins remain green.

Calcium: New leaves mishape or stunted. Existing leaves remain green.

Potassium: Yellowing at the tips and edges, usually in younger leaves. Dead or yellow patches develop on leaves.

Carbon Dioxide: White deposit on leaves. Stunted growth, and plants die back.

Phosphate: Leaves are darker than normal and loss of leaves.

and have an idea of what types of nutrients you're trying to deliver to the plants and soil.

Using bloodmeal and compost, along with other organic fertilizers, will improve the soil while feeding the plants. When possible, use organic fertilizers. Your garden will benefit from this in the long run. Think of synthetic fertilizer as a candy bar for the garden. It gives quick nutrients to the plants, but the effects are fleeting. Synthetic fertilizer doesn't benefit the garden over time.

Fertilizers all have a combination of nutrients in them. Most of them have the "Big Three" macronutrients, nitrogen (N), phosphorus (P), and potassium (K). Some fertilizers have micronutrients such as calcium, magnesium, manganese, and iron. Fertilizer labels include what is called an "analysis," which is the percentage of each nutrient contained in the product.

DIFFERENT TYPES OF FERTILIZER

You might have grown up only using packaged chemical-based fertilizers, but there are other choices.

LIQUID ORGANIC OR NATURAL FERTILIZER

Organic or natural fertilizers are usually made from kelp, fish emulsion, or a combination of each. Mix this type of fertilizer with water in watering cans to water into the soil. Some liquid organic or natural fertilizers are used as foliar feeds, diluted and sprayed on the leaves. Mix these fertilizers with water in a pressurized sprayer and spray the leaves of the plants. The plants will soak up the nutrients through their leaves. Organic fertilizers are smelly, so don't use them right before you have an outdoor barbecue. Organic fertilizers tend to have more micronutrients along with the "Big Three" (nitrogen, phosphorus, and potassium).

LIQUID CONVENTIONAL OR SYNTHETIC FERTILIZER

Synthetic fertilizers have nitrogen, phosphorus, and potassium in them in one combination or another (usually just these macronutrients). These fertilizers are formulated for different types of plants. You can buy houseplant fertilizers, fertilizers for acid-loving plants, vegetable fertilizers, and fertilizers formulated to encourage more blooms on plants. You can buy

---

Ready to Use

FERTIFEED
All Purpose Plant Food

12-4-8

FertiFeed Ready To Use All-Purpose Plant Food
Net Weight 4lb. 12oz. (2.15kg)

GUARANTEED ANALYSIS

Total Nitrogen (N)	12%
12.0% Urea Nitrogen	
Available Phosphate (P_2O_5)	4%
Soluable Potash (K2O)	8%
Manganese (Mn)	0.05%
0.05% Chelated Manganese (Mn)	
Zinc (Zn)	0.05%
0.05% Chelated Zinc (Zn)	
Inert Ingredients	76%

Information regarding the contents and levels of metals in this product is available on the Internet at http://www.regulatory-info-sc.com.

KEEP OUT OF REACH OF CHILDREN

Example of a typical fertilizer label.

conventional fertilizer in concentrated liquid forms and concentrated powder forms. In both cases, you need to mix the concentrate with water. Some brands of fertilizer have special attachments that will do the mixing for you.

GRANULAR FERTILIZER

Granular fertilizer is sometimes called slow-release fertilizer. They're really two different things. Granular types are pelletized. Some granulars are quick-release and break down immediately. Some granulars have a mixture of quick- and slow-release fertilizers. Sometimes granular fertilizer is combined with pre-emergent weed control in a weed-and-feed product. Don't use weed-and-feed products where you've just planted seeds, or they won't sprout.

ORGANIC NON-LIQUID FERTILIZER

These types of fertilizers are often called "tones." Bloodmeal, bone meal, and fish emulsion meal also fall into this category. These organic or natural fertilizers are made from different mixtures of natural, or non-synthetic, ingredients. Usually you will side-dress or mix these fertilizers into the soil. They break down over time and feed the microorganisms in the soil as much as the plants. If you want to build up the fertility of the soil, these tones and natural fertilizers are better to use than a quick shot of synthetic fertilizer.

There are some fertilizers (both organic and synthetic) that are mixed to provide nutrients for specific types of plants. For example, Holly-tone™ is an organic fertilizer that provides macro- and micronutrients specifically for acid-loving plants.

Lacewings are natural predators. Encourage the "good bugs" to take up residence in your garden.

CONTROLLING PESTS

Pests are a fact of life in the landscape. I tend to take a somewhat laissez-faire approach to pest control. I hardly ever have to use pesticides in my garden, primarily because I have a high tolerance for pest activity, and I also grow a lot of different types of fruits, vegetables, flowers, trees, and shrubs. Professor Douglas Tallamy explains why this matters in his book *Bringing Nature Home*. When you grow a biologically diverse garden and have a biologically diverse landscape, you support the beneficial insects that prey on harmful insects.

On a single tree in the forest, there could be 400 types of caterpillars, 400 types of insects eating the caterpillars, and thousands of bacterial organisms eating the insects. What this means is that ecosystems have their own checks and balances. When we use chemicals to control certain pests, we are messing with the checks and balances, and that can have consequences.

BENEFICIAL INSECTS

You can encourage beneficial insects, such as ladybugs, lacewings, soldier beetles, wasps, and others, to live in your yard by limiting the use of broad-spectrum (kills everything) chemicals and by cultivating a diverse landscape. Chemicals that kill everything kill the insects that are working for you too.

INTEGRATED PEST MANAGEMENT

I selected plants for this book based on the fact that many of them don't have significant pest problems.

However, it's unrealistic to think that you'll never have an issue that needs to be dealt with. When deciding what to do, follow the principles of Integrated Pest Management (IPM) to have the lowest impact on the rest of the environment.

There are four pillars of IPM:

- **Set action thresholds:** You don't have to spray at the first sight of an insect. Decide what amount of damage you're willing to live with.
- **Monitor and identify pests:** Early detection leads to early action before much damage can be done.
- **Prevention:** Do what you can to prevent pest and disease problems. Plant resistant varieties, use barriers to keep pests from reaching the plants, and provide plants with the best care possible so that they can withstand pest problems.
- **Control:** After all of the other steps, you can decide how to control the pests. Controls can be organic or synthetic, involve treating the pests, or pulling out the affected plants.

ORGANIC VERSUS SYNTHETIC CONTROLS

There's a misconception that if you use an organic pesticide, you're not putting yourself or your plants in any danger. That is false. There are organic pesticides made from naturally occurring ingredients that are just as deadly as pesticides that are made in a lab. When deciding to use a pesticide to control

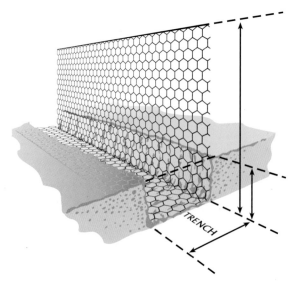

Bury the chicken-wire fencing to prevent mammals from burrowing into the garden.

weeds, insects, or diseases, always read the label and follow the instructions for dosage, protective equipment, re-entry timing, and harvest windows.

CONTROLLING MAMMALIAN PESTS

Deer, rabbits, chipmunks, and squirrels are all problems in the edible garden. The most effective way to control these pests is with barriers. Fencing, repellents, and netting are just about the only way to keep these pests out of the garden. If you're growing vegetables in rows, think about using row covers to keep pests away.

DESIGNING THE GARDEN

Once you have a good handle on the growing conditions where you live, you can start to think about design. I'd encourage you to think about your landscape as a whole—not just the vegetable gardens or the flowerbeds or the lawn—but as a functioning ecosystem and a stage for family activities (even if your family is you and your dog or you and your husband and your mother-in-law).

If you have children, you will want some lawn areas planted with grass that can withstand heavy foot traffic. If you like to lounge outside, shade

will be of utmost importance. Like to cook? Tending a vegetable or herb garden will bring you joy and delicious ingredients. Thinking about how one aspect of the landscape will affect another will save you problems in the long run. For example, I enjoy butterfly bushes, but they attract the cabbage white moth that wreaks havoc on cole crops in the vegetable garden. So, I don't plant butterfly bushes in my yard because I want to harvest healthy cabbages.

As you read through chapters describing how to grow certain types of plants, have your sketchbook handy to make notes or diagrams about how this type of shrub or tree works into the overall environment.

There are some design tips in the chapters and plant profiles, primarily dealing with selecting plants based on size, color, and bloom time. To take that information and put it to good use, you need to learn aspects of design. If you can master these concepts and then employ them with the information about individual plants, you will have a spectacular garden.

What makes this perennial border at Longwood Gardens so beautiful? The contrast! There are contrasting textures (ferny leaves with large, thick leaves), contrasting colors (pink and purple, chartreuse and burgundy), and contrasting forms (mounded plants and spiky plants).

This color combination is pretty, if fairly standard. All three plants are warm colors (shades of red, orange, and yellow).

In this grouping, the rust-colored coleus from the previous grouping has been switched with a silver-colored plectranthus. *Pow!* It really pops! The silver is a cool color that contrasts with the warmer colors of the ornamental grass and petunias.

Contrast is what keeps gardens and landscapes from looking like one giant blob. It's what leads the eye around the landscape and creates drama. To create contrast, try these contrasting combinations:

- Big leaves with small leaves.
- Textured leaves with smooth leaves.
- Cool-colored foliage or flowers with warm-colored foliage or flowers.
- Rounded leaves (hosta) with lance-shaped or long, skinny leaves (mondo grass).
- Light-colored leaves with dark-colored leaves.

THE BIG THREE: COLOR, FORM, AND TEXTURE

You can create contrast in the garden when you concentrate on selecting plants with differing colors, forms, and textures.

CONTRASTING COLORS

If design as a whole makes people nervous, color is probably the part people worry about the most. The main thing about color combinations is that if you like the way two plants look side by side, that's all that matters. Don't be afraid to try something unusual. That's what will make your plantings really stand out.

VARIEGATION: BUILT-IN CONTRAST

The most common variegation is two-toned green-and-white plants. The white is due to lack of chlorophyll (pigment that reflects green light, among other things) in certain areas of the plant. When you use these plants, you have built-in contrast! Green and gold is another variegation.

CONTRASTING FORMS

Form is basically the growth habit of plants. Plants can have upright forms, trailing forms, spiky forms, round forms, vase-shaped forms, and more. To add interest to the garden, look for plants with long, thin leaves and a vertical growth habit, or a plant with a trailing growth habit, instead of a "roundy moundy" habit.

CONTRASTING TEXTURES

It's easy to confuse form with texture. They're not the same thing. Leaf shapes and characteristics are what offer texture in most garden plants.

Hostas and ferns are often planted together for contrast. They also both have mounding habits. For example, Japanese painted ferns have highly dissected (incised) leaves, which contrast with the large, smooth hosta leaves.

Variegated plants have naturally occurring contrast.

When creating plant combinations or designing landscapes, think of contrast across all levels of the garden—from the ground level with annuals, perennials, and groundcovers to the mid level with shrubs and vines, to the top with trees.

REPETITION

Repetition adds cohesion to the landscape as a whole. Repeating a color in tree leaves, annual flowers, and the paint color on accessories ties everything together and makes the yard look less chaotic. When using the principle of repetition, think across plant types.

The Tennis Court garden at Chanticleer in Wayne, Pennsylvania, is one of the most beautiful gardens I've ever seen (opposite). Its designers have the color/form/texture contrast concept perfected. It's a textbook example of how to use those design concepts to create an interesting garden that encourages you to keep looking, rather than settling in one fixed spot.

This combination of *Hakonechloa* (ornamental grass on the left) and hosta (right) shows two plants with similar forms (mounding), but different textures. The skinny leaves of the grass contrast nicely with the wide leaves of the hosta. They also have good contrasting colors in their leaves!

The smooth leaves of the hosta (top) contrast with finely cut, dissected leaves of the fern (bottom).

The Tennis Court garden at Chanticleer Gardens in Wayne, Pennsylvania.

If you look closely at this picture, you'll notice something else: repetition. Colors, forms, and textures are repeated throughout the garden. The color chartreuse is a motif in this garden. It winds through the beds like a river. To repeat something like color, you don't have to use the same plants everywhere. You can see that they've used at least three different plants with chartreuse leaves to keep the color going throughout the garden. Silver is another color that's repeated, though in different plants with differing heights, textures, or growth forms.

CHOOSE PLANTS THAT "TALK" TO EACH OTHER

Plants that talk to one another means plants that have a similar color or colors running through each of the plants. Here's an example of that in a container garden (right).

You could also achieve this effect with texture by using a large plant and a small plant or plants, each with grassy-type leaves. Remember, repetition doesn't have to mean using the same plant over and over. You can repeat plant characteristics—the colors, forms, and textures—as well.

These are the very basics of gardening in the Mid-Atlantic. Anything plant specific will be described in the individual plant profiles. Now, let's get gardening!

Burgundy or chartreuse colors appear in each of the plants in this large container planting. The repetition between plants unifies the look.

ANNUALS
for the Mid-Atlantic

It's a shame I can't just say, "It's my favorite!" about all of the annuals in this chapter, because they're all great in the landscape, in containers, or both, or I wouldn't have included them. Annuals are garden staples for long-lasting color. They're always the first plants you see when you visit a garden center or home-improvement store—and that's on purpose. They're brightly colored, practically screaming "take me home!" Most annuals are grown because they bloom continuously throughout the growing season, but there are a few foliage annuals that are grown for the colors of their leaves, not the flowers. Coleus, Persian shield, and a few ornamental grasses fit that bill.

Some gardeners won't plant annuals, other than in containers, because they don't want to replant every year. I'm the opposite—I save room in my perennial gardens to pop in some plants for seasonal color. I leave room for shade annuals and sun annuals. While the perennials move in and out of bloom, annuals offer continuity throughout the landscape during the growing season.

Planting new annuals each year also allows you to change the look of your garden without giving it a complete renovation or having to commit long-term. Annuals are, by definition, plants that sprout, flower, and set seed—thus completing their entire life cycle—in one growing season. Then they're done. You can replant and repeat the color schemes the next year, or not. Gardening with annuals allows you to have fun and play more than any other type of plant material.

SOURCING ANNUALS

One of the reasons why gardening with annuals is so fun is that seeds and plants are relatively inexpensive. That means you can try growing a whole bunch of new varieties without breaking the bank. If something doesn't perform the way you wanted it to, you can yank it out, throw it on the compost heap, and not look back.

There are two ways to buy annuals: as seeds or as transplants. Which is better? That depends on what you want to grow and where you're growing it.

Use a sharpened pencil as a small dibber to make holes for sowing seeds in flats.

GROWING PLANTS FROM SEED INDOORS

Most annuals are fairly easy to grow from seed, but growing transplants inside for planting outside requires dedication and special equipment. If you plant lots of annuals and want to grow some unusual varieties, it's worth the investment.

To start seeds for annuals (and edibles) indoors, you need, at a bare minimum:
- Grow lights on chains or a frame (so that they can be moved)
- Heating mat
- Propagation flats

Seeds grown indoors without grow lights are spindly and weak. There's just no way around the grow light. Lights should be situated on chains or some sort of system that allows you to keep them a few inches above the plants at all times, meaning you need to move the lights *up* as plants grow.

A heating mat or propagation mat increases the soil temperature to favor germination. Most warm-weather annuals, in particular, need soil temperatures of at least 70 degrees Fahrenheit to grow happily. That can be difficult to achieve indoors during winter without a heating mat. The mat should be waterproof and designed specifically for growing plants.

Propagation flats make starting seeds easier. A propagation flat is usually composed of three parts: a flat for planting, a tray to catch water, and a dome to keep in moisture. You can rig your own propagation flat, but those three elements are important.

GROWING TIP

If you want to grow heirlooms, sourcing seeds is often your best option. See Resources on page 207 for unusual and heirloom mail-order seed sources.

Seed packets usually have a "time before last frost" date for recommended indoor sowing, so you know when to plant them. Always harden off transplants before planting outside.

DIRECT-SOWING SEEDS OUTDOORS

It's easier, if I'm growing plants from seed, to sow them directly into the garden. That only works for certain areas though. Seeds require enough attention and special care that I primarily only direct-sow the following:

- Annuals planted in or around the vegetable garden (nasturtiums and marigolds, primarily).
- Larger annuals that germinate quickly—sunflowers for example.
- Flowers sown for a cutting garden.

Annuals in the vegetable garden and annuals in the cutting garden are sown in rows or big clumps, so it's easy to find and water them. Big annuals, such as sunflowers, sprout quickly and are also easy to keep track of in the garden bed. They're also not expensive. If you're growing a specialty annual that comes 12 or 24 seeds to a packet, you aren't going to want to just throw them out into the garden bed and cross your fingers that they'll sprout. Those are better to baby along indoors.

GROWING ANNUALS FROM TRANSPLANTS

Annuals at garden centers are like gummies at a candy store. I can't buy one; I have to buy a hundred. That is enough to convince me to set up a big seed-starting operation in my guest room. While annual transplants aren't nearly as expensive as perennials, they still cost more than seeds. But here's why you should shop for plants versus seeds:

- **You want to grow new varieties.** Many new varieties are trademarked and not available

from seed. The only way to get them is to buy from garden centers that have bought them from licensed growers.

- **You want to plant large quantities of annuals and you don't have the space to produce them yourself.** I tend to plant several flats of the same annuals, and even if I wanted to grow them myself, I don't have a greenhouse, and I don't have anywhere I could set up to produce 20 flats of annuals.

- **You like instant gratification.** There is nothing wrong with this! You can go to the garden center, design on the spot, and come home with all of the trappings of an instant color explosion.

WHAT TO PLANT WHERE & WHEN

It's easy to find summer annuals that love the sun. What about annuals that thrive in shade—part shade to really deep shade? And how about annuals that you can plant when it's still a bit nippy outside? Most annuals grow well in containers, but some are particularly suited to it and/or need the good drainage provided by container gardens. Others have distinctive blooms that are best admired up close. To get the most out of your garden, choose the right plant for the right place and the right season.

ANNUALS FOR SHADE

- Begonias
- Caladium (annual bulb)
- Coleus
- Geranium
- Madagascar periwinkle
- New Guinea impatiens
- Persian shield
- Torenia

CONTAINER ANNUALS

- Alyssum
- Annual lobelia
- Bat face cuphea
- Calibrachoa
- Diamond Frost euphorbia
- Fuchsia hybrids
- Geranium
- New Guinea impatiens
- Sweet potato vine

COOL-WEATHER ANNUALS

- Alyssum
- Annual lobelia
- Calendula
- California poppy
- Dusty miller
- Nasturtium
- Ornamental cabbage or kale
- Pansy
- Snapdragon
- Viola

DESIGNING WITH ANNUALS

Design is a mix of proper location, proper timing, and plant groupings. When you've determined which area you're planting for which season, you can start to pick out plants.

MASS PLANTINGS

When you think about mass plantings of annuals, you probably think of the shopping mall parking lot. I am not advocating that you turn your yard into Disney World. There is, however, a happy medium between buying a 6-pack of marigolds (not enough unless you're planting one pot) and buying 60 flats of marigolds. Mass planting has its place in the home garden. Think about massing:

- Around the mailbox.
- Along the sidewalk.
- In a landscape bed facing the street.
- In a landscape bed toward the back of your property.

Mass planting provides big impact from a distance. When I mass plant pansies or violas in the front garden facing my street, I'm ecstatic when I drive home and see my pretty flowers. That sounds ridiculous, but don't underestimate the joy a big bunch of color can bring. Let's say you have a landscape bed near the back of your yard that you can see while you stand at the kitchen window. A big sweep of salvias, melampodium, Madagascar periwinkle, and rudbeckia will really light up the yard, and you don't have to get right up on the garden to appreciate it.

INTEGRATED IN PERENNIAL GARDENS

Annuals have a place in the perennial garden. By changing out annuals here and there each season you can keep the garden fresh and interesting. In my front garden I have three "zones" where I plant annuals.

- By the sidewalk leading from the driveway to the front door. That way there's always something colorful in an area where I walk most frequently. I tend to mass plant here.
- The front of the bed that faces the street. Those plants greet me when I drive home. The neighbors like them too. This is another mass planting zone—something different every season.

A mix of annuals and perennials surround a lush lawn.

- The main perennial bed. I use plants like coleus or Persian shield throughout the perennial garden to provide color transitions between areas. I might plant a few tall cleome here and there to give some height and color at waist-level.

IN THE VEGETABLE GARDEN

Marigolds and nasturtium are staples in the vegetable garden, but I've been known to throw a handful of zinnia or alyssum seeds in there too. The first two are for pest control and the second two are to attract pollinators. Plus, flowers growing with the veggies just make the garden prettier!

CONTAINER GARDENS

You can grow other types of plants in container gardens, but this is where annuals really shine.

The typical container garden recipe is "thriller, filler, spiller." Plant one or two of something spectacular, fill in around the thriller with multiples of one, two, or three different types of plants (depending on how large the container is), and plant something that will trail or spill over the edge.

Cool-weather sun: Geranium (thriller), Diamond Frost euphorbia (filler), annual lobelia (spiller)

Warm-weather sun: Jade Princess millet (thriller), annual rudbeckia (filler), black ornamental sweet potato vine (spiller)

Warm-weather shade: Pentas (thriller), coleus (filler), torenia (spiller)

When grouping plants in containers, pair like with like. That means same sun needs, same water needs, and similar growth rates.

CARING FOR ANNUALS

To grow all out for as many as five months, annuals require extra care. Biologically, annuals are driven to flower and produce seed. The way we care for the plants is like throwing a stick in a bike wheel—it slows down or stops the process, which, for gardeners, means a longer show.

WATERING

Watering properly is the most important aspect of plant care. Too much water or too little water can have equally devastating effects. Know your plants. Portulaca requires about one-fourth of the water that papyrus needs. To encourage deep rooting, water as infrequently and deeply as possible. Direct the water at the soil, not on the plant leaves. You'll learn when you need to water by looking at your plants. Many plants take on a kind of grayish tinge and get droopy when they need water.

DEADHEADING

Deadheading serves an important biological function beyond just cleaning up the looks. By removing dead flowers, you're preventing the plant from setting seed, which is the end of its life cycle. To keep annuals blooming, deadhead frequently unless the plants don't require it. You don't have to deadhead angelonia. You do have to deadhead zinnias.

PINCHING

Pinching is basically breaking off or cutting off the top of a plant to spur buds to break lower on the plant. It results in a bushier plant. Some plants do better with pinching or require pinching, while others don't. Coleus, Persian shield, and melampodium grow best when routinely pinched. Angelonia and Madagascar periwinkle don't require it.

FERTILIZING

Annuals burn through a lot of resources to put on a continuous show. The amount of fertilizing needed

Pinch coleus several times during the summer to encourage bushy growth.

depends a lot on your soil. Hopefully, you amended it with compost before planting. Even if you did, you'll still need to fertilize every two weeks to once a month. I'm a fan of side-dressing with a Plant-Tone type food or watering with a liquid organic fertilizer. Though they're smelly, they're effective and they feed the soil microorganisms as well as the plants.

MULCHING

No special techniques for mulching annuals, but it is a good idea to mulch around the plants with finely shredded hardwood or compost to keep weeds down and roots cool. Don't let the mulch touch the plant stems.

ALTERNANTHERA
Alternanthera ficoidea

Why It's Special—You can find *Alternanthera* (also called Joseph's coat) plants in almost every color. They are excellent for mass plantings or borders in landscape beds and perfect to perk up container gardens. Because they don't flower, unlike coleus, you'll spend less time on care.

How to Plant & Grow—Select varieties that will mature to heights that match the planting locations. You can grow from seed, but colors can be unpredictable. It's better just to buy transplants and plant them in full sun to partial shade after danger of frost has passed. Combine with newer varieties of coleus that like sun.

Care & Problems—*Alternanthera* has few pest problems. Some varieties stay small, but if your plants get leggy, just get out the scissors and cut it back to just above a leaf.

Bloom Color(s)—Grow *Alternanthera* for its variegated foliage, which comes in almost every color combination from green to pink to yellow to orange.

Bloom Period/Peak Season—Spring through fall, but it thrives in warm weather.

Mature Size (H x W)—6–24 inches x 6–24 inches

Water Needs—Medium, even moisture

ALYSSUM
Lobularia hybrids

Why It's Special—We're *not* talking about standard seed-grown alyssum here. I recommend planting Snow Princess® or one of the other hybrids in that series. They are vigorous, cool-weather-flowering annuals that have been bred to withstand some heat. In the Mid-Atlantic they'll keep growing all summer; most types won't.

How to Plant & Grow—You can grow Snow Princess® from frost to frost, though you might have to shear it back in summer. Use this plant as a filler in containers or as a border in landscape beds. Space plants 8 to 12 inches apart.

Care & Problems—Snow Princess® has few problems other than being so vigorous that it can take over a container. Seedling alyssum varieties can be prone to botrytis if it's cold and wet. Shear plants in summer if they get leggy. Water and fertilize after shearing to encourage new growth.

Bloom Color(s)—White, pink, purple

Bloom Period/Peak Season—Frost to frost

Mature Size (H x W)—Seedling varieties: 4 inches x 6 inches

Snow Princess® hybrids: 8 inches x 18 inches

Water Needs—Medium moisture. Does not like wet feet.

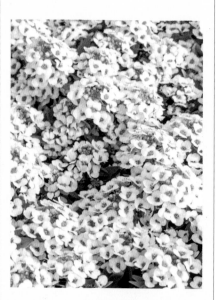

ANGELONIA
Angelonia angustifolia

Why It's Special—Some people call this the "summer snapdragon" because its flowers resemble those of snapdragons (several individual flowers borne on spikes), but, unlike snapdragons, angelonia keeps blooming profusely throughout the summer without a lot of care. It grows equally well in the landscape and in containers. It's deer-resistant and not fussy. I *love* this plant!

How to Plant & Grow—It's easier to find transplants than seeds. Plant outside when the danger of frost has passed and nighttime temperatures are at least 60 degrees Fahrenheit. It grows well in full sun but will still perform in partial shade. Space plants 12 inches apart.

Care & Problems—Angelonia is a fairly problem-free plant. You don't have to deadhead it, but if you want to encourage bushier plants, you can shear them in summer. Flowering will decline as the days get shorter and the nights cooler. It's a true summer bloomer.

Bloom Color(s)—White, purple, pink, burgundy

Bloom Period/Peak Season—Summer to frost

Mature Size (H x W)—18–24 inches x 12 inches

Water Needs—Drought-tolerant once established. Keep soil evenly moist.

BAT FACE CUPHEA
Cuphea llavea

Why It's Special—Bat face cuphea produces masses of red flowers with purple centers that look a little like faces. Birds and butterflies enjoy sipping nectar from the blooms. It is an excellent container plant because it invites close inspection, but it is also great for massing in the landscape. If you're not growing it in a container, plant in multiples of three to five for best effect.

How to Plant & Grow—You can start seeds 12 weeks before you plan to plant outside or pick up transplants from the garden center. If you plan to mass-plant, it will be more cost-effective to grow your own. Leave 6 to 12 inches between plants in the ground (less in containers).

Care & Problems—This is a low-maintenance plant. Water regularly after transplanting. If it gets leggy during summer, just cut the plant back by half, water, and fertilize to encourage new growth. Once the plant is established, you can water less frequently.

Bloom Color(s)—Red with purple center

Bloom Period/Peak Season—Summer

Mature Size (H x W)—12–18 inches x 12–18 inches

Water Needs—Low to medium

BEGONIA
Begonia spp.

Why It's Special—Begonias are incredibly versatile in the garden—especially the Dragon Wing® begonias. They can grow into enormous plants in the shade. They're drought tolerant and won't wilt in the summer heat.

How to Plant & Grow—Plant outside when danger of frost has passed and nighttime temperatures are consistently above 50 degrees Fahrenheit. They do best in partial sun to full shade, preferring morning sun to afternoon. Leave 12 to 18 inches between plants. Combine with caladium for a pop of color in shady corners.

Care & Problems—Dragon Wing® begonias don't have many problems. You don't have to deadhead, but if they outgrow their space you can cut them back in midsummer and fertilize to encourage new growth. If planted too early, begonias can be affected by botrytis that thrives during cool, wet weather. The solution is to plant when the nights are truly warm. Fertilize once a month with liquid fertilizer.

Bloom Color(s)—Pink, white, red

Bloom Period/Peak Season—Summer

Mature Size (H x W)—Depends on the variety. 6–18 inches x 8–18 inches

Water Needs—Low water once established.

BLUE DAZE
Evolvulus glomeratus

Why It's Special—I won't ever forget the first time I saw what blue daze could do. It's a trailing plant that grows well in containers or as an annual groundcover. It's also drought tolerant to the max, thrives in poor soil, and has the most gorgeous true blue flowers. It's especially well-suited to dry areas next to driveways and sidewalks. Pair with 'New Gold' lantana for a bright display.

How to Plant & Grow—Plant in full sun when nights are consistently over 70 degrees Fahrenheit. Leave at least 12 inches between plants in the landscape or plant as a spiller in containers. They are ramblers once they start growing.

Care & Problems—Water to establish, but once established, provide supplemental irrigation only when the soil is dry. Fertilize once a month with liquid organic fertilizer. Trim it if it grows out of bounds. It has few pest problems.

Bloom Color(s)—Blue

Bloom Period/Peak Season—Summer to fall. Blooming declines as temperatures drop; it is not a cold-tolerant plant.

Mature Size (H x W)—4 inches x 12–18 inches

Water Needs—Low once established.

BLUE SALVIA
Salvia farinacea

Why It's Special—Plant blue salvia to instantly evoke the feeling of an English cottage garden around your home. Vertical bluish purple flower spikes attract butterflies and hummingbirds while adding a specific design element to the garden. They're excellent for use as cut flowers too.

How to Plant & Grow—Start seeds indoors 12 weeks before the last frost. Plant blue salvia in full sun when danger of frost has passed and nighttime temperatures are consistently warm. Space plants 6 to 12 inches apart in the garden bed. Deadhead to encourage constant blooming. Combine with orange cosmos for an electric display.

Care & Problems—These plants are fairly pest-free but can be susceptible to powdery mildew during hot, humid weather. This problem usually resolves itself. Water to establish plants. They can tolerate some drought once they've been in the garden for a while. Fertilize once a month with liquid fertilizer.

Bloom Color(s)—Blue (white and purple also available)

Bloom Period/Peak Season—Summer through frost

Mature Size (H x W)—Up to 3 feet x 2 feet.

Water Needs—Medium to low

CALENDULA
Calendula officinalis

Why It's Special—Calendula is well known for its medicinal properties, but its bright, sunny flowers are gorgeous (and underutilized, in my opinion) in the flower garden. They're a good stopgap between bulbs and summer annuals and perennials. Calendula are excellent flowers for cutting gardens, particularly the taller varieties.

How to Plant & Grow—Start from seed indoors six to eight weeks before last frost. Harden off after the last frost and plant into the garden or containers in full sun to part shade. Leave 8 to 12 inches between plants in the garden. Grow near the vegetable garden to deter pests. A late summer planting pairs well with *Crocosmia* 'Lucifer'.

Care & Problems—It has few pest problems. Occasionally, aphids and whiteflies visit when the plants get stressed from heat. Cut back in midsummer or replant in September for fall growing. Fertilize monthly with liquid fertilizer. Stake plants if they start to flop over. Deadhead to encourage blooming.

Bloom Color(s)—Yellow, orange, gold

Bloom Period/Peak Season—Mid-spring through early summer, fall

Mature Size (H x W)—12–24 inches x 12 inches

Water Needs—Low once established

CALIBRACHOA
Calibrachoa hybrids

Why It's Special—Petunia lovers everywhere rejoiced when calibrachoas hit the market because these plants (which look like little petunias but which are *not* little petunias) actually thrive in the heat, unlike petunias. They are available in many different color combinations and as single or double flowered.

How to Plant & Grow—Calibrachoa plants absolutely need full sun and well-drained soil. They grow best in containers, but can be used as bedding plants if the soil dries out quickly. Plant these when nighttime temperatures are consistently above 65 degrees Fahrenheit. They'll bloom until frost.

Care & Problems—Provided they're planted in full sun and well-drained soil, these plants are fairly trouble-free. If they're not growing or the leaves are off-color, check the soil pH. Calibrachoa plants grow best in slightly acidic soil. Fertilize every other week in summer. Cut back if they get leggy. They are self-cleaning—no deadheading required.

Bloom Color(s)—Every color, including multicolor

Bloom Period/Peak Season—Planting to hard frost

Mature Size (H x W)—6 inches x 12 inches

Water Needs—Low, but consistent once established. Does not like wet feet.

CELOSIA
Celosia cristata or *spicata*

Why It's Special—Celosia flowers are so saturated with color that planting even a few can make a big impact. They are striking in containers, easily filling the role of the "thriller." There are plants with crested or spiked flowers. Crested varieties are good for drying and both make great cutting flowers.

How to Plant & Grow—Start seeds indoors four to six weeks before the last frost date. Wait until soil temperatures are at least 60 degrees Fahrenheit before hardening off and planting outside in full sun in well-drained soil. Crested types are taller than spike types. Leave 18 inches between crested and 8 to 12 inches between spiked types.

Care & Problems—If you're growing taller varieties (anything over 16 inches), you'll likely have to stake individual plants or set up a lattice of string and stakes for the plants to grow through. Few disease problems unless planted too early in cold, wet soil. Fertilize once a month with liquid fertilizer.

Bloom Color(s)—Red, pink, orange, white, yellow

Bloom Period/Peak Season—Summer

Mature Size (H x W)—13–14 inches x 12–18 inches

Water Needs—Medium to low

COLEUS
Solenostemon spp.

Why It's Special—You could plant an entire garden of coleus with different leaf sizes, shapes, colors, and textures. There are now coleus that tolerate full sun. Use coleus to pull your entire garden design together.

How to Plant & Grow—Start seeds indoors eight weeks before last frost. They are easy to grow from seed. Newer varieties, however, might only be available as transplants from garden centers. Plant in partial sun (ideally) after last frost. Color is best-developed (not washed out) when planted in partial sun. Plant with fuchsias, impatiens, and annual vinca for a colorful combo. Leave 12 inches between plants.

Care & Problems—Pinch or cut back to a leaf to encourage compact growth. Plants in deep shade can get leggy and need more pinching. Plants in full sun will need to be watered more frequently to prevent wilting.

Bloom Color(s)—Coleus is grown for colorful foliage. It's usually variegated in shades of chartreuse, purple, burgundy, pink, orange, and red.

Bloom Period/Peak Season—Summer

Mature Size (H x W)—24 inches x 12 inches

Water Needs—Medium. Likes evenly moist soil.

COSMOS
Cosmos bipinnatus

Why It's Special—Cosmos are ridiculously easy to grow from seed and make wonderful cut flowers. Butterflies love them. You'll most commonly see white, pink, and red varieties, but orange cosmos is an easy-care alternative to zinnias, which sometimes struggle with powdery mildew.

How to Plant & Grow—Sow seed indoors four weeks before the last frost or directly into the garden after the last frost. They grow best in full sun in well-drained soil. If planting transplants, leave 18 inches between plants. If sowing seeds, sow thinly because they have a high germination rate.

Care & Problems—If you grow single plants, they might need to be staked so they don't fall over. Deadhead to prolong bloom, but stop deadheading in late August and let the plants go to seed so you get volunteers the next year. Cosmos do not require fertilizing. Water when soil is dry. It's drought tolerant once established.

Bloom Color(s)—White, pink, red, lavender, orange, burgundy

Bloom Period/Peak Season—Summer through frost

Mature Size (H x W)—2–4 feet x 2 feet

Water Needs—Low to medium

DIAMOND FROST® EUPHORBIA

Euphorbia 'Diamond Frost'

Why It's Special—Diamond Frost® gives you a big bang for the buck. Use it as a filler in container gardens or to add texture to the landscape bed. It has an airy, open growth habit with delicate white flowers.

How to Plant & Grow—This is a trademarked plant available only as a transplant. Plant outdoors after the last frost in well-drained soil or containers in full sun to partial sun. Leave 12 to 18 inches between plants.

Care & Problems—This plant basically grows itself. It's a euphorbia, just like poinsettias, and has a milky sap that causes allergic reactions in some people. If you have latex sensitivity, wear gloves when handling. It does not require fertilizer. Water when soil is dry. If it grows out of bounds, you can trim it back. About the only time you'll have a problem with Diamond Frost® is if it doesn't get enough sun or stays too wet. Vigorous growers can sometimes crowd it out in containers.

Bloom Color(s)—White

Bloom Period/Peak Season—Early summer to frost

Mature Size (H x W)—18 inches x 18 inches

Water Needs—Low once established

DUSTY MILLER

Senecio cineraria

Why It's Special—Grow dusty miller for its soft, silvery gray leaves that contrast well with other flowers in shades of blue, purple, and magenta. It's a cool-weather annual that grows best from early spring through early summer and again in fall through early winter. Dusty miller makes a fantastic and unusual filler plant when used in combination with apricot-colored flowers.

How to Plant & Grow—Plant in full to part sun in well-drained soil. They can take cool weather so long as it isn't deep and prolonged. You can grow them in containers as a filler or in the landscape bed as a border. Leave 8 inches between plants in the landscape border.

Care & Problems—Dusty miller is fairly carefree. If it survives the winter, it will bloom during the second season. Water when soil is dry. It does not need supplemental fertilizer.

Bloom Color(s)—Grown for silver foliage

Bloom Period/Peak Season—Cold-hardy in Zones 7 and higher. Early spring through frost.

Mature Size (H x W)—12 inches x 8 inches

Water Needs—Low once established

FLOWERING TOBACCO

Nicotiana alata and hybrids

Why It's Special—Flowering tobacco plants range from relatively short (12 inches) to huge (4 feet) depending on the variety grown. The species *N. alata* gets huge, with big white flowers. It's stunning in the garden. Hybrids have colorful flowers and shorter growth habits. Birds and butterflies love to sip nectar from the flowers, which are fragrant in the afternoon hours.

How to Plant & Grow—Sow seeds indoors eight weeks before the last frost. Harden off and plant outside after the last frost. Plant in full sun to partial shade. If growing in the landscape leave 12 to 18 inches between hybrid plants and 24 inches between species plants. They will flower most reliably during the cooler weather of early spring through early summer and again in fall.

Care & Problems—Water regularly to keep the soil evenly moist. These plants appreciate afternoon shade in warmer climates. They are fairly pest-free and don't require deadheading.

Bloom Color(s)—Red, pink, yellow, white

Bloom Period/Peak Season—Spring, early summer, fall

Mature Size (H x W)—1–3 feet x 1–2 feet

Water Needs—Medium

FUCHSIA
Fuchsia hybrids

Why It's Special—Fuchsia flowers are flashy! They're brightly colored in shades of pink, purple, and, well, fuchsia. If you have a plant on the porch or patio, you'll always be visited by hummingbirds. This plant is a thriller all the way. You can bring them inside for winter.

How to Plant & Grow—Most hybrids are propagated through cuttings, so you'll generally find fuchsias available as large, lavishly grown hanging baskets. Plant in container gardens in partial shade after the last frost. Fuchsias bloom best in cooler weather, so they'll provide sparkle in the garden after the bulk of spring blooming has finished but before summer flowers are at peak.

Care & Problems—Use insecticidal soap to take care of insects that attack during hot, dry weather and move the plants into an area with more protection from the sun. Keep the soil moist. Fertilize every two weeks with liquid fertilizer.

Bloom Color(s)—Red, purple, white, pink. Many two-toned varieties.

Bloom Period/Peak Season—Spring through fall

Mature Size (H x W)—12–24 inches x 12–18 inches

Water Needs—Medium

GLOBE AMARANTH
Gomphrena globosa

Why It's Special—Globe amaranth flowers are old-fashioned cutting garden flowers. Kids love them because of their gumball shape. They work well when planted among perennials because their bright, globe-shaped flowers are borne on tall thin stems. They add height and movement to the garden. You can also cut and dry them. 'Strawberry Fields' has bright red flowers. 'Fireworks' flowers are purple-pink and spiky (like fireworks exploding).

How to Plant & Grow—You can sow seeds directly into the garden after the last frost, start seeds indoors six to eight weeks before the last frost, or purchase transplants from the garden center. Plant in well-drained soil in full sun. Leave 8 inches between plants. Create a hot combo with black-eyed Susans and taller varieties of ageratum.

Care & Problems—Keep soil evenly moist as plants are establishing. Deadhead to prolong bloom. Feed with liquid fertilizer once a month during the summer. Pinch or cut back to encourage branching and bushier plants.

Bloom Color(s)—Purple, red, pink, yellow, orange, white

Bloom Period/Peak Season—Summer

Mature Size (H x W)—6 inches x 24–30 inches

Water Needs—Medium

HELIOTROPE
Heliotropium arborescens

Why It's Special—Plants with deep purple flowers are some of my favorites, and heliotrope is no exception. They have small individual flowers that make up mounded, clumping, fragrant inflorescences reminiscent of hydrangea flowers, but these beauties have a light vanilla fragrance too! While purple is the most common color, there are white varieties. 'Alba' is a fragrant white variety. This is another old-fashioned cottage garden flower.

How to Plant & Grow—Start seeds indoors eight to twelve weeks before the last frost. Harden off and plant transplants outside when nighttime temperatures are regularly above 60 degrees Fahrenheit. Leave 12 inches between plants. They grow best in full sun, but can use afternoon shade in Zones 7 and higher. Heliotrope makes a stunning container plant when grown along with creeping Jenny. The chartreuse leaves of the trailing creeping Jenny make the purple heliotrope flowers pop.

Care & Problems—Heliotrope requires regular water. Do not let the soil dry out. Pinch to encourage bushy growth.

Bloom Color(s)—Purple, lavender, white

Bloom Period/Peak Season—Summer

Mature Size (H x W)—12–24 inches x 8–18 inches

Water Needs—High

LANTANA
Lantana camara

Why It's Special—Lantana is so easy to grow; birds and butterflies flock to it, deer hate it, and it's drought tolerant. What's not to love? There are now many different color choices available too. 'New Gold' is a fairly cold-hardy yellow selection. 'Lavender Swirl' has light purple flowers.

How to Plant & Grow—Plant lantana in the landscape or container garden in full sun and well-drained soil. Wait until nighttime temperatures are at least 60 degrees Fahrenheit before planting transplants from the garden center.

Care & Problems—Lantana is a tough plant. Water to establish plants, but then cut back. Once plants are established, they'll need little to no supplemental water (in the landscape) and little water (in containers). You do not need to feed the plants or deadhead them. If they grow out of bounds, just cut them back and they'll grow back out again.

Bloom Color(s)—Yellow, orange, red, pink, lavender, white (often multiple colors on one plant)

Bloom Period/Peak Season—Summer to frost

Mature Size (H x W)—6–24 inches x 12–36 inches

Water Needs—Low

LOBELIA
Lobelia erinus

Why It's Special—This lobelia is a cool-weather annual with delicate deep blue flowers. There are trailing and upright forms, not to be confused with the upright *Lobelia cardinalis* that has red flowers. Use as a spiller or filler in container gardens and hanging baskets. It's a standard choice for combining with geraniums and alyssum.

How to Plant & Grow—Lobelia is difficult to grow from seed. Plant transplants outside after the last hard frost. (It's hardy to 35 degrees Fahrenheit.) Grows best in full sun to partial shade, with more shade needed the hotter the climate. Leave 6 to 8 inches between in-ground plants. It needs well-drained soil.

Care & Problems—If planted in well-drained soil and watered consistently, lobelia is largely problem-free. Feed with liquid fertilizer once a month. It will often decline during the hot summer, so you can cut it back and grow it out in the fall or take them out. It's also deer resistant.

Bloom Color(s)—Dark blue, light blue, white

Bloom Period/Peak Season—Early spring through early summer, fall

Mature Size (H x W)—6 inches x 12–18 inches

Water Needs—Medium

MADAGASCAR PERIWINKLE
Catharanthus roseus

Why It's Special—This plant is special to me because my mother always grew it. It's sometimes called annual vinca because the flowers are similar in shape to those of vinca vines. Madagascar periwinkle is an easy-to-grow bedding plant that instantly brightens the garden.

How to Plant & Grow—Plant in full sun to partial shade in well-drained soils. Wait to plant until nighttime temperatures are consistently 65 degrees Fahrenheit or above. Leave 12 inches between plants in the ground. You can also use it as a thriller in containers.

Care & Problems—Vinca requires almost no care. The most important thing is planting it in the right place (full to partial sun and well-drained soil) at the right time (when nights are warm). After that, water regularly when the soil dries out, but avoid overhead watering. Feed with liquid fertilizer once a month. It does not require deadheading.

Bloom Color(s)—Shades of pink, red, white, lavender. Some have yellow centers.

Bloom Period/Peak Season—Summer to early fall

Mature Size (H x W)—12–18 inches x 12 inches

Water Needs—Low to medium

MARIGOLD
Tagetes spp.

Why It's Special—Marigolds are garden workhorses. They're easy to grow from seed or transplants, they are deer and rabbit resistant, and they repel pests when planted in the vegetable garden. The flowers are edible too. 'Lemon Gem' and 'Tangerine Gem' are heirloom varieties with thumbnail-sized flowers that cover the plants over lacey green foliage.

How to Plant & Grow—Plant in full sun after the last frost. Soil temperatures should ideally be in the high 60s for plants to germinate from seed. Even when planting transplants, wait until nights are warm. Spacing depends on the size. French marigolds (*T. patula*) are shorter and smaller—you can get away with 12 inches between plants. Taller African marigolds (*T. erecta*) need more space—18 to 24 inches—between plants.

Care & Problems—Use Neem oil to treat powdery mildew. Let the soil or container dry out before watering. Deadhead to encourage bloom and feed with liquid fertilizer once a month in summer.

Bloom Color(s)—Various shades and combinations of orange, white, and red

Bloom Period/Peak Season—Summer

Mature Size (H x W)—8–36 inches x 12–18 inches

Water Needs—Low to medium

MELAMPODIUM
Melampodium divaricatum

Why It's Special—Melampodium is sometimes called the "butter daisy." It is in the aster (daisy) family and blooms with bright yellow, nickel-sized flowers on lime-green stems. Though the flowers are small, they're prolific and bloom almost continuously from planting to frost. Grow it in combination with angelonia Angelface® Blue or blue salvia for a high-contrast display. Celosia and globe amaranth combine with melampodium for hot color.

How to Plant & Grow—Plant melampodium in full to partial sun after the last frost. Know whether you are planting dwarf or species types because, while dwarf plants will stay compact, species will grow to heights and spreads of 2 feet and you want to space appropriately. These plants do best in well-drained soil.

Care & Problems—Melampodium is a fairly problem-free plant. Water regularly during summer, keeping the soil evenly moist. If growing the species, plan to stake taller plants or cut them back to encourage more compact growth.

Bloom Color(s)—Yellow

Bloom Period/Peak Season—Summer

Mature Size (H x W)—12–24 inches x 12–18 inches

Water Needs—Medium to low

MEXICAN SUNFLOWER
Tithonia rotundifolia

Why It's Special—I'm a big fan of herbaceous plants that get really big. Mexican sunflower plants can grow to heights of 5 or 6 feet—all in the span of one season. Plant these along a fence line or in the middle or back of the perennial garden for some extra height. Mix seeds with those of cosmos, zinnias, and sunflowers for a wild cutting garden of riotous color.

How to Plant & Grow—Mexican sunflowers are easy to grow from seed. Sow seeds directly into the garden or plant transplants when soil temperatures are at least 60 degrees Fahrenheit. Leave at least 24 inches between transplants. You can plant seeds 12 inches apart and let them grow up together to support each other.

Care & Problems—These are easy-care plants. Unless they are growing among a lot of other plants, you might need to stake them so they don't fall over. Let the soil dry out between waterings. Deadhead the plants to prolong bloom.

Bloom Color(s)—Orange

Bloom Period/Peak Season—Midsummer to fall

Mature Size (H x W)—Up to 6 feet x 2 feet

Water Needs—Low to medium

NASTURTIUM

Tropaeolum spp.

Why It's Special—When the light shines through nasturtium flowers, they absolutely glow in shades of red, orange, and yellow. There are bush-type varieties and vine-type varieties, but, honestly, they perform similar functions in the garden. I like to plant them around the edges of my raised bed vegetable gardens for color and pest deterrence. They also make beautiful cool-weather hanging baskets.

How to Plant & Grow—Nasturtium seeds have a thick seed coat. Nick the coat with a pair of nail clippers before planting to encourage fast germination. (I've used my teeth for this. I don't recommend that.) Direct-sow outside in full sun after the last frost. Plant two seeds per hole, leaving 6 inches between.

Care & Problems—Do not fertilize nasturtiums. Keep the soil evenly moist and let them grow. The flowers are edible. In the summertime, they might take a break from blooming. Cut them back, and they may grow out in fall.

Bloom Color(s)—Orange, yellow, red, white, variegated

Bloom Period/Peak Season—Early spring, early summer, fall

Mature Size (H x W)—8 inches x 12 inches

Water Needs—Medium

NEW GUINEA IMPATIENS

Impatiens hawkeri

Why It's Special—New Guinea impatiens have to replace bedding impatiens (*Impatiens walleriana*) in the mid-Atlantic landscape because impatiens downy mildew makes it all but impossible to grow the formerly standard bedding plants. You can find varieties of New Guinea impatiens with burgundy or green leaves. Some variegated types are equally as attractive when out of flower as in flower, but once they start blooming, they'll provide color up until frost.

How to Plant & Grow—Plant transplants outside in partial sun to shade after the last frost and when the soil has warmed to at least 50 degrees Fahrenheit. Leave 12 to 18 inches between plants or plant in containers. For a big splash as a bedding plant, combine with caladium bulbs.

Care & Problems—Water consistently so that the soil remains evenly moist, but not soaking wet. Fertilize once a month with liquid fertilizer. Sprinkle diatomaceous earth around plants if you see signs of slug damage. This plant is self-cleaning.

Bloom Color(s)—Pink, red, lavender, white, orange, salmon, variegated

Bloom Period/Peak Season—Summer

Mature Size (H x W)—18 inches x 18 inches

Water Needs—Medium to high

PANSY

Viola × wittrockiana

Why It's Special—Pansies can withstand hard freezes and will bounce back and flower. Plant them in masses for winter-long color in Zones 6 and higher or in containers to spruce up the front doorstep.

How to Plant & Grow—Plant pansies starting in September for fall color. They flower best in full sun but can take some afternoon shade. You can grow from seed, but garden centers always have tons of colors available for purchase. Plant close together (4 inches between plants) for the biggest show.

Care & Problems—In zones 7 and 8, you'll get consistent color throughout winter. In zone 6, the plants will overwinter but won't bloom much from December until March when it starts to warm up again. In zone 5 and lower, you'll have to plant in fall and again in spring. In spring, as the weather warms and the plants begin to grow again, you can increase watering and fertilize every two weeks with liquid fertilizer.

Bloom Color(s)—Blue, purple, maroon, orange, pink, burgundy, white, yellow, and variegated/multicolored varieties

Bloom Period/Peak Season—Fall through spring

Mature Size (H x W)—8 inches x 12 inches

Water Needs—Medium

PAPYRUS
Cyperus papyrus

Why It's Special—Papyrus is just a cool plant. Use it as a thriller plant in containers or plant in the landscape with elephant ears, cannas, and other water-loving plants. It looks like a grass, but it's in the sedge family.

How to Plant & Grow—Plant in full sun in moist soil when soil temperatures are 60 degrees Fahrenheit or higher. Where you plant it depends on the eventual size; there are dwarf varieties that top out at 12 to 24 inches, but Graceful Grasses® King Tut® is a giant variety that can reach heights of 6 feet or more. Tutankhamun, known in the trade as Little Giant Papyrus, grows to be 2 to 3 feet and has fluffy, threadlike flowers at the top of the plant.

Care & Problems—Keep the plant well watered while it is establishing itself. It will tolerate a bit more drought once is has established roots, though. Overwinter this plant in a warm basement. Place the plant in a container in a bucket with water in the bottom.

Bloom Color(s)—Grown for foliage

Bloom Period/Peak Season—Summer

Mature Size (H x W)—18–72 inches x 12–24 inches

Water Needs—High

PENTAS
Pentas lanceolata

Why It's Special—Pentas is quite possibly the perfect annual flower. It grows well in sun to shade (just not deep shade); butterflies love it; it looks stunning in containers; and it blooms from planting until a hard frost. Plant fuchsia pentas with yellow melampodium for hot color.

How to Plant & Grow—Start seeds eight to ten weeks before the last frost. Plant outdoors when the soil temperature is at least 60 degrees Fahrenheit. Pentas grow fast, so leave at least 4 inches of space when planting in containers and 12 inches of space when planting in the ground.

Care & Problems—Pentas are easy-care annuals. They don't require deadheading, but you can cut them back if they get leggy and to encourage branching. Fertilize once a month and keep the soil evenly moist but not soggy. If plants are stressed, aphids and spider mites can be a problem. Use Neem oil or insecticidal soap to control the insects.

Bloom Color(s)—Pink, red, lavender, white, salmon, purple

Bloom Period/Peak Season—Summer to frost

Mature Size (H x W)—18 inches x 12 inches

Water Needs—Medium

PENNISETUM, JADE PRINCESS
Pennisetum glaucum 'Jade Princess'

Why It's Special—This annual ornamental grass is a knockout. It has bright chartreuse leaves and burgundy flower stalks that look like fluffy cattails. Use it as a thriller in container gardens or as a bright background in the landscape. It combines well with burgundy or burgundy and lime bicolor coleus. For a tropical look, plant with cannas and elephant ears. The lime-colored leaves of this grass make a perfect backdrop for sun-loving plants with fuchsia or purple flowers.

How to Plant & Grow—Sow indoors 14 weeks before the last frost or purchase transplants. Plant outside in the garden after the last frost. Leave 12 to 18 inches between plants if massing.

Care & Problems—The flowers of this plant are sterile, so they're not invasive, unlike some other pennisetum varieties. Water to establish the plant and then water only when the soil is dry. If the plant grows out of bounds, the only way to trim is to cut individual stalks back to the ground.

Bloom Color(s)—Chartreuse foliage, burgundy flower stalks

Bloom Period/Peak Season—Summer

Mature Size (H x W)—36 inches x 18 inches

Water Needs—Low once established

PERSIAN SHIELD
Strobilanthes dyerianus

Why It's Special—Persian shield is an excellent alternative to coleus in the garden. The purple leaves have a different texture—they're shiny and rough. You could call them variegated because of prominent green veins. They can also grow quite tall—up to 3 feet. If you need a cool-colored plant for your combination, try *Strobilanthes*.

How to Plant & Grow—Buy transplants from the garden center and plant in moist, well-drained soil after the last frost. Leave 12 to 18 inches between plants because they can get big. Plant with dusty miller and other gray-leafed plants to emphasize the silvery highlights of the leaves.

Care & Problems—This is a fairly trouble-free plant. Pinch throughout the growing season, the way you'd pinch coleus, to encourage branching. It doesn't need extra fertilizer. Keep soil evenly moist, but not soggy. In Zones 7 to 8, don't pull up the plants until spring. The roots might overwinter, and the plants could resprout.

Bloom Color(s)—Silvery purple foliage

Bloom Period/Peak Season—Summer

Mature Size (H x W)—Up to 36 inches x 24 inches

Water Needs—Medium

PORTULACA
Portulaca grandiflora

Why It's Special—Looking for a groundcover annual for full sun? Portulaca is the perfect plant to add a pop of color to the front of borders or rock gardens. You can also use it as a "spiller" in sun container gardens. I like to plant it along my front walk because it thrives in hot sun, poor soils, and with little water. Portulaca will also self-sow if allowed to remain in the garden until frost.

How to Plant & Grow—Start seeds indoors 12 weeks before the last frost. (Seeds are tiny; it is easier to just buy transplants.) Plant in full sun in well-drained soil when the soil temperatures are at least 60 degrees Fahrenheit. Leave 8 to 12 inches between plants because they do spread.

Care & Problems—Keep portulaca on the dry side. If they sit in water, they'll develop root rot. Flowers won't open on cloudy or rainy days—that's normal, so don't get worried.

Bloom Color(s)—White, pink, orange, red, yellow, salmon

Bloom Period/Peak Season—Summer

Mature Size (H x W)—6 inches x 12–18 inches

Water Needs—Low

RUDBECKIA 'PRAIRIE SUN'
Rudbeckia 'Prairie Sun' and annual varieties

Why It's Special—Annual rudbeckias are special because they are just gorgeous. There's nothing brighter and more cheerful for the garden. 'Prairie Sun' has palm-sized, two-toned, daisylike yellow flowers with greenish eyes (centers). Other annual varieties have large yellow petals with black centers, burgundy petals with black centers, and other color combinations. Plant a mix of cultivars together *en masse* or dot individual plants throughout the perennial garden. 'Prairie Sun' is stunning when planted with 'Fireworks' fountain grass, another annual.

How to Plant & Grow—Technically these plants are biennial, but will bloom from seed the first year they are planted, and therefore are considered to be annuals. Start seeds indoors 12 weeks before the last frost and plant outside in full sun in well-drained soil after the last frost. Leave 12 inches between plants.

Care & Problems—Deadhead plants throughout summer to encourage continuous bloom. They are drought tolerant, but do best with regular water; they do not, however, like to sit in soggy soil. Fertilize midway through summer.

Bloom Color(s)—Yellow, burgundy, dual tones

Bloom Period/Peak Season—Summer

Mature Size (H x W)—24–30 inches x 12–18 inches

Water Needs—Medium

SCAEVOLA
Scaevola aemula

Why It's Special—Scaevola, sometimes called "fan flower" because of its, well, fan-shaped flowers, is a low-growing, vining annual that thrives in hot, humid weather. It has few pest and disease problems. It's a favorite for use in containers or as a groundcover bedding plant. It is also salt-tolerant for those of you gardening by the sea. Scaevola combines well with lantana.

How to Plant & Grow—Plant outside when soil temperatures are at least 60 degrees Fahrenheit and nighttime temperatures are at least 60 degrees Fahrenheit. These plants thrive in hot, humid weather. Plant close together as the spillers in container gardens or leave 8 to 12 inches between plants to use them as groundcover in the landscape.

Care & Problems—Keep soil evenly moist and fertilize a couple of times during summer. If the plant grows out of bounds or flowering declines, cut the plants back and let them grow out. They have few pest problems. This plant is self-cleaning.

Bloom Color(s)—Purple, white, pink (purple is most common)

Bloom Period/Peak Season—Summer

Mature Size (H x W)—6 inches x 18 inches

Water Needs—Medium

SNAPDRAGON
Antirrhinum majus

Why It's Special—Snapdragons are old-fashioned annual flowers that grow well in the cool weather of late spring and early summer. They add a striking vertical element to the garden. There are semi-trailing varieties that look great in container gardens. Taller types make great cut flowers.

How to Plant & Grow—Sow seeds indoors 12 weeks before the last frost. Harden off and plant outside in full sun after the last frost. Snapdragons can handle some cool weather. In Zones 7 and higher, you can plant outside in September and leave them in the garden through winter. Leave 6 to 8 inches between plants.

Care & Problems—Snapdragons will stop flowering when the weather is hot. Cut them back and leave them in the garden; they'll bloom again in fall. Keep soil evenly moist. After a big bloom, cut the plants back hard, water, and fertilize to encourage repeat blooming. Stake taller varieties.

Bloom Color(s)—Pink, orange, yellow, white, lavender, salmon, peach, red, burgundy

Bloom Period/Peak Season—Late spring to early summer, fall

Mature Size (H x W)—6–24 inches x 6–12 inches

Water Needs—Medium

SPIDER FLOWER
Cleome hassleriana

Why It's Special—Spider flowers offer a different texture in the garden than many tall annuals. They have delicate, spidery-looking flowers borne at the top of leafy stems. Newer hybrids are thornless and have a more compact growth habit, so are easier to handle. The species of this plant can self-seed liberally. It's a must-have if you want to attract butterflies and hummingbirds to the yard.

How to Plant & Grow—Plant in full sun after the last frost. You can grow from seed sown directly in the garden or visit the garden center for transplants of newer, more compact hybrids. You can use plants as thrillers in containers. They're also stunning as mass plantings. Leave 12 inches between plants.

Care & Problems—Keep soil evenly moist. Fertilize once, in midsummer. You can cut flowers for bouquets, and the remaining plant will branch. This plant has few pest problems and will often reseed.

Bloom Color(s)—White, pink, lavender

Bloom Period/Peak Season—Summer

Mature Size (H x W)—2–4 feet x 1–2 feet

Water Needs—Medium. Drought tolerant once established.

SUNFLOWER
Helianthus annuus

Why It's Special—Sunflowers have a nostalgic place in most gardener's hearts, mine included. There are now many different hybrids and varieties in almost every shade of orange, yellow, and burgundy. There are plants that top out at 2 feet and others that grow to 8 feet. 'Teddy Bear' is an interesting double variety. 'Mammoth' has large flowers that produce lots of seeds.

How to Plant & Grow—You can start seeds indoors for ease of keeping track where the plants are and to keep squirrels from eating the plants. You can also just direct sow into the garden after the last frost. Space seeds or plants according to the final expected size of the variety.

Care & Problems—Some sunflowers bloom once and that's it. Others are branching, so if you deadhead, they'll keep blooming. Rust and powdery mildew sometimes attack lower leaves—just cut them off. Stake taller varieties if they start to lean. Keep the soil evenly moist and do not fertilize.

Bloom Color(s)—Yellow, orange, burgundy

Bloom Period/Peak Season—Summer to fall

Mature Size (H x W)—2–7 feet x 1–3 feet

Water Needs—Low to medium

SWEET POTATO VINE
Ipomoea batatas

Why It's Special—If you need a large patch of ground covered quickly and cheaply, go for sweet potato vine. There are more varieties than when it was first introduced, with different leaf shapes and colors. Illusion series plants have lacy leaves. 'Tricolor' has pink, green, and white variegated leaves.

How to Plant & Grow—Purchase transplants and plant in full sun after danger of frost has passed. These grow from tubers, so they cannot be planted from seeds. Sweet potato vines can be used as spillers in containers or as groundcovers in the landscape. Leave 4 feet between plants if using as a groundcover, as they grow and spread quickly.

Care & Problems—These plants are easy to grow and have few pest and disease problems. Cut them back if they get ratty or grow out of bounds. Keep soil evenly moist.

Bloom Color(s)—Grown for chartreuse, dark burgundy, or variegated leaves

Bloom Period/Peak Season—Summer

Mature Size (H x W)—6–8 inches x 6 feet

Water Needs—Low once established

TORENIA
Torenia fournieri

Why It's Special—This is a grossly underused annual, as far as I'm concerned. It is an excellent container plant for partial to full shade areas. It thrives during the cool days of late spring and early summer and again in fall. Combine with caladium for interesting shade garden containers.

How to Plant & Grow—You can start seeds indoors six to eight weeks before the last frost or purchase transplants at the garden center. Plant outside after the last frost. Use as a spiller in container gardens or as an edging or border plant in the landscape. Space plants 8 to 12 inches apart if planting in the ground.

Care & Problems—Keep the soil moist, but not sopping wet. Cut the plant back and let it grow out if you have problems with powdery mildew. Fertilize container plantings every two weeks and in-ground plantings once a month.

Bloom Color(s)—The species is blue. There are cultivars with white, yellow, or pink flowers.

Bloom Period/Peak Season—Early summer, fall

Mature Size (H x W)—6–12 inches x 12–24 inches

Water Needs—Medium

ZINNIA
Zinnia elegans

Why It's Special—Zinnias are the easiest flowers to grow from seed, hands down. They are also the best cutting flowers—lasting up to a week in a vase. They come in a huge variety of colors and sizes, single and double flowered, and even multicolored variegated types. 'Candy Cane Mix' plants have speckled flowers that look like a paintbrush has been flicked over the blooms.

How to Plant & Grow—Sow seeds directly into the garden after the last frost or start indoors a month before the last frost. Plant in full sun. Leave 6 to 12 inches between plants. You can grow zinnias in containers, but they work better as landscape plants.

Care & Problems—The biggest problem with zinnias is that they are susceptible to powdery mildew. The answer to this is to plant resistant varieties. Otherwise, keep the soil evenly moist and feed once a month during the growing season. Deadhead routinely to keep plants branching and blooming.

Bloom Color(s)—Every color of the rainbow

Bloom Period/Peak Season—Summer

Mature Size (H x W)—12–36 inches x 8–18 inches (depending on the variety)

Water Needs—Low to medium

ANNUALS MONTH-BY-MONTH

JANUARY

- Order seeds now for the best selection. You're probably getting seed catalogs in the mail, or you're receiving fancy e-mail newsletters touting the best and brightest and newest plants available. Seeds for highly coveted varieties sell out fast, so this is the time to buy.

- Gather seed-starting materials. You'll need seedling mix, seed flats with covers, blank plant labels (you can use popsicle sticks or mailing labels), and a permanent marker for writing the labels.

- Construct a propagation area for starting seeds. At a bare minimum, you need a non-flammable surface on which to set a propagation mat or two and a set of grow lights mounted on chains over the mat. Mounting the lights on chains enables you to easily move the lights up as the seedlings grow taller.

FEBRUARY

- Start seeds of cool-weather annuals, including snapdragons, alyssum, bachelor's buttons, calendula, and nasturtium. Nick the seed coats of nasturtiums before planting.

- Make a table or spreadsheet listing those seeds you sowed, including the date and the number planted. This will help you stay organized and know what you planted where and when so you don't overlook anything.

- Check seeds daily to ensure they are receiving enough moisture and aren't experiencing problems with fungus gnats or damping off.

- Promote air circulation in the seed-starting area by running an oscillating fan on a low setting. This will result in seedlings with stronger stems and fewer problems with pests and diseases.

MARCH

- Transplant seedlings of cool-weather annuals up into larger pots so that they can continue growing. You'll likely need to raise the grow lights.

- When the ground is workable, prepare flowerbeds outside for cool-weather annuals. Rake last year's leaves and remove any annuals planted in fall to make way for new spring plantings.

- Repot and trim any tropical annuals or container plantings (such as geraniums) that you brought inside to overwinter. You can take cuttings from geraniums and coleus for rooting and planting out in summer.

APRIL

- Plant container gardens filled with cool-season flowers, including alyssum, nasturtium, pansies, violas, annual lobelia, geraniums, and calendula. Bring inside if a hard frost is predicted.

- Harden off and plant transplants of cool-season annuals. Cover at night if a hard frost is predicted.

- Stay on top of weeds in flowerbeds. Warmer weather makes them go crazy. Apply pre-emergent herbicide, but only after any new plantings have been in the ground for at least three weeks.

- Start seeds indoors for warm-weather annuals such as zinnias, melampodium, mealycup sage, and spider flower.

- Sow seeds of cool-weather annuals directly into the garden if you prefer to direct-sow.

MAY

- Feed cool-weather annuals growing in containers and flowerbeds with liquid fertilizer.

- Deadhead annuals in the landscape or containers to encourage continuous bloom.

- Transplant warm-weather seedlings up into larger pots, if you're starting inside.

- Keep an eye out for pests, particularly cutworms. Protect young plants by sinking "collars" into the soil, surrounding the plant. Toilet paper tubes can be used to make collars.

- Move overwintered tropical plants outside. Keep in a protected location at first to harden the plants off and acclimate them to weather changes outside. Plant annual bulbs, including tropicals such as elephant ears.

JUNE

- Switch out cool-season annuals for warm-season annuals in containers and in the landscape. Now is the time to harden off and plant out any warm-season annuals grown from seed. Direct-sow warm-season annuals, including zinnias and sunflowers.

- Step up the watering plan. June brings the heat for most of the Mid-Atlantic, so you'll need to check plants every couple of days to see if they need water. As plants in container gardens grow, they'll need to be watered more frequently as well.

- Fertilize annuals in the landscape and in containers every two weeks with liquid organic fertilizer.

JULY

- Water and fertilize regularly to keep plants healthy. July can be a hot, dry month. If you're going on vacation, get a plant babysitter and teach that person how to water properly. It doesn't matter if they do anything else, but they need to stay on top of watering.

- Deadhead annual flowers to encourage continuous blooming. Not all annuals require deadheading, but zinnias, marigolds, and many cutting flowers bloom more profusely when regularly deadheaded.

- Shear back any annuals that have gotten overly leggy. Melampodium is a prime candidate for a midsummer haircut. Lantana often benefits from a summer trim too.

- Pests can be active. If any annuals are destroyed by chomping insects, yank the plants up and compost them or throw them away. Honestly, it's not worth the effort to mount a major spraying campaign for annual plants.

- Direct-sow another round of warm-season cutting flowers (including sunflowers) so you'll have bouquets through frost.

AUGUST

- It's time to start seeds inside again! If you're planning on using seed trays and pots that you used in spring, clean and disinfect them by washing in a solution of 9 parts water to 1 part bleach. Sow seeds for cool-weather annuals such as lobelia, alyssum, calendula, and pansies for fall planting.

- Continue watering, fertilizing, deadheading, and weeding.

- Take cuttings of plants you want to overwinter inside. Salvia, begonias, coleus, and geraniums are good candidates for winter growing.

- Move cool-weather annual seedlings up to a larger-sized pot so they can grow a bit more before being planted out.

- Harvest seeds to save for the next season. Allow them to dry fully on a paper towel and then store in individually labeled envelopes.

SEPTEMBER

- Change out the garden! Pull up spent warm-weather annuals and replace them with cool-weather annuals, including flowering kale, Swiss chard, alyssum, and violas. Compost the annuals you removed, unless they show symptoms of disease.

- Plant transplants of cool-weather annuals outside after hardening off. (Just because it's warm outside doesn't mean you don't need to take the time to get plants used to different growing conditions.)

- Bring tropical plants inside for winter.

- Purchase mums at garden centers and pop them into the ground or into containers for seasonal color. Keep a close eye on plants, as they tend to dry out quickly. You might have to water daily.

OCTOBER

- Water and fertilize cool-weather annuals planted outside, including those in containers.

- Deadhead annuals growing outside. The more energy they put into growing root systems now, the more likely they are to make it through winter. (Don't be alarmed if they don't, though.)

- Enjoy potted chrysanthemums while they bloom. When they're finished, plant them in the garden. Sometimes they will overwinter.

NOVEMBER

- Make notes about what did and did not grow well in the garden. Few people actually do this, but it helps planning next year's garden.

- Keep an eye on annuals you've moved indoors. Look for signs of stress such as dropping leaves or pest problems. Move plants around so they receive more light and pay careful attention to watering.

DECEMBER

- Not much is happening in the garden in the coolest regions.

- Keep an eye on winter annuals in warmer regions. Deadhead. Water only if daytime temperatures routinely rise above 50 degrees Fahrenheit and there's no rain.

BULBS
for the Mid-Atlantic

In some ways, bulbs are quite like annuals, providing a showy flower display during a particular season. In other ways, they're like perennials because most come back each year. Some bulbs are grown as annuals either because they're not hardy in the Mid-Atlantic (caladium) or because their performance declines after the first bloom (tulips). The bulbs featured here, even if they're annuals, add enough color, texture, and interest to the garden to warrant your effort to plant them. Bulbs are the finishing touch on the garden.

DESIGNING WITH BULBS

Incorporating bulbs into a garden design allows you to add layers of color and texture to areas of the garden that might be kind of staid without them. There are short, early bloomers such as crocus or winter aconite. There are tall season-bridging bulbs such as alliums and surprise lilies. Then there are the highly saturated colorful blooms of daffodils or tulips that provide a much-needed splash when there's not much else happening. When designing with bulbs, ask yourself, "What is this going to add that I can't achieve with another plant?"

ANNUALS VERSUS PERENNIALS

Some bulbs are not hardy in the Mid-Atlantic, but they're still worth growing because they are spectacular. Nothing can provide the big splash that dinnerplate dahlias do or the true blue color of agapanthus, but both require special winter care. Other bulbs, such as tulips, are cold-hardy, but their performance suffers after the first year, so they're usually grown as annuals. And then there are bulbs that you plant with the plan that they'll come back year after year. Explore tender bulbs to add excitement to the garden, even though they require more work, because the tender bulbs highlighted in this chapter provide interest that you can't get with anything else.

GROWING TIP

This chapter covers all plants with bulbous roots. There are true bulbs, but also corms, rhizomes, and tubers. If the plant grows from an enlarged underground root or stem structure, it's categorized as a bulb. Regardless of the morphology, their care is quite similar.

NATURALIZING

In some of the bulb profiles you'll see "naturalizes well" or something similar. That essentially means that the bulb will come back year after year and will spread. Daffodils, crocus, and winter aconite are good candidates. Plant bulbs that naturalize under trees or in lawn areas where you can wait to mow until their foliage dies back.

INCORPORATING BULBS WITH ANNUALS

In the ground and in containers, you can layer bulbs with cool-season annuals. Plant daffodils 6 to 9 inches deep, and then plant pansies or violas over them. You'll enjoy the annuals all winter and then get an extra show in the spring when the bulbs bloom.

To plant bulbs, dig a hole and use your trowel to measure the depth. Plant most bulbs at least three times as deep as the bulb is tall. For example, plant a 2-inch-tall bulb 6 inches deep.

Plant bulbs with the pointy end up. If you're not sure which side is the top of the bulb, lay the bulb on its side and cover.

HOW TO PLANT BULBS

There are two main bulb planting seasons: Late spring for bulbs that bloom during summer, and fall for bulbs that bloom in spring. Just because a bulb blooms in summer doesn't mean it is cold hardy. Pay attention to packaging and planting instructions when you buy the bulbs so that you plant at the right time. (There are a few late spring bloomers that you plant in the early spring. Instructions are noted on plant profiles.)

A general rule of thumb for bulb planting is to plant three times the height of the bulb. If a bulb is 2 inches tall, plant it 6 inches deep. Irises are an exception. They grow from rhizomes and should planted so that the top of the rhizome is aboveground. For most bulbs, corms, and tubers, plant so that the pointy end is up and the flat end is down. If you can see dried-up roots on the bulb, put that side down.

Spacing depends entirely on the bulb. Most bulbs put on the best show when planted in groups of five, ten, or fifteen bulbs. Crocus, daffodils, grape hyacinths, alliums, and surprise lilies fall into that category. Other bulbs, such as elephant ears, produce enormous amounts of foliage and flowers and require a lot of space. Requirements are listed on individual plant profiles.

Pests can be an issue for bulbs throughout the growing season, but the time when they are most vulnerable is right after planting and during winter. Small mammals absolutely love to dig them up and eat them. Try shaking ground red pepper on the bulbs and on top of the soil where you plant. There are also repellants you can spray on the bulbs. If you have severe problems with animals digging up the bulbs, you can also construct a cage from chicken wire that you bury and plant the bulbs in. (The gauge of holes must be smaller than the bulbs, but large enough for the leaves and stems to grow through.) That is a lot of work though, and not something you can do for mass plantings.

CARING FOR BULBS

Bulbs are pretty fuss-free, but they have some specific care requirements because of the way they grow.

STAKING

Some bulbs require staking. Dahlias can grow enormous flowers that require support. Push a single stake into the ground about 2 inches from the plant stem. Use twine or foam-covered wire to loosely tie the stem to the stake in several places. A lattice system is a good way to keep bulbs grown for cutting purposes—such as gladiolus or a row of multiple dahlias—from falling over. Create a lattice by weaving string around several stakes spaced in the ground, creating a crisscross pattern. Do this before the plants have started growing so that they can grow up through the lattice.

POST-BLOOM CARE

- Remove flower stalks by cutting them to the ground.
- Fertilize with a bulb-specific or general-purpose fertilizer right after the plants stop blooming.
- Allow foliage to die (turn brown or yellow) before cutting back. This is one of the most important aspects of bulb care. They have to be able to photosynthesize and store nutrients in order to bloom the following year.
- Divide (if necessary) after foliage dies back. Dig up the bulbs and carefully separate clusters. Replant immediately.

OVERWINTERING TENDER BULBS

Gladiolus, dahlias, elephant ears, and other bulbs are tender and won't survive the winter in most areas of the Mid-Atlantic. Is it worth saving these bulbs to plant the next year? That depends on what it is. I prefer to compost gladiolus and buy new bulbs because they're inexpensive and easy to find. A prized or rare dahlia, on the other hand, would be worth the effort to keep it over winter. Use this technique for lifting and overwintering tender bulbs.

- Dig up before the last frost.
- Cut off leaves and trim roots. Brush off soil.
- Leave outside to cure for a day.
- Bring indoors and pack in wood shavings or peat moss.
- Keep in a cool, dark, dry place for winter.
- Replant outside in spring.

PESTS & PROBLEMS

The main problems you'll encounter are animals eating the bulbs—either at the time of planting, during winter, or, most frustratingly, right when the bulbs are about to open and bloom—or the bulbs rotting in the ground during the growing season or off season.

To deter animals, use repellents or plant resistant types. For example, most animals leave daffodils alone. To avoid rotting, plant bulbs in well-drained soil and do not provide extra water except during the growing season if it's dry.

AGAPANTHUS
Agapanthus africanus

Why It's Special—These plants are worth the effort for their spectacular blue flowers. Individual flowers cluster together to form a loose sphere borne at the top of a long stem. They are definitely specimen plants.

How to Plant & Grow—Agapanthus grow best when slightly potbound or crowded, and they make the biggest impact if you plant several close together. Plant outside in well-drained soil in full sun to partial shade after the danger of frost has passed. Spacing between plants depends on the eventual size of the variety you're growing—generally 12 to 18 inches.

Care & Problems—Keep these plants on the dry side. If you're going to overwinter agapanthus in a container, bring it into the garage or basement and cut down on watering.

Bloom Color(s)—Dark blue, lavender, purple, white

Bloom Period/Peak Season—Summer

Mature Size (H x W)—(With flower stalk) 2–4 feet x 1–2 feet

Hardiness—Hardy in Zones 6 and higher. (Depends on the variety. Hardiness varies between Zones 5 to 10.)

Water Needs—Medium

ALLIUM
Allium spp.

Why It's Special—Alliums are ornamental flowers in the onion family. They have globe-shaped inflorescences composed of many separate flowers on top of a long stalk. They're a great plant to provide garden color between spring perennials and summer flowers.

How to Plant & Grow—Plant allium bulbs in fall in well-drained soil, sited in full sun. The foliage of these plants dies back midsummer, so plant them where they can grow up through other perennials so they don't leave holes in the garden bed. Plant several close together to create a statement.

Care & Problems—Allium won't bloom if they're planted in shade or if their foliage is covered up by other plants before it dies back. They also do not do well in wet soil. Otherwise, they're fairly trouble-free. Remove the foliage after it dies back.

Bloom Color(s)—Blue, purple, pink, white

Bloom Period/Peak Season—Late spring to early summer

Mature Size (H x W)—(With flower stalk) 1–4 feet x 6–12 inches

Hardiness—5 (for most varieties) to 8 or 9

Water Needs—Low to medium

CALADIUM
Caladium bicolor

Why It's Special—I always plant white-and-green variegated caladiums in my front garden because they really pop in the darker areas of the flower bed.

How to Plant & Grow—Plant caladium outside in the shade after the last frost and when the soil has warmed to at least 50 degrees Fahrenheit. You can buy bulbs or plants that have already started growing. Leave 12 to 24 inches between plants. Plant individually throughout the garden or make big, dramatic sweeps. They're beautiful either way.

Care & Problems—Caladiums are pest-free for the most part. Keep the soil moist. Remove shaggy leaves. Use diatomaceous earth around plants to prevent slug damage. You can lift these bulbs for winter storage. If you have an unusual or hard-to find variety, definitely lift them. If you're growing more common types, it's easier to just compost. If you're overwintering them, remove all foliage and store in a cool, dry place.

Bloom Color(s)—Grow for the foliage in shades of green, white, pink, red, and variegated.

Bloom Period/Peak Season—Summer foliage

Mature Size (H x W)—24 inches x 24 inches

Hardiness—Hardy in Zones 9 and higher; grow as annual in the Mid-Atlantic

Water Needs—Medium

CAMASSIA
Camassia leichtlinii

Why It's Special—Camassia is a must-grow if you are trying to get the cottage garden look in your landscape beds. The plants have star-shaped blue flowers on tall spikes and straplike foliage. It tolerates fairly moist soil, so plant as an accent plant at the edge of bog gardens. It's native to the Pacific Northwest, but camassia will grow just fine in the Mid-Atlantic.

How to Plant & Grow—Plant in rich soil in full to partial sun. Camassias put on the best show when planted in clumps of 10 to 20 bulbs in the border. After flowering, the foliage starts to die back, so plant where they can bloom and then be out of the way or covered up by perennials that are late to leaf out.

Care & Problems—These plants need evenly moist soil. They don't require fertilizing. Cut back the flower stalks after blooming. You can cut back the leaves after they turn brown, in midsummer.

Bloom Color(s)—Blue

Bloom Period/Peak Season—Late spring

Mature Size (H x W)—3–6 feet x 2–4 feet, clumping

Hardiness—5–9

Water Needs—Medium

CANNA
Canna generalis

Why It's Special—Cannas are probably one of the easiest plants to grow. They tolerate nearly every type of soil, including wet, boggy soils. If you can only plant one variety, go for *Canna* Tropicanna®, which has stunning variegated burgundy foliage and tangerine flowers. It looks great from spring to frost.

How to Plant & Grow—Plant in full sun. You can grow these plants in boggy soils or containers, but they get to be large, so if you're container growing, choose a big container! Plant outside when soil temperatures are at least 50 degrees Fahrenheit.

Care & Problems—Cannas are easy-care. Water frequently during summer so that the soil stays moist. In fall, if growing in Zones 6 or lower, lift bulbs and cut off all of the foliage. Store the bulbs in a cool, dry location in peat moss.

Bloom Color(s)—White, yellow, orange, red, pink

Bloom Period/Peak Season—Summer

Mature Size (H x W)—4–7 feet x 3–6 feet

Hardiness—7 and higher; can be lifted and stored in cooler climates

Water Needs—High

CLIVIA
Clivia miniata

Why It's Special—The flowers on this tender bulb are just spectacular, and they bloom from December through April. They're worth their trouble, honestly. Grow them inside as houseplants and move them outside during summer as greenery in a shady container garden combo.

How to Plant & Grow—Grow clivia in pots. They bloom best when slightly potbound. Move plants outdoors once the weather warms up, and site them in dappled shade. Bring the pots inside before the first frost and keep them in a sunny location.

Care & Problems—Feed with half-strength liquid plant food every other week in summer. Stop watering plants October 1 when you bring them indoors. Keep clivia at 55 degrees Fahrenheit (a garage window is ideal) for eight weeks, then bring indoors to a sunny window and start watering again. Once you start watering, only water when the soil dries out. Don't let it stay soggy. When given this dormant cold treatment, the plants should flower.

Bloom Color(s)—Primarily orange or red with some multicolored varieties.

Bloom Period/Peak Season—Winter

Mature Size (H x W)—18–24 inches x 18–24 inches

Hardiness—9 and higher

Water Needs—Low

COLCHICUM
Colchicum autumnale

Why It's Special—When you think of little flowering bulbs, you probably think "spring," but *Colchicum* are autumn crocuses. They naturalize well in flower beds or even in turf areas. Plant them in clumps of 10 or more for the best effect. They're special because they bloom when you're least expecting flowers like they have. Colchicum are also deer resistant, unlike many other flowering bulbs.

How to Plant & Grow—Plant in full sun in well-drained soil. These bulbs, like most others, don't like to have wet feet. Plant in clumps for the biggest impact. The plants grow foliage in spring that dies back in summer, so plant the bulbs where the foliage dieback won't detract from the landscape.

Care & Problems—These are easy-care plants. You can remove foliage after it turns brown in summer. Dig up and divide clumps after the foliage dies back in summer every three to four years.

Bloom Color(s)—Lavender-pink

Bloom Period/Peak Season—Fall

Mature Size (H x W)—4–6 inches x 4–6 inches

Hardiness—4–10, depending on the variety

Water Needs—Low to medium

CRINUM
Crinum spp.

Why It's Special—Crinum lilies are another group of tropical bulbs that have to be brought indoors during winter in most of the Mid-Atlantic, but they're so spectacular that they're worth it. Add a tropical touch around the pool or make a statement near the front door.

How to Plant & Grow—Plant in pots with 2 inches of space between the bulb and the edge of the pot. Leave the neck of the bulb exposed. Set the pot outside after the last frost. In Zones 7 and higher, some varieties can overwinter outdoors in the ground. Plant those outside in moist soils.

Care & Problems—Keep the soil evenly moist but not wet. In fact, keep the soil on the dry side so that the bulbs don't rot if they are growing in containers. Do not repot until the bulbs are completely potbound. Move inside for winter and place in a bright, cool spot. Cut down on water.

Bloom Color(s)—White, red, pink, bicolor

Bloom Period/Peak Season—Summer

Mature Size (H x W)—24–48 inches x 24 inches

Hardiness—7 and higher (depending on variety)

Water Needs—Low to medium

CROCOSMIA
Crocosmia 'Lucifer'

Why It's Special—Crocosmia looks tropical but it's hardy. I think that's most of its mystique. Bright red trumpet-shaped flowers are borne on gracefully arching stems surrounded by straplike foliage. They are statement plants in the garden when they bloom. Hummingbirds love to sip nectar from the flowers.

How to Plant & Grow—Plant in well-drained soil in full sun to part shade. These plants make the biggest impact when planted in clumps of eight or more bulbs. In cooler Zones (5 to 6) plant in a south-facing landscape bed (the warmest spot in the garden).

Care & Problems—Water to establish. Fertilize after flowering. Spider mites are the biggest problem for crocosmia plants, attacking the foliage, sometimes to the extent that they affect the blooms; use insecticidal soap to control them. Crocosmia can spread rampantly when they're happy. If they get out of hand, dig up the clumps and divide them, passing along extras to a friend.

Bloom Color(s)—Red

Bloom Period/Peak Season—July and August

Mature Size (H x W)—18–24 inches x 24 inches

Hardiness—5–9

Water Needs—Medium

CROCUS
Crocus vernus

Why It's Special—Crocus are often the first bulbs to bloom in spring, and when their purple, yellow, pink, or white flowers open, they're a sight for sore eyes. They're easy to grow and naturalize well in the lawn and landscape.

How to Plant & Grow—Plant in full sun to partial shade in well-drained soil. You can plant them in the lawn or on hillside berms for color if you're willing to let the foliage die back before mowing for the first time in spring. Plant in clumps of 10 or more for the best effect. They also look good in rock gardens.

Care & Problems—The biggest problem with these bulbs is that squirrels will sometimes dig them up as soon as you finish smoothing the soil over a new planting. Spray repellents to deter these pests. You can also plant bulbs in buried chicken wire cages. Leave foliage until it turns brown or yellow.

Bloom Color(s)—Purple, white, yellow, pink

Bloom Period/Peak Season—Early spring

Mature Size (H x W)—6 inches x 6 inches

Hardiness—3–8

Water Needs—Low

DAHLIA
Dahlia x hybrida

Why It's Special—Dahlias have gorgeous, big, exuberant flowers up to dinner plate-size in rich, striking hues. They're not hardy in all of the Mid-Atlantic, but they're easy to keep from year to year.

How to Plant & Grow—Plant in full sun two weeks before the average last frost. Planting depth depends on the plant size you're growing. Smaller bulbs that grow to 2 to 3 feet can be planted 3 to 4 inches deep. Larger bulbs or varieties should be planted 6 to 8 inches deep. Space according to mature size expected as well.

Care & Problems—Water regularly throughout summer. Stake taller varieties. Deadhead to encourage repeat blooming. After a killing frost, dig up the tubers and cut off the foliage. Allow to dry out in the sun for a few days. Dust with fungicide and store in a dark, cool location in damp (but not wet) peat.

Bloom Color(s)—Every color imaginable

Bloom Period/Peak Season—Midsummer to frost

Mature Size (H x W)—1–6 feet x 1–3 feet

Hardiness—7–10

Water Needs—Medium to high

ELEPHANT EARS
Colocasia esculenta

Why It's Special—Though they're not hardy in the Mid-Atlantic, elephant ears add a lot to the landscape, and they're easy to overwinter. 'Black Magic' has dark purple, almost black leaves. 'Mojito' is a green-and-black speckled variety. They're native to Southeast Asia, where the roots are used to make an edible paste.

How to Plant & Grow—Plant in rich, moist soil in full sun to partial shade after the last frost. Leave 4 to 6 feet between bulbs. You can plant them as margin plants along a pond (in up to 6 inches of water).

Care & Problems—Elephant ears are largely problem-free as long as you keep the soil moist throughout the growing season. If leaves get ratty, simply cut them back to the ground. In fall, lift the bulb, cut off all of the foliage, and let it dry for a day. Then store in a cool, dark location in wood shavings (a basement is good).

Bloom Color(s)—Grown for foliage in shades of green, white, purple, and variegated.

Bloom Period/Peak Season—Summer

Mature Size (H x W)—4–6 feet x 4–6 feet

Hardiness—8 and higher; overwinter in the Mid-Atlantic

Water Needs—High

FRITILLARIA
Fritillaria meleagris

Why It's Special—These bulbs have elegant flowers that look like gracefully nodding checkered tulips. When a plant has such an exotic-looking flower, I always think it should be difficult to grow, but these are not. Plant them and forget them until they bloom in April and May. Let them naturalize under a tree or in the perennial garden. They are deer resistant.

How to Plant & Grow—Plant outdoors in rich, evenly moist soil in partial shade for best results. Plant bulbs 3 inches deep in clusters of three to six, leaving 3 to 4 inches between bulbs. Water in fall to encourage rooting. Unlike many bulbs, these actually thrive in moderately damp soil.

Care & Problems—These are easy-care bulbs. Water when they start flowering in spring if you're not getting regular rainfall. Fertilize with multipurpose fertilizer after they finish flowering and allow the foliage to turn yellow before cutting back.

Bloom Color(s)—Burgundy with a checkered pattern, or white

Bloom Period/Peak Season—April to May

Mature Size (H x W)—12–18 inches x 6 inches

Hardiness—3–8

Water Needs—Medium

GLADIOLUS
Gladiolus

Why It's Special—My mother always said she didn't like gladiolus because "they're funeral flowers." And while it is true that these are often found in less-expensive funeral sprays, that doesn't negate the fact that they are wonderful in the garden. Almost nothing is easier to grow than gladiolus, and, well, they *do* make good cut flowers. You can find gladiolus in almost every color imaginable. Plant a mixture for bright summer color.

How to Plant & Grow—Plant bulbs 3 inches deep, 4 to 6 inches apart in full sun after the last frost. You can plant groupings every two weeks for a succession of flowers through summer. They make the biggest impact in mass plantings.

Care & Problems—Gladiolus bloom stalks can become heavy and fall over. Consider constructing a lattice system for the bulbs to grow up through, using stakes and twine to create a crisscross pattern. Pull up and compost after they bloom.

Bloom Color(s)—Every color imaginable

Bloom Period/Peak Season—Summer

Mature Size (H x W)—24–36 inches x 4 inches

Hardiness—7–10; grow as an annual in much of the Mid-Atlantic

Water Needs—Medium to low

GRAPE HYACINTH
Muscari armeniacum

Why It's Special—Grape hyacinths are old-fashioned bulbs that look right at home in the cottage garden, interplanted with pansies and violas, or massed in containers for a big impact in the spring. They naturalize well in the landscape, and are ideal for creating sweeps of color. They get their common name from the look of the flower clusters—like small bunches of grapes.

How to Plant & Grow—Plant in full sun to partial shade, 3 to 4 inches deep, in fall. Plant bulbs in clusters of ten or more, leaving 2 to 3 inches between each bulb. These are most effective when planted in clumps or masses. You can pot up some Muscari and leave them in the garage for a cooling treatment. Bring them indoors in January, set them in a sunny spot, and enjoy their blooms.

Care & Problems—Water after planting to encourage rooting. These bulbs are fairly carefree. Make sure to let the foliage yellow before cutting back in early summer. Bulbs may sprout new foliage in fall.

Bloom Color(s)—Blue, purple

Bloom Period/Peak Season—Spring

Mature Size (H x W)—6 inches x 2 inches

Hardiness—4–8

Water Needs—Low

HYACINTH
Hyacinthus orientalis

Why It's Special—Hyacinths are some of the most fragrant flowers you can grow. Some people really enjoy the fragrance, while others find it off-putting. If you want to have a cottage garden, hyacinths are a must. A fun fact: hyacinths are one of the few plants that will grow under a black walnut tree.

How to Plant & Grow—Plant bulbs in fall, 5 inches deep and 4 to 6 inches apart, in full sun to partial shade. Water to encourage bulbs to grow a strong root system. For the best effect, plant these in groups of five to seven bulbs.

Care & Problems—Water while the bulbs are sprouting in spring. Deadhead after flowering and allow foliage to persist during spring until it turns yellow, at which point you can cut it back to the ground. Fertilize after bloom while foliage is still green. Hyacinths perform best with some water during their active growing season, but soil should remain on the dry side while these bulbs are dormant.

Bloom Color(s)—Pink, white, purple

Bloom Period/Peak Season—April

Mature Size (H x W)—8–12 inches x 4 inches

Hardiness—4–8

Water Needs—Low

IRIS, BEARDED
Iris germanica

Why It's Special—Bearded iris is the plant on this book's front cover. These gorgeous perennials come in almost every imaginable color and color combination. I have a dear friend who collects them. They're spectacular!

How to Plant & Grow—Plant iris outside July to September in full sun to partial shade (afternoon shade in hotter climates) in well-drained soil. The top of the iris rhizome should just barely peek out of the soil. Space at 12 inches.

Care & Problems—Dig up the entire clump in July to September and divide by breaking apart the rhizomes. Trim the foliage back to 4 to 6 inches, cut off any rotten or shriveled rhizomes, and reset. Water to establish the plants, but stop watering once established unless your area is experiencing drought. Iris borers hatch in spring. Keep an eye out for small white caterpillars and crush them before they can burrow into the plants.

Bloom Color(s)—Every imaginable color

Bloom Period/Peak Season—Late spring to early summer

Mature Size (H x W)—Plant heights are between 12–24 inches. Plants naturalize into clumps up to 2–3 feet wide.

Hardiness—Hardy Zones 3 and higher

Water Needs—Low once established

IRIS, SIBERIAN
Iris sibirica

Why It's Special—Siberian irises display the best characteristics of Japanese iris and bearded iris, combined. The flowers look like more delicate versions of bearded iris, but they have the same grasslike foliage that characterizes Japanese iris. Their bright blue or purple flowers blend well with other water-loving perennials. 'Butter and Sugar' is a yellow-and-white-flowering cultivar. 'Ceasar's Brother' has dark blue-purple flowers and blooms in June. 'Chilled Wine' blooms with dark burgundy red flowers.

How to Plant & Grow—Plant in spring or fall in full sun in rich, moist soil. Space plants 12 to 18 inches apart. Water to establish. These plants make the biggest impact when planted in masses.

Care & Problems—These plants are fairly trouble-free. Keep the soil moist as they're becoming established. They can be divided in fall if the clumps outgrow the space allotted in the garden.

Bloom Color(s)—Shades of purple and blue

Bloom Period/Peak Season—Late spring to early summer

Mature Size (H x W)—12–36 inches x 12–24 inches (when grown in clumps)

Hardiness—3–8

Water Needs—High

NARCISSUS
Narcissus spp. and cultivars

Why It's Special—Narcissus (also called daffodil or jonquil) is the definitive harbinger of spring. When these bulbs start blooming, you know there's light at the end of the tunnel. They're easy to grow and deer resistant. Plant early-, mid-, and late-flowering varieties so that you have some blooming from mid-March through mid-May.

How to Plant & Grow—Plant narcissus outside in full or part sun in fall. Plant bulbs at a depth of three times the height of the bulb. These make the most impact when planted in clumps of three or more bulbs.

Care & Problems—Daffodils have few pest and disease problems. After the bulbs flower, fertilize with a multipurpose fertilizer and cut the flower stalks back to the ground. Allow leaves to yellow before cutting them back. Lift and divide clumps after flowering every four to five years.

Bloom Color(s)—Yellow, white, orange, peach, pink, bicolors, tricolors

Bloom Period/Peak Season—Mid-March through early May

Mature Size (H x W)—6–18 inches x 2–4 inches (for individual plants)

Hardiness—4–8; select varieties that grow in your hardiness zone.

Water Needs—Low

IRIS, JAPANESE
Iris ensata

Why It's Special—All iris are showy and beautiful. Japanese iris grow best in moist soils and can even be grown in pots in water gardens. Their straplike foliage is quite similar to that of an ornamental grass, but with the added bonus of lovely summer blooms. The flowers are clearly iris, but flat-topped as opposed to vertical in nature.

How to Plant & Grow—Plant in full sun to partial shade after the last frost in spring. Plant the rhizomes 2 inches deep and 6 inches apart. Japanese iris do best with wet feet in summer, but drier conditions in winter. They grow well at the edges of bog gardens.

Care & Problems—Provide extra water during summer. Divide plants every three years in fall by digging up the whole plant and using a clean, sharp knife to cut apart the rhizomes, leaving at least one fan of leaves per rhizome and replanting.

Bloom Color(s)—Blue, purple, white, bicolors

Bloom Period/Peak Season—Summer

Mature Size (H x W)—36 inches x 6 inches (individual plants, but they're usually grown in clumps)

Hardiness—4–9

Water Needs—Medium to high

ORIENTAL LILY
Lilium 'Stargazer'

Why It's Special—Oriental lilies, particularly 'Stargazer', seem almost too good to be true in the garden. They're fragrant, with large, upward-facing flowers the size of a salad plate. They make excellent cut flowers, but they're splashy when planted among other perennials too. You'd think they'd be difficult to grow, but they're not. If you cut them to bring inside, pinch the pollen capsules off so they don't stain your counters red.

How to Plant & Grow—Plant bulbs outside in full or part sun in early summer or fall. (If you plant in early summer, the bulbs will flower the same year you plant them.) Leave 8 to 12 inches between bulbs and plant bulbs 6 to 8 inches deep.

Care & Problems—Water bulbs after planting to encourage rooting. Before flowers open, place stakes to support stems. Fertilize after flowering. The bulbs and the flowers are highly attractive to small mammals. Spray with repellents.

Bloom Color(s)—'Stargazer' is pink and white. Other Oriental lilies are orange, yellow, red, or white.

Bloom Period/Peak Season—Summer

Mature Size (H x W)—4 feet x 8 inches

Hardiness—5–9

Water Needs—Medium to low

RANUNCULUS
Ranunculus asiaticus

Why It's Special—Ranunculus are popular wedding bouquet flowers. Their very form is so romantic—rosettes of hundreds of petals, almost peony-like. They hold up well as cut flowers. Though you have to grow these bulbs as annuals, they're so pretty and striking, they're worth the effort.

How to Plant & Grow—Plant outside, 6 inches deep, in well-drained soil in full sun three weeks before the last frost. They are easy to grow as long as they are not in waterlogged soil. You can also plant in containers at the same time for a spring bloom. They make the biggest impact when planted in clusters of 10 or more. Space 3 to 6 inches apart.

Care & Problems—The trick is to plant ranunculus early enough that they have the chance to grow and bloom before summer heat sets in. Water to keep the soil moist, but not soggy. When plants are finished blooming, pull them up and compost.

Bloom Color(s)—White, yellow, pink, burgundy, red, orange, bicolors

Bloom Period/Peak Season—Spring

Mature Size (H x W)—12–24 inches x 12–24 inches

Hardiness—8–10; grow as an annual

Water Needs—Medium

SNOWDROPS
Galanthus nivalis

Why It's Special—Snowdrops are some of the earliest-blooming bulbs, making their appearance from late February through late March. They naturalize into clumps in the perennial garden, underneath trees, or in the lawn. They're deer resistant and not particularly attractive to squirrels, so if you want early blooms but have problems with critters eating your crocus bulbs, try planting snowdrops.

How to Plant & Grow—Plant outside in full sun to part shade in fall along with other spring-blooming bulbs. Snowdrops make the biggest impact when planted in clusters of five to ten bulbs in several places around the garden. Plant bulbs 3 to 4 inches deep. They look stunning when emerging from dense green groundcovers.

Care & Problems—Allow bulbs to naturalize. Do not cut back foliage until it has turned yellow. You can dig bulbs up and divide clumps every four to five years after the bulbs finish blooming in spring. Fertilize with a multipurpose fertilizer after flowering.

Bloom Color(s)—White

Bloom Period/Peak Season—Late winter

Mature Size (H x W)—Individual plants 6 inches x 2–3 inches

Hardiness—3–7 (In Zone 8, plant leucojum instead.)

Water Needs—Low to medium

SPANISH BLUEBELLS
Hyacinthoides hispanica

Why It's Special—Some bulbs are fussy, not hardy, require overwintering indoors, or they fade out after a couple of years, but Spanish bluebells are none of those things. They're easy to grow and bloom with hyacinth-like spikes of blue flowers in spring. I love plants that give you a big show for little work. They're also deer resistant. Bonus!

How to Plant & Grow—Plant bulbs in full sun to partial shade in fall. Plant 4 to 6 inches deep and 4 inches apart. They will naturalize well under a tree or in a landscape border. You'll often see these bulbs growing in huge sweeps. Because their foliage dies back, plant masses where the lack of greenery won't be a problem during the summer. Water to establish.

Care & Problems—These plants are easy to grow and largely problem-free. Feed with an all-purpose fertilizer at the conclusion of the spring bloom. Wait until foliage turns brown to cut back. If clumps get large, you can divide and reset them after flowering in spring, or wait until fall.

Bloom Color(s)—Blue, pink, and white

Bloom Period/Peak Season—Spring

Mature Size (H x W)—8–18 inches x 8–12 inches

Hardiness—3–8

Water Needs—Medium

SQUILL
Scilla siberica

Why It's Special—As one of the first bulbs to bloom in spring, Siberian squill flowers are a welcome sight. They're resistant to deer—always a plus. Plant them in broad sweeps and let them naturalize in the lawn, border, or under trees. For a truly eye-catching display, plant in combination with winter aconite. These bulbs spread via offsets and self-seed.

How to Plant & Grow—Plant in fall in full sun to partial shade. Plant bulbs 3 to 4 inches deep and 3 to 4 inches apart. Create drifts within the garden or landscape, when possible. These are excellent for rock gardens. Water at planting to encourage roots to establish.

Care & Problems—These bulbs have few pest problems. Let foliage die back before trimming in spring. If you're letting them naturalize in the lawn, plant somewhere that you can wait to mow until the plants go dormant. Dig up and divide clumps after flowering every four to six years.

Bloom Color(s)—Blue

Bloom Period/Peak Season—Late winter to early spring

Mature Size (H x W)—6 inches x 6 inches

Hardiness—2–8

Water Needs—Low

SURPRISE LILY
Lycoris squamigera

Why It's Special—Sometimes called "naked ladies" or "resurrection lilies," surprise lilies bloom in summer, seemingly out of nowhere. The leaves sprout in spring and then die back, so you're forgiven if you forget they're there. Flowers emerge in late summer on long, "naked" stems. They make for a fun surprise in the perennial garden.

How to Plant & Grow—Plant in fall in full sun in well-drained soil. Leave 6 inches between bulbs and plant 6 inches deep. Water at the time of planting to encourage rooting. Water when foliage appears, but stop when it dies back before the flower stalk sprouts. For best effect, plant among perennials with nice foliage. While the naked stems are a novelty, they're not the most attractive.

Care & Problems—Mark the planting spot with a golf tee. That way you won't accidentally plant something on top of them. Cut the foliage back after it turns brown and dries up.

Bloom Color(s)—Light pink

Bloom Period/Peak Season—Late summer

Mature Size (H x W)—2 feet x 6 inches

Hardiness—5–9

Water Needs—Medium

TULIP
Tulipa spp. and cultivars

Why It's Special—There is almost nothing more beautiful than a big sweep of tulip flowers in spring. If you are organized about your selections, you can enjoy tulips blooming for up to six weeks. There are standard tulips with smooth, round petals. Parrot types have color breaks and ruffled petals. Doubles are usually short with peony-like blooms.

How to Plant & Grow—Plant in fall in full sun in moist, well-drained soil. Plant bulbs 4 to 6 inches deep and leave 4 to 6 inches between bulbs. Tulips really look best when mass-planted. Water at the time of planting to encourage rooting.

Care & Problems—Tulips require a cold treatment to bloom. If growing in warmer areas (Zones 7 and 8), select varieties that have proven track records in those zones. If growing as annuals, pull up after flowering. If they're being allowed to perennialize, let foliage yellow before cutting it back.

Bloom Color(s)—Every color imaginable, including bicolors

Bloom Period/Peak Season—Spring

Mature Size (H x W)—6–24 inches x 4 inches (individual flower)

Hardiness—3–8, but unless growing the species, easier to grow as annuals

Water Needs—Medium

WINDFLOWER
Anemone coronaria

Why It's Special—Windflowers are striking when mass-planted in the landscape. These are perfect flowers to bridge the gap between spring bloomers and summer color. They're hardy in Zones 7 and higher, but they can be grown as container plantings or annuals in the rest of the Mid-Atlantic.

How to Plant & Grow—Plant outside in fall in Zones 7 and higher. Plant in pots or outside in early spring (April) in Zones 6 and lower for an early-summer bloom. Bulbs are small (about the size of grapes), so plant shallowly (1 to 2 inches deep) and in masses. You can dig a 12-inch-wide hole or trench and sprinkle several bulbs in it.

Care & Problems—Plant, water, and wait for them to sprout. Once they're finished flowering, in Zones 6 and lower, pull them up and toss them in the compost. They'll perennialize in warmer areas, but not reliably. You can always just replant.

Bloom Color(s)—Purple, blue, red, white, lavender, bicolors

Bloom Period/Peak Season—Late spring to early summer

Mature Size (H x W)—24 inches x 8–12 inches

Hardiness—7 and higher

Water Needs—Medium

WINTER ACONITE
Eranthis hyemalis

Why It's Special—The cheerful yellow blooms of winter aconite signal the coming end to winter and the arrival of spring. They are some of the first bulbs to bloom, after snowdrops. They are easy to grow and naturalize well in the landscape, especially because they're deer resistant. You can see an absolutely spectacular display of these flowers along the hillsides of the gardens at Winterthur in Delaware.

How to Plant & Grow—Soak tubers overnight and plant outside in fall. Select a location that has full sun in later winter, but increasing shade throughout summer. (These bulbs thrive under trees.) Plant 3 inches deep with 3 to 4 inches between tubers. Water at planting to encourage establishment.

Care & Problems—Water bulbs as foliage sprouts in spring, through flowering. Allow foliage to yellow before cutting back. You can fertilize with an all-purpose fertilizer after flowering. Do not move or divide—simply allow them to spread in the garden.

Bloom Color(s)—Yellow

Bloom Period/Peak Season—Late winter to early spring

Mature Size (H x W)—4–6 inches x 4–6 inches

Hardiness—3–7

Water Needs—Medium

BULBS MONTH-BY-MONTH

JANUARY

- Force some bulbs into bloom to beat the winter blahs. Paperwhites are easy to grow. Spread a shallow layer of gravel in a dish. Fill with water so that the top of the water just reaches the top of the rocks. Set paperwhite bulbs on top of the rocks. Place the bulbs in a cool, dark location. Once they've grown roots, bring them out to a sunny windowsill. Keep the water level constant.

- If you have any amaryllis that haven't started growing yet, stop watering them and move them to a bright location. They will most likely start to sprout. You can start to water sparingly once the flower stalk starts growing. If the bulbs don't sprout, chuck them in the compost pile!

- Cut the flower stalks off any amaryllis that have stopped blooming and allow the leaves to grow. Water once with half-strength liquid fertilizer, then let the soil dry out. Water only when dry.

FEBRUARY

- Order summer- and fall-flowering bulbs. Oriental lilies, fritillaria, dahlias, and gladiolus are summer bloomers. Colchicum are fall-bloomers. Check out specialty bulb catalogs for unusual varieties.

- Compost paperwhites after they finish blooming.

- Take a walk around the garden. You might start seeing the earliest bloomers starting to pop up out of the ground. Snowdrops, winter aconite, and crocus are likely candidates for early emergence. You can gently pull dead leaves and debris away from foliage to let sunlight in.

- Bring potted bulbs inside to begin forcing into bloom.

MARCH

- Pot up summer-flowering bulbs to give them a head start. Tuberous begonias, caladium, and dahlias will all put on a bigger show in the garden if they are already growing by the time they get outside. Keep the soil barely damp until the plants start to sprout leaves.

- Check areas where bulbs are planted in the garden. If you're growing bulbs that deer and small mammals enjoy munching, be vigilant about spraying repellents as soon as the foliage starts growing. Reapply every two weeks as the bulbs grow.

- Remove mulch and winter debris from around spring bulbs only if temperatures are regularly above freezing.

APRIL

- Fertilize bulbs immediately after they finish flowering. Cut back flower stalks and allow leaves to grow, storing food in the bulb for next year's bloom.

- Begin watering bulbs that have not bloomed as they start actively growing.

- Remove any remaining mulch cover from around and above spring-flowering bulbs.

- Spray deer repellent on emerging tulip foliage.

- Apply insecticides to control iris borers.

MAY

- Dig up, divide, and transplant any spring-blooming bulbs that you want to move around.

- Allow foliage to persist until it turns yellow. You can cut back any bulb foliage that has declined.

- Start planting gladiolus every two to three weeks. By staggering the plantings, you'll be able to enjoy the blooms for a longer period.

- Plant tropical foliage bulbs outside for the summer, including elephant ears and caladium.

- These tropical plants grow to be large, so give them plenty of room to spread out. Elephant ears, caladium, and cannas all like fairly moist soil. They pair well with hardy bananas and papyrus, which also thrive in moist conditions.

JUNE

- Harden off and transplant the summer-flowering bulbs you potted up in April into garden locations.

- Plant one more row or clump of gladiolus bulbs for late-summer flowering.

- Trim back the last of the foliage from spring-flowering bulbs. Try not to directly water spring-blooming bulbs during the summer. If they sit in water, they will rot.

- Pull up tulips and discard them.

- Pinch the growing tips from dahlia plants to encourage branching. Stake tall flowering bulbs before flowers open so the plants don't flop open.

- Continue to spray deer and rabbit repellent to bulb foliage.

JULY

- Plant fall-blooming bulbs and water them to encourage rooting.

- Cut stems of lilies (before the flowers open) to enjoy inside. Cut dahlias when the flowers are fully open and gladiolas when you can see the flower color but before the flowers are open.

- Order spring-blooming bulbs for fall planting. Most spring bulbs put on the biggest show when planted in masses. Instead of ordering 20 daffodils, order 100! It seems like it will be a lot of work to plant, but the show next spring will be so worth it.

- Continue applying deer repellent.

AUGUST

- Divide iris. Dig up the plants, trim the leaf fans back by half and use a sharp knife to separate rhizomes. Discard any rotten or shriveled rhizomes. Replant, ensuring that the top of the rhizome is barely visible above the soil. Water to encouraging rooting.

- Deadhead summer-flowering bulbs to encourage the plants to continue to bloom (dahlias) or put energy into storage for next year's bloom (lilies).

- Cut off scraggly foliage from elephant ears, caladium, and other tropical bulbs.

- If you're planning to discard gladiolas rather than overwinter them, pull up the corms as they finish flowering.

SEPTEMBER

- Dig up tender tropical bulbs and prepare them for storage. Cut off all leaves and brush off the soil. Allow to cure in the sun for a day. Then pack in wood shavings or peat moss for winter.

- Dig up and pot bulbs to overwinter. Tuberous begonias, caladium, and calla lilies will grow well indoors through winter.

- Bring clivia inside for winter.

- Stop watering amaryllis bulbs and allow them to go dormant.

OCTOBER

- Plant spring-blooming bulbs now. If deer or squirrels are a problem, spray repellents on the bulbs when planting. Water to encourage the bulbs to establish roots.

- Pull up any tender bulbs that you aren't planning to overwinter and compost them.

- Take some time to admire fall-blooming bulbs such as colchicum. We can get so caught up in garden cleanup that we forget to enjoy what is still putting on a show.

- Keep amaryllis bulbs outside in a protected location to get a cold treatment, or bring inside to the garage. Cut off old foliage.

NOVEMBER

- Pot up spring-blooming bulbs for forcing. Daffodils, hyacinth, tulips, crocus, and grape hyacinth are all good candidates. Plant them in lightweight potting soil and water until the soil is barely moist to encourage rooting. Store in a cool (35 degrees Fahrenheit), dark place. Covered in the garage is a good place for these bulbs.

- Mulch outdoor bulb beds for winter protection.

DECEMBER

- Pot up amaryllis for holiday blooming. Bring the amaryllis you forced into dormancy back into the house and observe it. As soon as it starts pushing up a flower stalk you can begin to water sparingly.

- Put together pots of paperwhite bulbs for holiday gifts. You can plant paperwhites in shallow pots or you can assemble decorative dishes of bulbs resting on smooth, polished pebbles or glass stones. Include a card with watering instructions. Bulbs planted in soil should be kept barely damp. Bulbs resting on top of pebbles can be watered so that the water just barely touches the bottoms of the bulbs resting on the stones.

PERENNIALS &
ORNAMENTAL
GRASSES
for the Mid-Atlantic

erennials are—or should be—the backbone of every garden. They live for a long time, require less care (in general) than annuals and bulbs, and come in an amazing variety of colors, textures, shapes, and sizes. I've grouped ornamental grasses with perennials in this chapter because, for the most part, ornamental grasses are used in the landscape as perennials or with perennials. They have similar maintenance requirements as well. So unless specified, consider the maintenance issues discussed in relation to perennials to be the same for ornamental grasses.

The perennials featured are plants that have stellar reputations. They provide long-season interest, are easy to care for, grow with little fuss, are pest resistant, or offer a combination thereof. It would be hard to choose a favorite. My problem (and maybe yours too) is that I don't have room to grow them *all* at the same time.

Some of these plants are listed by their species with some notable cultivars mentioned. There are a lot of unique cultivars for almost all species of perennials—some offer variegated leaves, others a different, usually smaller size, or unusual flower color. There isn't room to list them all here, but do some digging when you're plant shopping to see what you can find.

SOURCING PERENNIALS

You can buy seeds for perennial plants. If possible, though, I'd recommend buying 4-inch, quart-, or gallon-sized plants from the garden center or home-improvement store. Perennials have fairly particular requirements for germination, including a period of cold, a period of cold and damp, actual freezing, scarification (nicking the seed coat), or soaking before planting. Because the plants live a longer time, you can basically amortize the cost over a period of years.

The one exception to growing perennials from seed is to winter-sow seeds in a cutting garden or wildflower garden and let them be. I've ended up with some beautiful purple coneflowers, among other things. You can also sow seeds in the summer and hope for them to sprout the next spring.

A mixed perennial border.

When planting a new perennial garden, measure to ensure that you purchase enough plants and mulch to eventually fill the bed.

Before digging holes, set plants in the garden where you plan to plant them so that you can adjust their spacing, if necessary.

You can buy perennials in garden centers, home-improvement stories, or via mail order. Read the reviews carefully before mail ordering. Sometimes all you'll get is a root. I have had good success with a few companies, and they're listed in the resources section.

If you purchase a perennial to grow in a pot or window box, remember to subtract a zone from the plant's marked hardiness. Without the insulating factor of in-ground soil, the plant will be slightly less cold hardy.

DESIGNING WITH PERENNIALS

Some perennials bloom continuously for three to six weeks and then are done for the year. Others can be deadheaded and coaxed into blooming for a little bit longer. There are some that you can cut back to encourage a second bloom later in the season, and others bloom twice on their own. That makes designing with perennials a bit more challenging, because you want to create a garden that has interesting blooms or foliage throughout most of the spring, summer, fall, and even a smidge for the winter. (Ornamental grasses really up the *ooooh* factor for gardens in the winter.) You'll still apply the same principles of color, form, and

Dig a hole that is just as deep as the plant's rootball and 1½ times as wide. Backfill with the same soil you removed from the planting hole. Do not amend the soil.

texture (also see page 18) when designing with perennials, but you have to factor bloom time into your plans.

I like to think of design in terms of creating plant combos like you'd do for a container garden, but with perennials, the plants are in the ground, not in a pot. Try to mix colors, forms, and textures within the combos.

Here's an example:

A burgundy heuchera, apricot-flowered agastache, and silver-blue fescue will combine well. All of the plants can take sun, and need well-drained soil. The heuchera has a coarser texture, with larger leaves, the agastache adds some height, and the blue fescue adds some fluffy, wispy texture.

You can repeat this combo throughout a garden bed to create a border, or you can add on to the combo by repeating the attributes displayed in the first few plants you selected.

Introduce some more apricot color through sun coleus or heuchera with apricot leaves. That also repeats the coarse texture. Add more height and continue the silver-blue color by planting some Russian sage. Almost nothing adds the same sort of texture that ornamental grasses provide, but there are some gold-brown-colored sedges that blend well with apricot- or rusty-colored flowers that can add additional texture.

While you're adding, think about when the plants you're selecting will be interesting in the garden. Foliage plants look great all summer. Blooming perennials, unless they have interesting foliage, should be integrated based on bloom time. When possible, get plants that do double duty in the garden, such as *Amsonia hubrichtii*, which has gorgeous blue flowers in spring, and the foliage turns rusty gold in fall, putting on a great show when most everything else is slowing down. Well, this is that plant's way of slowing down, but it goes out with a bang!

Design the plants to "talk" to each other with compatible colors, but select plants that repeat an element or two in one of the other plants in the design. You'll quickly achieve a harmonious look.

PLANTING PERENNIALS

There are two main planting seasons for perennials: spring and fall. When possible, avoid planting during the heat of summer. Fall is an excellent time to plant because you can often get plants on sale. They'll become established and then, the next spring, will be as large as they would have been if you'd planted them the previous spring, but at half the price! Unless indicated in the plant description, wait until after the last frost when spring planting.

There is no need to fertilize or backfill the planting hole with compost. Dig a hole that is one and a half times the rootball of the plant and just as deep. Plant, then backfill with the same soil you took out of the hole, making sure that the crown of the plant (where the roots meet the stem) is aboveground (otherwise the plant can rot). Water to establish.

CARING FOR PERENNIALS

Perennials don't require much care, but they do require specific care at certain times during their growth cycle. From pruning to deadheading to cutting back and dividing, here's how to keep perennials healthy.

Deadhead perennials regularly (remove the spent flowers) to keep the plants blooming longer and to encourage plants to put energy back into growing strong root systems, as opposed to producing seeds.

DEADHEADING

Deadheading perennials is as much about cosmetic value as it is for keeping blooming going. Some plants simply don't rebloom. Peonies are an example: they bloom in the spring, and when they're done, they're done. We deadhead to improve the appearance of the plant, not so that it will rebloom. Some perennial salvias are the opposite. Their flower heads are actually attractive, so it wouldn't be bad to leave them on the plants, but if you deadhead, you can spur a repeat bloom later in the season.

PRUNING

Pruning is different than deadheading. You can prune perennials to control size and delay flowering. Some people like to prune and others don't. I think it's a matter of personal preference. I have some enormous perennial sunflowers that grow to be upward of 7 feet tall. If I prune them in July, they'll stay more compact at 4 to 5 feet and they'll bloom later. Sometimes I prune a few of the plants and let some of the others go for staggered bloom times and sizes. The year I pruned them all

You can create your own lattice for staking with string and bamboo stakes.

I missed my fall-blooming giants. The plants were too well behaved—they still bloomed profusely, but they were much shorter and less blowsy and floppy. If you want more compact perennials, then prune. If you like them to be a little wild, don't.

In general, if you want to prune to control size and flowering, cut the plants back by one-third two months before they would normally flower. Always cut back to just above a leaf.

STAKING

Perennials with tall flower stalks and heavy flowers sometimes need staking. For the record, if you prune perennials, they are less likely to need staking. That's not necessarily the best reason to prune, though.

When you stake, avoid the "cinched belt" look. Do not just tie a string around the outside of the plant and yank it tight. Here are some alternatives:

- Lattice: This is discussed in the introduction to the bulbs chapter. You can create a lattice of twine and stakes for the plants to grow through. They'll have support, but they'll still have a natural look.
- Single stake per plant (star method): Push a bamboo stake into the ground. If the plant has one main flowering stem, loosely tie the stem to the stake. If it has multiple flowering stems, you can use individual strings looped from the stems to the stake to allow the plant to still have a more open appearance.

DIVIDING

Some perennials will bloom happily for years without being divided, while others need to be dug up every three to five years. If you notice a plant starting to die out in the center, it has outgrown its space, or blooming is declining overall, dig it up, chop it in half, and replant. You can gift the extra piece to a friend. The best times to divide are spring and fall, just like the best times to plant. If a plant has unique requirements for dividing, those are listed in the profiles.

PESTS

The perennials in this chapter are here, for the most part, because they aren't big pest magnets. I find that if you grow a variety of plants, pests aren't a huge problem. Snails, slugs, Japanese beetles, aphids, deer, and small mammals are the main pest problems for perennials.

You can combat slugs with diatomaceous earth sprinkled around the plants. Try repellents for deer and mammals. Aphids can sometimes be blasted off with a strong spray of water or treated with insecticidal soap. Japanese beetles are the most difficult to control. Some people swear by traps, while others say the traps just attract more beetles to the yard. Sometimes you just have to wait it out.

Create a slug trap by pouring beer into a shallow lid sunk into the ground next to the plant.

Go beyond the sunny garden border. Here are some perennials for tricky areas and times of the year.

PERENNIALS THAT LIKE WET FEET

Cardinal flower
Cordgrass
Hardy hibiscus
Ligularia
Rodgersia
Siberian iris
Spiderwort
Toad lily
Turtlehead

SHADE PERENNIALS

Astilbe
Coral bells
False solomon's seal
Ferns
Foam flower
Goats beard
Hosta
Lenten rose
Lungwort
Siberian bugloss
Solomon's seal
Toad lily

FALL BLOOMING PERENNIALS

Boneset
Joe-pye weed
Liriope
Ornamental grasses
Russian sage
Sedum 'Autumn Joy'
Swamp sunflowers
Toad Lily

AGASTACHE

Agastache spp.

Why It's Special—If I were to select a favorite perennial, it would be *Agastache*. Two different types are commonly grown: anise hyssop (*Agastache foeniculum*) has more tender green leaves and purple or white flowers, while hummingbird sage (*Agastache aurantiaca*) has smaller, gray-tinged leaves and peachy pink flowers. They're all drought tolerant and deer resistant. As plants in the mint family, its flowers and foliage are fragrant and can be cut for bouquets.

How to Plant & Grow—Plant outside in spring after frost. Anise hyssop can grow in part shade in moderately moist to dry soils. Hummingbird sage should be planted in full sun in well-drained to dry soils. Leave 18 inches between plants.

Care & Problems—Let soil dry out between watering. Neither type needs fertilizer. Deadhead to prolong bloom. Wait until midwinter to cut back, when you know the plants are fully dormant.

Bloom Color(s)—Peach, pink, white, purple

Bloom Period/Peak Season—Mid- to late summer

Mature Size (H x W)—12–36 inches x 12–18 inches

Hardiness—*A. foeniculum*, Zone 5 and above; *A. aurantiaca*, Zone 6 and above

Water Needs—Medium to low

AMSONIA

Amsonia spp.

Why It's Special—Amsonia is a three-season perennial that could stand to see more use in the garden. All species and cultivars have gorgeous true blue flowers and yellow fall leaf color. *Amsonia hubrichtii* has threadlike foliage that adds an interesting texture to the garden. Individual stalks look like fluffy branches on a miniature white pine tree. This type looks absolutely spectacular in fall when grown *en masse* on a hillside.

How to Plant & Grow—Plant in full sun to partial shade after the last frost. Plants are happiest in moist but well-drained soils. Leave 18 to 24 inches between plants.

Care & Problems—Amsonia has few pest problems. Water regularly to establish. After its first year, plants are much more drought tolerant. Leave the plants standing in fall and winter for their golden foliage. Cut back in spring before new foliage begins growing. Then, cut the plants back by one-third after they finish blooming to encourage them to grow into compact mounds.

Bloom Color(s)—Shades of blue

Bloom Period/Peak Season—Early summer

Mature Size (H x W)—1–3 feet x 1–3 feet

Hardiness—4–9 depending on species

Water Needs—Medium to low

AROMATIC ASTER

Symphyotrichum oblongifolium

Why It's Special—Aromatic asters are natives that put on a spectacular show in fall. Purple flowers cascade in mounds, creating a big splash when mass-planted. Because they're late bloomers, the flowers provide an important source of food for pollinator insects at a time when buffet choices are limited. It's also the host plant for the endangered silvery checkerspot butterfly. 'October Skies' is a compact-grower with light lavender flowers.

How to Plant & Grow—Plant in full sun in well-drained soil after the last frost. Leave 24 inches between plants. Plant with rudbeckias, boneset, and other prairie wildflowers. It tolerates heavy clay soils but doesn't do well with constantly wet feet.

Care & Problems—Water to establish, but after establishment, provide supplemental water only during drought. Do not fertilize. These plants are fairly trouble-free; they might require staking if they grow tall and flop over. Cut back in winter after a plant is fully dormant.

Bloom Color(s)—Purple

Bloom Period/Peak Season—Late summer to early fall

Mature Size (H x W)—3 feet x 3 feet

Hardiness—3–8

Water Needs—Low

ARTEMISIA 'POWIS CASTLE'

Artemisia 'Powis Castle'

Why It's Special—The feathery silver foliage of 'Powis Castle' adds beautiful texture to the perennial garden. Pair with the apricot flowers of hummingbird sage and the needlelike foliage of blue fescue for a stunning combination. As with all silver-leafed plants, it makes a splash when paired with plants that have burgundy leaves. It is deer resistant and has fragrant foliage.

How to Plant & Grow—Plant in full sun after the last frost. Artemisia grows best in well-drained soils. It can be susceptible to root rot in poorly drained soils, and will stretch out and flop over in shady conditions. Leave 12 to 18 inches between plants.

Care & Problems—Water to establish. Plants are much more drought tolerant after they are well rooted and will not need supplemental water unless drought conditions persist. Cut back by one-third partway through the summer. Do not cut all the way to the ground. In spring, wait for new growth to emerge before trimming off old, dead growth.

Bloom Color(s)—Grown for silver foliage

Bloom Period/Peak Season—Summer

Mature Size (H x W)—2 feet x 2 feet

Hardiness—6–9

Water Needs—Low

ASTILBE

Astilbe spp.

Why It's Special—Any plant that thrives in full shade is a winner to me. Astilbe blooms with plumy flower spikes on top of deep green, glossy leaves. *Astilbe japonica* 'Deutschland' has feathery flower spikes that resemble goatsbeard. *Astilbe chinensis* 'Visions' blooms with dense, fluffy flower clusters that look like they're made from chenille. Mass-plant for a striking show or interplant with other shade perennials, including hosta, goatsbeard, and ferns.

How to Plant & Grow—Plant in partial to full shade in spring after the last frost or in early fall (leaving time for the plants to root before the first frost). Leave 12 to 18 inches between plants.

Care & Problems—Keep soil evenly moist. Cut flower stalks back to the ground after they're finished blooming to tidy up the plant. You can cut the entire plants back midwinter when they're fully dormant. Fertilize with 10-10-10 in fall.

Bloom Color(s)—White, pink, red, lavender

Bloom Period/Peak Season—Spring to fall, depending on species or cultivar. (No species blooms that long, but different types have different bloom times.)

Mature Size (H x W)—1–3 feet x 1–2 feet

Hardiness—4–8

Water Needs—Medium to high

AUTUMN SAGE

Salvia greggii

Why It's Special—I'm an equal-opportunity salvia lover. Birds and butterflies love this plant too. Also called "Texas sage" or "bush sage," autumn sage is a woody perennial salvia native to the Southwest. It's deer and rabbit resistant and drought tolerant. 'Furman's Red' has scarlet flowers. 'Lipstick' flowers are bubble-gum pink.

How to Plant & Grow—Plant in full sun in well-drained soils after last frost. Leave 12 to 18 inches between plants. It can also be grown in containers.

Care & Problems—Water to establish, but once established, let soil dry out before watering again. Plants do not like wet feet. No extra fertilizer is required. Deadhead to prolong bloom. Prune back in spring once new growth appears. Autumn sage can be killed back to the ground in colder clients. Wait awhile after the weather warms before pulling up the plant because it could resprout.

Bloom Color(s)—Red, white, purple, bicolors

Bloom Period/Peak Season—Midsummer to fall

Mature Size (H x W)—1–3 feet x 1–3 feet

Hardiness—6–10 (depends on the cultivar; check before buying. 'Furman's Red' is the most cold tolerant)

Water Needs—Low

BAPTISIA
Baptisia australis

Why It's Special—This native perennial blooms in spring with blue flower spikes that resemble smaller, looser lupine flower stalks. *Baptisia alba* is a closely related species with white flowers. *Baptisia sphaerocarpa* has yellow flowers. After blooming, seedpods form that rattle when blown by the wind, adding an element of sound. It is drought tolerant, rabbit resistant, and easily grows in poor soils. Baptisia attracts butterflies.

How to Plant & Grow—Plant in full sun to partial shade after the last frost or in fall, leaving enough time for a plant to establish roots before the first frost. Leave 18 to 24 inches between plants, as the plant clumps can grow to be quite large.

Care & Problems—Do not overwater after establishment. You can trim off the flowers after blooming to maintain a compact growth habit and prevent the plants from reseeding prolifically, but you won't get the nifty sound from the seedheads if you do. It's fairly pest-free. Baptisia does not require fertilizer.

Bloom Color(s)—Purple, white, yellow

Bloom Period/Peak Season—Early summer

Mature Size (H x W)—2–3 feet x 2–3 feet

Hardiness—3–9

Water Needs—Low once established

BEEBALM
Monarda didyma

Why It's Special—Beebalm is almost absurdly easy to grow. The species can have problems with powdery mildew, but newer cultivars have been bred to be resistant; 'Jacob Cline' is one of the most resistant. Birds and butterflies *love* the flowers, which bloom over a long period. When it's happy it can spread. It's a member of the mint family and its fragrant leaves are used medicinally. The name "beebalm" comes from the use of the leaves as a salve to soothe bee stings.

How to Plant & Grow—Plant after the last frost in full sun to partial afternoon shade in moist soils. Beebalm is a heavy drinker. Leave 18 to 24 inches between plants.

Care & Problems—Keep the soil evenly moist to prevent plants from getting stressed. (Stressed plants are more likely to have powdery mildew problems.) Deadhead to prolong flowering. Divide clumps every three to four years to prevent the plants from taking over the garden.

Bloom Color(s)—Red, pink, purple, white

Bloom Period/Peak Season—Midsummer through fall

Mature Size (H x W)—1–3 feet x 2–3 feet

Hardiness—4–10

Water Needs—High

BLACK-EYED SUSAN
Rudbeckia fulgida

Why It's Special—Black-eyed Susans are native perennials that will grow in almost any type of soil, bloom profusely, and are easy to maintain. They are deer resistant, drought resistant, and attract butterflies. It pairs well with ornamental grasses, tall (not creeping) sedum, asters, shrub roses, and coneflowers. 'Goldsturm' is a popular cultivar.

How to Plant & Grow—Plant in full sun after the last frost or before the first frost in early fall, leaving plants enough time to establish roots. Plants tolerate a bit of dappled afternoon shade, but they bloom best in full sun. Space at 18 to 24 inches.

Care & Problems—These are largely carefree plants. Deadhead to prolong bloom throughout summer and then leave the last round of flowers on the plants to set seed. Birds will appreciate the gesture, and you'll probably get a few volunteer plants for your efforts as well. Leave plants standing through winter and cut back in spring.

Bloom Color(s)—Deep yellow-gold with black eye

Bloom Period/Peak Season—Mid- to late summer

Mature Size (H x W)—2–3 feet x 2 feet

Hardiness—3–9

Water Needs—Low once established

BLEEDING HEART
Dicentra eximia

Why It's Special—I love this little shade plant because the leaves have a wonderful, ferny texture to them, so it's interesting all summer. And we're talking about the small woodland perennial that blooms until about July, not the larger shade perennial that blooms in spring and goes dormant. 'Alba' has white flowers. 'Luxuriant' has red flowers and is more heat tolerant than the species.

How to Plant & Grow—Plant in spring or fall in partial to full shade in moist, well-drained soil. Bleeding heart will continue to bloom during spring and early summer, and might push a second flush in early fall. Water to establish.

Care & Problems—Ideally, keep the soil moist during summer, but not during winter. Bleeding heart has few problems and requires little extra care, but you can deadhead to prolong the bloom. If you have issues with slugs, sprinkle diatomaceous earth around plants as a barrier.

Bloom Color(s)—Pink

Bloom Period/Peak Season—Early spring to early summer, fall

Mature Size (H x W)—12–18 inches x 12–18 inches

Hardiness—3–9

Water Needs—Medium

BLUE FESCUE
Festuca glauca

Why It's Special—Blue fescue is an ornamental grass that is equally at home in the rock garden as it is the perennial garden. It is short (6 to 12 inches) with thin gray-blue leaves throughout summer and tall, plumy flowers in midsummer. 'Sea Urchin' is even shorter than the species and resembles its namesake.

How to Plant & Grow—Plant in full sun in well-drained soil in the spring or fall, after the last frost or before the first frost in fall. Leave 12 inches between plants. Blue fescue will not tolerate wet feet.

Care & Problems—This is a clumping plant, so it won't spread much beyond a mature width of 12 inches. Some people like the flowers, while others cut them off to let the foliage shine. Allow the leaves and flowers to persist past frost for winter interest. Cut back to 3 to 4 inches tall in late winter. Bonus for coastal residents: It's salt tolerant.

Bloom Color(s)—Grown for silvery-blue foliage.

Bloom Period/Peak Season—Summer, fall, winter

Mature Size (H x W)—Without flowers, 8 inches x 8 inches; with flowers, 12 inches x 8 inches

Hardiness—4–8

Water Needs—Low

BUTTERFLY WEED
Asclepias tuberosa

Why It's Special—Butterfly weed is the most important food source for monarch butterflies. It is pretty and looks good in the garden, but the big reason to grow it is that monarchs need all the help they can get. It's deer resistant.

How to Plant & Grow—Plant outside, 8 to 12 inches apart, after frost in full sun in dry or well-drained soils. Try to install transplants and then leave the plants alone once they're planted. Water to establish.

Care & Problems—Do not be surprised when you see caterpillars all over the leaves, chowing down. That is one of the reasons you plant butterfly weed—to feed the butterfly larvae. Don't be alarmed if the plants get chewed almost to the ground. They usually come back, but if they don't, know that you've done your good garden deed for the year. Provide extra water only during droughty times (no rain for over two weeks). Leave seedpods to ripen and disperse. Cut plants back in midwinter.

Bloom Color(s)—Red-orange bicolor

Bloom Period/Peak Season—Summer through fall

Mature Size (H x W)—3 feet x 1 foot

Hardiness—3–9

Water Needs—Medium

CARDINAL FLOWER
Lobelia cardinalis

Why It's Special—Cardinal flower got its name because its flowers reminded Linnaeus of the red robes worn by Roman Catholic cardinals. It blooms later than many perennials, so it is a nice plant to add a late summer-fall pop of color in the garden. It is a water garden staple, but will grow in the perennial border if the soil is kept adequately moist. It's a good choice for rain gardens too, and attracts hummingbirds and butterflies.

How to Plant & Grow—Plant in full sun to partial shade (particularly in warmer areas) in moist, rich soil. Space 12 to 18 inches between plants. Water to establish.

Care & Problems—Keep soil evenly moist throughout the growing season. Plants bloom from July to September. They're pest-free as long as they're well cared for. Cut back in midwinter. Divide in spring or fall every 3 to 4 years. You can propagate through layering. Bend a stem down and anchor it to the soil, covering up the area that touches the soil: it will root.

Bloom Color(s)—Red

Bloom Period/Peak Season—Summer through fall

Mature Size (H x W)—2–4 feet x 12 inches

Hardiness—3–9

Water Needs—Medium to high

CATMINT
Nepeta × faassenii 'Walker's Low'

Why It's Special—Catmint is a garden workhorse. It's easy to grow and not fussy, as long as it's planted in well-drained soil. Spikes of lavender-blue flowers cover the plant from summer through fall. It is deer resistant and drought tolerant. It makes a stunning display when mass-planted. 'Walkers Low' is a naturally more compact growing selection (but still benefits from some pruning). Plant drifts in the landscape with pink-flowering shrub roses for continuous color.

How to Plant & Grow—Plant in full sun in well-drained soil after the last frost. Leave 18 inches between plants. Water to establish, then cut back once plants are well rooted.

Care & Problems—Shear plants, cutting back by one-third, once a month or so to stimulate compact growth and continuous flowering. Bump up the water after shearing to help the plants recover. Cut back in midwinter after plants are fully dormant. Fragrant foliage makes this plant a great addition to cut flower bouquets.

Bloom Color(s)—Lavender

Bloom Period/Peak Season—Early summer through fall; will rebloom

Mature Size (H x W)—18 inches x 12–18 inches

Hardiness—5–9

Water Needs—Low

CAMPANULA
Campanula spp.

Why It's Special—The genus *Campanula* has several different species and cultivars, but all have one thing in common—their flowers are shaped like bells, hence their nickname "bellflowers." These are old-fashioned cottage-garden flowers that are at home in any perennial border. *Campanula punctata* 'Rubriflora' has unusual tubular red flowers. 'Cup and Saucer Mix' is a popular selection with large pink, purple, or white flowers. *Campanula poscharskyana* 'Blue Waterfall', or Siberian bellflower, has star-shaped purple-blue flowers. There are some creeping varieties that grow well in rock gardens.

How to Plant & Grow—Plant in spring in full sun to partial afternoon shade. Leave 12 to 18 inches between plants. Water to establish.

Care & Problems—Keep soil consistently moist throughout the growing season. Cut back flower stalks to the ground after flowering to tidy the plant. Bellflower will spread through underground rhizomes, but you can divide clumps every three to four years to keep the size in check. It does not require fertilizer.

Bloom Color(s)—Purple

Bloom Period/Peak Season—Midsummer

Mature Size (H x W)—18–28 inches x 12 inches

Hardiness—5–9

Water Needs—Medium

COLUMBINE
Aquilegia × hybrida

Why It's Special—Columbine is the essential cottage garden flower. They bloom in spring and early summer, lighting up the shade garden. There are native species with red and yellow flowers that are easy to grow that will self-seed all over the garden. Hybrids offer larger sizes and a wider range of colors. 'Red Hobbit' has red petals and a white center cup. 'Black Barlow' has stunning black double flowers.

How to Plant & Grow—Plant outside in spring after the last frost, but while the nights are still cool. Allow 12 to 18 inches between plants. Water to establish.

Care & Problems—Columbine needs to grow in soil that is kept evenly moist. Flower stalks on larger plants might require staking. You can cut back foliage in mid- to late summer if it browns or is attacked by leafminers. Deadhead to prolong blooming, but as blooming slows allow some seedheads to mature so the plants can self-sow.

Bloom Color(s)—Pink, yellow, purple, blue, red, white, bicolors

Bloom Period/Peak Season—Spring to early summer

Mature Size (H x W)—1–3 feet x 1–2 feet

Hardiness—3–8

Water Needs—Medium. More sun equals more water.

CORAL BELLS
Heuchera

Why It's Special—There are over 100 cultivars of heuchera available with leaves in various shades of purples, silvers, chartreuse, apricot, and more. They look great when mass-planted, but also when mixed in a perennial border. Little Cutie™ series plants bloom continuously with flowers that *do* add interest. MARMALADE™ series plants have ruffled leaves and hold their color well during winter.

How to Plant & Grow—Plant in full sun to shade (more afternoon shade the higher the growing zone) in spring after the last frost. Heuchera grows best in rich, moist soils. Leave 6 to 12 inches between plants (check the expected mature size before planting). Water to establish, and mulch to keep roots cool and moist.

Care & Problems—Heuchera roots will sometimes heave up in colder areas, resulting in the need to dig up, divide, and replant in spring. Keep soil evenly moist throughout the growing season. Flowers on most cultivars are not showy.

Bloom Color(s)—Primarily grown for foliage in burgundy, green, silver, apricot, chartreuse, and multicolored

Bloom Period/Peak Season—Summer, fall

Mature Size (H x W)—6–12 inches x 8–18 inches

Hardiness—4–8

Water Needs—Medium

DAYLILY
Hemerocallis cultivars

Why It's Special—There are so many different colors and shapes of flowers available now. If you choose wisely, you can have daylilies in bloom from mid-May through July. There are repeat blooming varieties as well. ('Happy Returns', with yellow flowers, is one of the most common repeat bloomers.) When not in bloom, their grasslike leaves add texture to the garden.

How to Plant & Grow—Plant in full sun to partial shade after the last frost. Leave between 12 to 24 inches between plants, depending on the eventual mature size and the effect you're trying to achieve. (Use less space if you're massing, more if you're growing among other perennials.) Water to establish.

Care & Problems—Daylilies are drought tolerant once established, but will remain nicer looking if watered during dry periods. Cut back bloom stalks to the ground after all flowers have opened. If foliage looks ratty, you can cut it back to the ground. Divide them every three to four years.

Bloom Color(s)—White, orange, red, burgundy, pink, peach, lavender, bicolors, purple

Bloom Period/Peak Season—Summer

Mature Size (H x W)—12–24 inches x 12–24 inches

Hardiness—3–9

Water Needs—Medium to low

DIANTHUS
Dianthus spp.

Why It's Special—Dianthus is a fragrant cutting flower of the old-fashioned cutting garden variety. Taller varieties are most commonly called carnations, while the shorter varieties go by "pinks" because of the toothed flower edges that look like they've been cut with pinking shears. 'Bath's Pink' (my favorite) has light pink flowers. 'Ruby Sparkles' has two-toned dark pink flowers with red centers.

How to Plant & Grow—Plant dianthus in spring in full sun and well-drained soil. It is especially important that the soil be fast-draining in winter; otherwise, the plants will rot. Dianthus spreads, forming a mat. Individual plants will eventually fill one square foot. Leave 12 inches between plants.

Care & Problems—Dianthus will suffer from crown rot if planted too deep or in moist soil. Deadhead frequently during blooming to encourage a longer flowering period. Most pinks will bloom heavily in May or June, and then sporadically during the rest of the summer. Count on them for early summer blooms only, though.

Bloom Color(s)—Pink, white, lavender, fuchsia, burgundy, multicolored

Bloom Period/Peak Season—May through July

Mature Size (H x W)—12 inches x 12 inches

Hardiness—3–9

Water Needs—Low

FEATHER REED GRASS
Calamagrostis × acutiflora 'Karl Foerster'

Why It's Special—Feather reed grass has one of the most strongly upright forms out of all of the popular ornamental grasses. In summer, tight inflorescences arise from the middle of a plant. These open to fluffy flowerheads that look beautiful when the sun shines through them. Plants don't have spectacular fall color, but will remain upright during winter, turning tawny brown and offering some winter interest. A concern with some introduced ornamental grasses is that they'll reseed prolifically and become weedy. This cultivar is sterile, so that's not a worry.

How to Plant & Grow—Plant outside after the last frost in full sun in moderately wet to wet soils. Leave 18 to 24 inches between plants.

Care & Problems—Keep the soil moist throughout summer; do not let it dry out fully. Let the foliage and flowers persist through until late winter, at which point you can cut the grass back using loppers, hand pruners, or hedge trimmers.

Bloom Color(s)—Tan

Bloom Period/Peak Season—Summer

Mature Size (H x W)—3–5 feet x 1–2 feet

Hardiness—5–9

Water Needs—High

FERNS
Various genera

Why It's Special—There are many varieties of ferns with different leaf shapes and colors. Some are suited to deeper shade than others. Regardless of individual specifics, ferns add marvelous texture to a shade garden and do put on a big show when mass planted.

How to Plant & Grow—Specific requirements vary by genus. For the most part, ferns need partial to full shade and moist, rich soil. Plant in spring after the fiddleheads (leaves) have started to unfurl. Water to establish. Spacing depends on the expected mature size of the plant.

Care & Problems—Unless otherwise specified, keep the soil moist. Trim off ratty leaves. Slugs and small mammals can be a problem for ferns. Sprinkle diatomaceous earth around the plants to prevent slug damage and use repellents to prevent deer and small mammals from eating the plants.

Bloom Color(s)—It's all about leaf color with ferns. Most come in different shades of green, but a few have a pretty rust fall color. Japanese painted ferns are purple, green, and white.

Bloom Period/Peak Season—Summer

Mature Size (H x W)—Varies from 6–36 inches x 6–36 inches

Hardiness—Varies

Water Needs—High

FOXGLOVE
Digitalis purpurea

Why It's Special—Foxgloves are striking plants. They have completely upright inflorescences made of thumb-sized, bell-shaped flowers that gradually open from the bottom of the stalk, up. When planted in masses, their effect is breathtaking. **Caution:** Though it is used medicinally, all parts of the plant are poisonous in their natural form.

How to Plant & Grow—Plant outside in early spring, up to three weeks before the last frost (as long as you harden the plants off before planting). Leave 8 to 12 inches between plants. Water to establish.

Care & Problems—Never pull out a foxglove! Foxglove is a biennial. Leave the seedheads to mature after flowering so it self-seeds. Once the majority of the seeds have opened, snap off the flower stalk and wave it around, shaking the seeds out into the garden. You'll notice babies sprouting over summer and into fall. Rarely do the plants need staking. The flower stalks are big but the stems are sturdy.

Bloom Color(s)—Pink, lavender, white

Bloom Period/Peak Season—Spring to early summer

Mature Size (H x W)—2–4 feet x 12–18 inches

Hardiness—4–8

Water Needs—Medium

GAILLARDIA
Gaillardia spp. and hybrids

Why It's Special—Gaillardia is a great perennial to grow in dry, well-drained sections of the garden. You will see the species flowers growing on windswept sand dunes at the beach. It's a tough, short-lived perennial that adds tons of color to the garden. Bees and butterflies love it too. 'Arizona Sun' is a compact grower. 'Lemons and Oranges' has bright yellow and orange flowers.

How to Plant & Grow—Plant in full sun after the last frost. These plants require well-drained soil and will rot if planted in areas that stay perpetually wet. Some types are more compact than others. Leave between 8 to 18 inches between plants, depending on the variety.

Care & Problems—Deadhead to keep gaillardia plants blooming. Gaillardia will bloom themselves to death, so be aware that they can be somewhat short-lived. Cut the plant back by half in midsummer, fertilize and water, and allow it to grow back out. It has few pest problems.

Bloom Color(s)—Combinations of orange, yellow, and red

Bloom Period/Peak Season—Summer

Mature Size (H x W)—12–24 inches x 12–18 inches

Hardiness—3–10

Water Needs—Low

GARDEN PHLOX
Phlox paniculata

Why It's Special—Garden phlox is a later-blooming garden perennial that adds height and color from midsummer through fall. Butterflies and hummingbirds love it. 'David' is a white-flowering cultivar with good mildew resistance. 'Laura' has pinkish-purple flowers with white eyes. 'Bright Eyes' has light pink flowers with dark pink centers. 'Blue Paradise' flowers open blue, turn violet during the day, and revert back to blue at night.

How to Plant & Grow—Plant in full sun to part shade in moderately moist, well-drained soils. The eventual height and spread of the plant depends highly on the cultivar. Leave 12 to 24 inches between plants.

Care & Problems—Powdery mildew and root rot are the two worst problems with this perennial. Plant in well-drained soil to prevent root rot. The only way to avoid powdery mildew is to plant resistant varieties. You can dig up the clumps and divide after flowering in fall or in spring after new growth appears.

Bloom Color(s)—White, pink, lavender, red, a few bicolor choices

Bloom Period/Peak Season—Late summer to early fall

Mature Size (H x W)—2–4 feet x 1–3 feet

Hardiness—4–8

Water Needs—Medium

GAURA
Gaura lindheimeri

Why It's Special—Gaura blooms almost nonstop and requires little care. It attracts butterflies and hummingbirds and adds wispy, floaty texture to the garden with its butterfly-shaped, thumbnail-sized, pink-tinged white flowers blooming along tall, wire-thin stems. 'Crimson Butterflies' has red foliage and dark pink flowers. It's more compact than the species.

How to Plant & Grow—Plant in full sun in well-drained, almost dry soil after the last frost. Some are more compact, while others are sprawling, so the spacing depends on which one you're growing—generally between 12 to 24 inches.

Care & Problems—Gaura will pitch a mighty fit if it is watered from overhead. You cannot turn the automatic sprinklers on this plant. Water to establish, and then provide water at the base of the plant only when there's no rain for more than a couple of weeks. Aphids can sometimes be a problem. Spray with insecticidal soap—according to package instructions—to eliminate these pests.

Bloom Color(s)—White, pink, bicolors

Bloom Period/Peak Season—Summer to fall

Mature Size (H x W)—1–3 feet x 6 inches–2 feet

Hardiness—5–9

Water Needs—Low to medium

74

GOAT'S BEARD
Aruncus dioicus

Why It's Special—Goat's beard gets its name because the plumy white flowers look like, well, a goat's beard. It is a shade garden staple, and it gets pretty big. After it's done blooming in spring, the foliage makes a nice backdrop for other shade plants.

How to Plant & Grow—Plant in moist soils in full sun to partial shade in early spring or fall. (The warmer your growing zone, the more afternoon shade the plant needs.) Leave 2 to 3 feet between plants. Water to establish.

Care & Problems—Keep the soil moist throughout the growing season. The leaves will scorch if the soil around the plant is allowed to fully dry out. Cut the flower stalks back to the nearest leaf after they're finished blooming to tidy the plant's appearance and prevent rampant self-seeding. Allow the foliage to persist. Cut the entire plant back in midwinter once it is fully dormant. Goat's beard is fairly pest-free.

Bloom Color(s)—White

Bloom Period/Peak Season—Spring

Mature Size (H x W)—2–4 feet x 2–4 feet

Hardiness—4–8

Water Needs—High

GOLDENROD
Solidago rugosa 'Fireworks'

Why It's Special—Species goldenrod is gorgeous in the fall garden, but 'Fireworks' is a newer cultivar with the same golden flowers and an arching growth habit that looks like fireworks exploding in the sky. Goldenrod gets a bad rap because it blooms at the same time as ragweed, the cause of allergies for many people. Goldenrod takes the blame because it's showier than ragweed, which sort of blends into the background.

How to Plant & Grow—Plant goldenrod in moist, well-drained soil in full sun. You can plant in spring or late summer, as long as you keep it watered. Leave 12 to 18 inches between plants.

Care & Problems—This plant is deer resistant, which makes it attractive if you have a rural garden. When it's happy, it spreads, so be ready to divide it and give pieces to friends. The soil must be kept evenly moist to wet throughout the growing season, not just during fall when it is blooming. Leave the plant to set seed and cut back in midwinter.

Bloom Color(s)—Yellow

Bloom Period/Peak Season—August to September

Mature Size (H x W)—24 inches x 24–36 inches

Hardiness—4–8

Water Needs—High

HAKONE GRASS
Hakonechloa macra 'Aureola'

Why It's Special—This is one of a handful of ornamental grasses that grows well in partial to full shade. 'Aureola' has chartreuse-and-green striped leaves, which brighten up darker corners of the garden nicely. There's a bigger contrast between the green and gold striping in shadier locations. More sun equals yellower leaves. This grass is deer resistant.

How to Plant & Grow—Plant in moist, well-drained soil in partial shade after the last frost. Hakone grass spreads by underground rhizomes, so it can develop a large patch or clump. Leave 12 to 24 inches between plants to allow for growth.

Care & Problems—Hakone grass will burn out in full sun, so make absolutely sure it has afternoon shade or partial shade all day. Keep the soil moist throughout the growing season. You can dig it up, divide, and replant if the clump starts to get too large. Cut back in midwinter. It's relatively pest-free.

Bloom Color(s)—Grown for chartreuse foliage

Bloom Period/Peak Season—Summer

Mature Size (H x W)—12–18 inches x 12–24 inches

Hardiness—5–9

Water Needs—Medium

HARDY HIBISCUS
Hibiscus moscheutos

Why It's Special—Hardy hibiscus is related to tropical hibiscus, but this type can take a hard winter. They are firmly in the "gigantic herbaceous perennial" category, growing to heights of up to 7 feet in just one summer, only to die back to the ground for winter. They're excellent plants for slow-draining areas and they have huge, beautiful flowers when other perennials are starting to throw in the towel.

How to Plant & Grow—Plant after the last frost in moist soil and full sun. These plants get huge, so leave lots of room—at least 3 to 4 feet between plants.

Care & Problems—Hardy hibiscus need continuously moist soil, so plant somewhere that stays wet (such as near a drain pipe), or water frequently. Fertilize monthly during the growing season. Do not cut back hardy hibiscus in spring until you see emerging new growth. They are usually some of the last perennials to start leafing out, so don't worry if it takes time.

Bloom Color(s)—White, pink, red, yellow, bicolors

Bloom Period/Peak Season—Late summer to fall

Mature Size (H x W)—3–5 feet x 4–7 feet

Hardiness—5–10

Water Needs—High

HOLLYHOCK
Alcea rosea

Why It's Special—Hollyhocks are biennials, growing a rosette of leaves during their first summer, overwintering, and blooming the next summer. They have tall flower spikes, up to 7 to 8 feet, that bloom for several weeks at a time, with new flowers opening from the bottom, up. The leaves are the larval food for the painted lady butterfly. 'Appleblossom' has fully double flowers that look like peonies. 'Nigra' has single black flowers.

How to Plant & Grow—Plant transplants outside in full sun in spring; sow seeds in the garden in late summer. The plants will have a few months to grow leaves and store some energy for winter. Leave 12 to 28 inches between plants.

Care & Problems—Stake to prevent stalks from falling. Rust is a big problem; cut off affected leaves. For that reason, it's a good idea to plant hollyhocks where other things can grow up and around them to camouflage their leafless stems.

Bloom Color(s)—White, red, pink, peach, yellow, lavender, burgundy, black

Bloom Period/Peak Season—Early summer

Mature Size (H x W)—5–7 feet x 1–2 feet

Hardiness—2–10

Water Needs—Low

HOSTA
Hosta spp.

Why It's Special—Hostas are the workhorses of the shade garden. There are hundreds of cultivars with a huge variety of leaf shapes and colors. You could plant an entire shade garden with nothing but hostas, and it would be gorgeous all summer. 'Praying Hands' is a variety that looks more like a peace lily, with dark green, somewhat folded leaves. *Hosta plantaginea* species has huge, white, fragrant flowers.

How to Plant & Grow—Plant after the last frost in full shade in rich, well-drained soil. Hostas do not really emerge until the soil starts to warm up. They're one of the last perennials to emerge. Spacing depends on the variety.

Care & Problems—Hostas are drought tolerant once established. They don't require fertilizer. Slugs love to eat hostas. So do deer. Sprinkle diatomaceous earth around the plants to keep the slugs at bay. Spray plants with deer repellents to prevent deer from munching them.

Bloom Color(s)—White or purple, but the main attraction is foliage

Bloom Period/Peak Season—Summer

Mature Size (H x W)—6–18 inches x 8–36 inches

Hardiness—3–9

Water Needs—Low

JAPANESE ANEMONE
Anemone hupehensis

Why It's Special—This is a pretty woodland garden perennial that flowers later in summer. Many woodland plants bloom in early spring, before trees leaf out, so to find one that looks good during late summer and early fall is a treat. Masses of daisy-shaped pink or white flowers with yellow centers bloom atop thin, wiry stems. The foliage is dark green and attractive as a backdrop before the flowers bloom. It's deer resistant.

How to Plant & Grow—Plant in partial shade in moist, well-drained soil after the last frost. If you have room, establish a large colony under shade trees in the yard. Water to establish. Leave 18 to 24 inches between plants. Individual plants will spread through underground rhizomes.

Care & Problems—Japanese anemones can be slow to establish, but, once happy, will take off and spread. Keep the soil evenly moist throughout the growing season. Cut back in midwinter.

Bloom Color(s)—Shades of pink or white

Bloom Period/Peak Season—Late summer to fall

Mature Size (H x W)—18–36 inches x 12–18 inches

Hardiness—4–8

Water Needs—Medium

LAVENDER
Lavandula angustifolia

Why It's Special—Lavender is too pretty and too fragrant to be consigned to the herb or vegetable garden. If you have a well-drained sunny spot in the garden, make room for a few plants. When they're not in bloom, the gray-green foliage is attractive too.

How to Plant & Grow—Plant English lavender in a sunny, well-drained location after the last frost. Leave 12 to 18 inches between plants, as plants will spread. Water to establish, but cut back quickly once the plants are well-rooted.

Care & Problems—There are two major rules to growing lavender. First, do not cut the plants back in spring until after they have started to sprout and you can see signs of new growth. Second, do not let the plants sit in water—ever—not during summer and not during winter. Follow those, and you'll be fine. If you want to cut lavender to dry, snip the stems where they meet the leaves before the flowers start to open.

Bloom Color(s)—Lavender to purple

Bloom Period/Peak Season—Early summer

Mature Size (H x W)—12–24 inches x 12–24 inches

Hardiness—5–8

Water Needs—Low

LAMB'S EAR

Stachys byzantina

Why It's Special—Grow lamb's ear for the soft silver foliage that feels like a lamb's ear. Lamb's ear ends up being a groundcover. When it's happy, it spreads, but that's not necessarily a bad thing—just something to be aware of when you plant it. 'Silver Carpet' is a popular cultivar because it doesn't produce many flowers.

How to Plant & Grow—Plant after the last frost in full sun in well-drained soil. Drainage is essential. Lamb's ear will rot if it stays wet for any length of time—particularly if it's wet during winter. Leave 12 to 18 inches between plants because they spread.

Care & Problems—Water to establish and then stop, unless there is a prolonged dry period. I cut off the flower stalks when they appear because I think they're ugly, but you can leave them. Divide in spring or fall if the plant starts to outgrow its location.

Bloom Color(s)—Grown for silver foliage

Bloom Period/Peak Season—Summer

Mature Size (H x W)—6–12 inches x 12–18 inches

Hardiness—4–8

Water Needs—Low

LADY'S MANTLE

Alchemilla mollis

Why It's Special—Lady's mantle is an excellent shade garden perennial that is usually underutilized. It blooms with yellow flowers in late spring to early summer. It has green leaves with a bit of a silver tinge to them. When it rains, water beads up on the leaves, looking like little diamonds rolling around on the plants.

How to Plant & Grow—Plant in partial shade to full shade after the last frost. It does best in fairly moist, rich soils. Leave 12 to 18 inches between plants. It pairs well with other shade garden plants including ferns, astilbe, and hosta. The unique foliage texture of lady's mantle creates interesting contrast with smooth-leafed plants.

Care & Problems—Cut flower stalks back to the ground after the plant finishes blooming. It can self-sow somewhat aggressively, so deadhead before the plant sets seed to prevent that. Water regularly throughout the growing season. This perennial has few pest problems.

Bloom Color(s)—Yellow

Bloom Period/Peak Season—Blooms in spring, but leaves are attractive throughout the summer.

Mature Size (H x W)—12–18 inches x 12 inches

Hardiness—3–8

Water Needs—Medium

LENTEN ROSE

Helleborus × hybridus

Why It's Special—Lenten roses are some of the first non-bulb perennial plants to bloom each spring. They have semi-evergreen foliage, under which papery flowers in shades of green, purple, white, and pink blooms. I think they always seem quite miraculous because they bloom when everything else is still dormant or under snow. During summer, the foliage makes a nice filler in the shade garden. To end up with a big variety of flower colors, purchase and plant when the flowers are in bloom. *Helleborus foetidus* 'Piccadilly' is a related species with highly dissected dark purple-blue foliage.

How to Plant & Grow—Plant hellebores in spring or fall in rich, well-drained soil in full shade. Spacing depends on the cultivar—some are bigger than others. In general, leave between 8 to 18 inches between plants. Japanese painted ferns make excellent companion plants to hellebores.

Care & Problems—These plants are fairly trouble-free and easy to grow. They will self-sow.

Bloom Color(s)—Shades of white, burgundy, purple, pink, or green

Bloom Period/Peak Season—Late winter, early spring

Mature Size (H x W)—12–36 inches x 12–18 inches

Hardiness—4–9

Water Needs—Medium to low

LIGULARIA
Ligularia dentata

Why It's Special—Ligularia look great whether or not they're blooming. They have dark green or burgundy leaves that form a symmetrical mound in the shade garden. In summer to early fall their yellow flowers open—either in daisy-shaped racemes or tall spikes with flowers up and down the stem. 'The Rocket' has tall spikes of yellow flowers. 'Britt Marie Crawford' leaves emerge burgundy. The undersides stay burgundy while the tops turn dark green.

How to Plant & Grow—Plant after the last frost in partial to full shade in moist soil. The warmer your growing zone, the more shade the plant needs.

Care & Problems—The soil has to stay consistently moist for ligularia to thrive. Slugs sometimes munch on the leaves. Just cut the leaves that have been eaten off the plant and use diatomaceous earth around them to prevent further damage. Ligularia will sometimes wilt in the afternoon of hot summer days. It's not dying and will perk up at night.

Bloom Color(s)—Yellow

Bloom Period/Peak Season—Summer to fall

Mature Size (H x W)—12–36 inches (with flower) x 12–18 inches

Hardiness—3–8

Water Needs—High

LILAC SAGE
Salvia verticillata

Why It's Special—This perennial salvia produces tall spikes of purple flowers above gray-green basal foliage in summer. It has a more open growth habit than some salvias, giving it a slightly "relaxed" look. The flowers look like a combination of beebalm and Mexican sage (not hardy here) flowers. They're borne in clusters circling the plant stem, but have a fuzzy texture.

How to Plant & Grow—Plant after the last frost in full sun and well-drained soil. Space at 12 to 18 inches.

Care & Problems—Soil must be kept relatively dry for plants to thrive. Only provide supplemental water after their first growing season if your area has been experiencing drought. Deadhead to encourage continuous blooming. Then, when blooming slows, cut the flower stalks back to the leaves. Cut the entire plant back in late winter to make room for new growth. Mulch during winter to prevent the roots from heaving out of the ground.

Bloom Color(s)—Purple

Bloom Period/Peak Season—Summer

Mature Size (H x W)—12–24 inches x 12–24 inches

Hardiness—5–8

Water Needs—Low

LITTLE BLUESTEM
Schizachyrium scoparium

Why It's Special—Little bluestem is a native prairie grass that looks equally at home in the landscape or perennial border. Its leaves are a silvery green; burgundy flowers emerge in midsummer. The whole plant turns a burgundy bronze in fall, persisting through winter. 'Standing Ovation' is a cultivar with a rigidly upright growth habit.

How to Plant & Grow—Plant after the last frost in full sun in well-drained to dry soil. It will tolerate heavy clay, but it doesn't do well in wet soil. Water to establish, but ease up once the plant has rooted. Leave 2 to 4 feet between plants—on the low end if you want to mass plant.

Care & Problems—This is a low-care ornamental grass. It has few pest problems. As long as it doesn't sit in water, it will be fine. Cut it back in late winter to early spring. New leaves emerge later than some grasses and perennials.

Bloom Color(s)—Burgundy

Bloom Period/Peak Season—Blooms late summer, but interesting year-round

Mature Size (H x W)—2–4 feet x 1½–3 feet

Hardiness—4–9

Water Needs—Medium-low

LUNGWORT
Pulmonaria officinalis

Why It's Special—Lungwort is one of the first perennials to bloom in spring. The little blue or pink flowers (depending on the variety) always surprise me. One day the plant is all leaves and the next it's blooming.

How to Plant & Grow—Plant outside in early spring after the ground has thawed. Lungwort needs at least partial shade, but will perform well in full shade. It thrives in moist, rich soils, but doesn't like to sit in standing water. Leave 6 to 12 inches between plants, on the lower end if plants are large when you install them, more if they're small.

Care & Problems—Lungwort is an easy-care plant. You can pretty much add it to the garden and forget about it, as long as you're getting adequate rain during the growing season. If it's in a prominent spot or you're using several plants as groundcover, cut the flower stalks back to the ground after blooming.

Bloom Color(s)—Blue or pink

Bloom Period/Peak Season—Flowers in early spring; leaves interesting spring to fall

Mature Size (H x W)—6 inches (without flowers)–12 inches (with flowers) x 12–18 inches

Hardiness—3–8

Water Needs—Medium

MISCANTHUS
Miscanthus sinensis

Why It's Special—Miscanthus is a large ornamental grass with narrow, thin leaves and a precise, tightly clumping, fountain-shaped growth habit. Its plumy flowers add fall and winter interest. 'Variegatus' has green-and-white striped leaves that are a little wider than the species.

How to Plant & Grow—Plant after the last frost in full sun in well-drained soil. Miscanthus will not grow well with wet feet. Space plants 3 to 5 feet apart, on the lower end if massing, the higher end if using as a specimen. Water to establish, but cut back once the plant is rooted.

Care & Problems—This is an easy-care plant; just keep it on the dry side. Leave the foliage and flowers through winter for height and color in the garden. Shear back to 4 to 6 inches above the ground in early spring. You might need to use a chainsaw when shearing large, old clumps. Leaves can be sharp. Wear gloves.

Bloom Color(s)—Brownish plumes in mid- to late summer; grown primarily for foliage

Bloom Period/Peak Season—Summer, fall, and winter

Mature Size (H x W)—4–7 feet x 3–6 feet

Hardiness—5–9

Water Needs—Medium

MUHLY GRASS
Muhlenbergia capillaris

Why It's Special—Muhly grass is a native species primarily grown for one reason: the cloud-like clusters of pink flowers that bloom in fall. The sun shining through a mass of these flowers is truly a spectacular sight. At times during the bloom, plants actually seem to glow. This grass is one of the finer textured of all of the ornamental grasses, so it does add summer interest to the garden, but its fall flowers are the big splash.

How to Plant & Grow—Plant after the last frost in full sun in well-drained soil. Take care to make sure muhly grass is not planted too deep. If the crown of the plant (where the roots meet the grass leaves) is underground, the plants *will* rot. Spacing is 18 to 24 inches between plants.

Care & Problems—This is an easy-care plant provided it is growing in well-drained soil. (If it is in wet soil, it will eventually just rot.) Once muhly grass has established, cut back on watering.

Bloom Color(s)—Pink

Bloom Period/Peak Season—Fall

Mature Size (H x W)—2–3 feet x 2–3 feet

Hardiness—6–9

Water Needs—Low to medium

79

NEW ENGLAND ASTER
Symphyotrichum novae-angliae

Why It's Special—This native flowering perennial bursts into bloom in fall when almost everything else is fading for the year. The species does get large, so plant it where it will have room to grow. It's especially at home around native rudbeckias, Joe-pye weed, and ornamental grasses. It's an important nectar source for migrating monarch butterflies in late summer.

How to Plant & Grow—Plant in full sun after the last frost. New England asters grow best in well-drained soil. If you're growing the species, allow space for it to spread out, or plant among shorter perennials that will support it.

Care & Problems—You can control the size of New England aster by cutting the plant back by one-third to one-half in July. That will slightly delay flowering. Powdery mildew can be a problem; try to plant these where there's good air circulation. Provide supplemental water during droughty summers.

Bloom Color(s)—Purple, pink, white

Bloom Period/Peak Season—Fall

Mature Size (H x W)—3–6 feet x 2–3 feet

Hardiness—4–8

Water Needs—Medium

PEONY
Paeonia lactiflora

Why It's Special—My grandmas always called peonies "Decoration Day" flowers because they bloom around Memorial Day. Peonies are remarkably resilient perennials. You can drive by abandoned homesteads or cemeteries and find peonies that were planted decades ago that still flower, spring after spring, without any care. They are fragrant and make beautiful cut flowers.

How to Plant & Grow—Plant peonies in fall in full sun to partial shade. Plant so that the top of the bulb or rootball is just *barely* underneath the soil. If you plant them too deep, they won't bloom. Peonies do best in well-drained soil. Leave 24 to 36 inches between plants. Water to establish.

Care & Problems—After peonies bloom, cut the flower stalks back to the ground but allow the foliage to remain until late summer. Peonies can be staked, but you don't have to. Do not divide plants if you can help it. Ants sometimes cover the flower; they won't cause any damage.

Bloom Color(s)—Shades of pink, white, lavender

Bloom Period/Peak Season—Late spring to early summer

Mature Size (H x W)—3 feet x 3 feet

Hardiness—3–7

Water Needs—Low

PENSTEMON
Penstemon digitalis 'Husker Red'

Why It's Special—There are many species, hybrids, and cultivars of penstemon, a native perennial, but 'Husker Red' is a standout cultivar because it grows and blooms reliably almost anywhere. Most penstemons do not grow well in wet soil, but 'Husker Red' can take it during summer—though not during winter. Its red foliage is also attractive, even when the plant isn't blooming. It's beloved by birds and butterflies.

How to Plant & Grow—Plant in full sun in well-drained soil after the last frost. It will tolerate a little bit of shade, but grows better in sun. Leave 12 to 18 inches between plants. Water to establish. Penstemon combines well with coreopsis, purple coneflower, ornamental grasses, salvias, and rudbeckias.

Care & Problems—Provide supplemental water if you're having a droughty summer. Generally, I don't have to stake this plant. Cut back the flower stalks after blooming. Cut back entire plant in mid-winter or early spring. It is deer resistant.

Bloom Color(s)—Reddish foliage, pinkish white flowers

Bloom Period/Peak Season—Early summer

Mature Size (H x W)—2–3 feet x 1–2 feet

Hardiness—3–8

Water Needs—Medium to low

PRAIRIE DROPSEED
Sporobolus heterolepis

Why It's Special—Prairie dropseed is a gorgeous native ornamental grass with hair-thin green leaves and clouds of pinkish brown flowers in late summer through fall. Birds love to munch on its seeds. While it flowers profusely, it doesn't reseed all over the place (a problem with some ornamental grasses). Few other plants can offer the same fine texture.

How to Plant & Grow—Plant after frost in well-drained soil in full sun. This grass tolerates heavy clay soils, but not wet feet, particularly during winter. Leave 2 to 3 feet between plants if massing, as the plants will gradually spread into bigger clumps.

Care & Problems—This is a low-care plant. Water to establish, but cut back once it roots in. Allow the foliage and flowers to persist through winter, but shear back to the 4 to 6 inches above the ground in early spring. If you want to divide the clump, dig it up once new growth has appeared, divide, and replant.

Bloom Color(s)—Pinkish brown

Bloom Period/Peak Season—Summer to fall

Mature Size (H x W)—2–3 feet x 2–3 feet

Hardiness—3–9

Water Needs—Low

PURPLE CONEFLOWER
Echinacea purpurea

Why It's Special—Purple coneflowers are easy to grow, add height to the garden, and attract butterflies (for nectar) and birds (which like to eat the seeds). There are a lot of new coneflowers available with flashy flowers, but beware—those can be short-lived. 'Tomato Soup' has red flowers and a proven track record. 'Kim's Knee High' has bright fuchsia flowers and a more compact growth habit that behaves well in a flower border. 'White Swan' is a large plant with white flowers.

How to Plant & Grow—Plant after the last frost in full sun in well-drained soil. Coneflowers will tolerate poor soil, but they don't do well with wet feet for extended periods of time, particularly in winter. Leave 18 to 24 inches between plants because they can get big. Water to establish.

Care & Problems—Coneflowers have few pest problems. Deadhead throughout summer to keep the plant tidy and encourage blooming. Stop deadheading in September and let the seedheads mature.

Bloom Color(s)—Pinkish purple, white, red

Bloom Period/Peak Season—Summer to fall

Mature Size (H x W)—2–5 feet x 1–2 feet

Hardiness—3–8

Water Needs—Medium to low

RODGERSIA
Rodgersia aesculifolia

Why It's Special—This is another huge plant! It has 12-inch-wide leaves that look like they should be dinosaur food. It blooms in late spring with 3- to 4-foot-tall stalks of creamy white flowers that look like larger cousin of astilbe. You have to have some space to grow rodgersia, but it looks spectacular in the perennial garden. Do not use as a foundation plant. It goes fully dormant in winter.

How to Plant & Grow—Plant outside after the last frost in part shade to full sun in moist soil. The more sun this plant gets, the more water it will need. Leave 3 feet between plants, as they do get big! Water to establish.

Care & Problems—You must keep the soil moist throughout the growing season for rodgersia to be happy. Cut off the flower stalks after they finish blooming. If leaves get ratty, prune them off. You can divide every three to four years in spring when new foliage emerges.

Bloom Color(s)—Creamy white, pink

Bloom Period/Peak Season—Late spring for flowers, summer for foliage

Mature Size (H x W)—3–4 feet x 3–4 feet

Hardiness—5–7

Water Needs—High

RUSSIAN SAGE
Perovskia atriplicifolia

Why It's Special—Russian sage adds texture to the perennial garden. It is a woody sage, part of the mint family, with a strong upright growth habit. The foliage is a silvery gray, so the plant contributes interest to the garden even when it isn't blooming. Purple flowers bloom in midsummer.

How to Plant & Grow—Plant after the last frost in full sun in well-drained soil. The more shade this plant gets, the floppier it gets. Skip the shade and plant in sun. Leave 2 to 3 feet between plants. I love seeing this planted with 'New Gold' lantana or in combination with fuchsia shrub roses and *Panicum* 'Dallas Blues'.

Care & Problems—A pretty, carefree plant, Russian sage might require staking if it is growing in the shade or gets tall and top-heavy. Cut back in spring before new growth appears. It does not need fertilizer, nor does it need supplemental water once established.

Bloom Color(s)—Purple

Bloom Period/Peak Season—Midsummer to fall

Mature Size (H x W)—2–4 feet x 2–3 feet

Hardiness—5–9

Water Needs—Low once established

SCABIOSA
Scabiosa cultivars

Why It's Special—Butterflies absolutely love to visit scabiosa flowers. Sometimes they're called pincushion flower because the flowers look like pincushions packed with tiny pinheads. The most common variety has blue flowers, but there are also pink-, white-, and burgundy-flowered types. The plant has low-growing leaves with flowers arising from thin, wiry stems. 'Beaujolais Bonnets' is a striking cultivar with light pink petals surrounding a burgundy center.

How to Plant & Grow—Plant in full sun to partial shade right around the last frost. (These plants can take some cool nights.) They do need well-drained soil to thrive, particularly in winter. Leave 6 inches between plants if massing.

Care & Problems—Scabiosa has few pests and will grow well if planted in well-drained soil. Deadhead to encourage continuous blooming. It's deer- and rabbit resistant. Cut back in late winter before new foliage emerges. It does not need extra fertilizer, but water if your area is experiencing a drought.

Bloom Color(s)—Blue, white, pink, burgundy

Bloom Period/Peak Season—Early summer, on and off through entire summer

Mature Size (H x W)—12 inches x 12 inches

Water Needs—Low

SEA HOLLY
Eryngium amethystinum

Why It's Special—Sea holly has a wonderfully unique appearance. The botanical name comes from the Greek word for thistle because its spiky green leaves and blue flowers resemble a thistle. When sea holly is in bloom, the flowers form a sort of spiny blue cloud above the foliage. This plant is native to the Mediterranean. Flowers add depth to fresh and dried arrangements.

How to Plant & Grow—Plant in well-drained soil and full sun after the last frost. Dry, fast-draining soil is non-negotiable for success with this plant. So is full sun. Once those two requirements are met, it's fairly easy to grow. Water to establish—that is *it*.

Care & Problems—Sea holly is fairly pest-free, but it may require staking. Water only if your area is experiencing a serious drought. Leave it standing for winter interest, particularly if planted around ornamental grasses, and cut back in early spring.

Bloom Color(s)—Blue

Bloom Period/Peak Season—Summer

Mature Size (H x W)—2–3 feet x 2–3 feet

Hardiness—4–9

Water Needs—Low

SEDUM
Sedum 'Autumn Joy'

Why It's Special—There are hundreds of types of sedum, including upright and creeping varieties, but 'Autumn Joy' is a popular upright-growing cultivar. There are other similar cultivars with slightly different flower colors or bloom times. But 'Autumn Joy' is drought tolerant, easy to grow, and just an overall staple of the perennial garden.

How to Plant & Grow—Plant after the last frost in full sun and in well-drained soil. *Sedum 'Autumn Joy'* is a clumping perennial that is slow to spread. Leave 12 to 24 inches between plants. Water to establish.

Care & Problems—This is probably *the* most low-maintenance plant you'll ever grow. Once it's established it doesn't need supplemental water. If it is grown in full sun, it won't flop. You can stagger the blooming of the various plants by cutting some of them back by one-third in midsummer. Leave it in the garden to provide winter interest and cut back in early spring.

Bloom Color(s)—Pink

Bloom Period/Peak Season—Late summer to fall

Mature Size (H x W)—2–3 feet x 2–3 feet

Hardiness—3–11

Water Needs—Low

SHASTA DAISY
Leucanthemum × superbum

Why It's Special—Shasta daisies are so easy to grow, they're almost a no-brainer for the perennial garden. Butterflies love them. They are also deer and rabbit resistant and tolerate dry soil. 'Becky' is the popular cultivar that grows a bit taller than the species. 'Snowcap' is a dwarf cultivar. 'Everest' is a monster that grows almost 4 feet tall. It would look spectacular when planted with native swamp hibiscus.

How to Plant & Grow—Plant in full sun in well-drained soil (though they can take partial shade in warmer areas). Water to establish. Leave 12 to 24 inches between plants.

Care & Problems—These plants are pest-free and don't generally require staking. Deadhead to encourage continuous bloom. Water if your area is experiencing drought. They do not require extra fertilizer. Shasta daisies spread, sometimes vigorously. Divide every three to four years to reinvigorate a plant. Cut back plants in early spring before new foliage emerges.

Bloom Color(s)—White with yellow center

Bloom Period/Peak Season—Summer to fall

Mature Size (H x W)—3 feet x 3 feet

Hardiness—5–9

Water Needs—Medium

SIBERIAN BUGLOSS
Brunnera macrophylla 'Jack Frost'

Why It's Special—Siberian bugloss, particularly the 'Jack Frost' cultivar, is a garden standout. The flowers look like forget-me-not flowers, but unlike the other blue spring-blooming flower, bugloss also has shiny silvery leaves that brighten up the shade garden, even after the plants stop blooming.

How to Plant & Grow—Plant in partial shade (the hotter your climate, the more shade needed) in moist, well-drained soils. Water to establish. Bugloss spreads through underground rhizomes.

Care & Problems—It's fairly pest-free *and* rabbit resistant. 'Jack Frost' is drought tolerant once established. Cut back the flower stalks after the plant finishes flowering to tidy the overall appearance. The leaves will brighten up the shade garden throughout summer. If slugs are a problem, sprinkle diatomaceous earth around the plants or set beer traps—shallow lids filled with beer and sunk into the ground near the plants. Cut foliage back in late fall after plants go dormant.

Bloom Color(s)—Blue; 'Jack Frost' also grown for silver leaves

Bloom Period/Peak Season—Blooms in spring

Mature Size (H x W)—12 inches x 12 inches

Hardiness—3–8

Water Needs—Medium

SNAKEROOT
Actaea racemosa

Why It's Special—Snakeroot has unusual undulating spikes of white flowers that "snake" through the garden in spring. It is sometimes called "bugbane" or "black cohosh." It has medicinal properties, but I grow it because it's a nice architectural addition to the shade garden, particularly with its mid- to late-season blooms. It is the larval host plant of the spring azure butterfly, so don't crush the caterpillars if you see them feeding on the plants.

How to Plant & Grow—Plant in partial to full shade after the last frost. Snakeroot thrives in moist, well-drained soils. Water to establish. Leave 2 to 4 feet between plants. It pairs well with hosta, astilbe, ferns, and other moist-shade-loving plants.

Care & Problems—Take care to keep the soil moist throughout the growing season. Sometimes the flower stalks will require individual staking. You can remove the stalks (and the stakes) after they finish blooming to tidy up the plant. Snakeroot can be slow to establish and doesn't like to be moved.

Bloom Color(s)—White

Bloom Period/Peak Season—Mid to late summer

Mature Size (H x W)—2–4 feet x 2–4 feet

Hardiness—3–8

Water Needs—Medium

SOLOMON'S SEAL
Polygonatum odoratum

Why It's Special—Solomon's seal creates a sea of undulating green when mass-planted in the shade garden. It makes the biggest impact when planted in multiples. It spreads through underground rhizomes. In spring, dainty, white, bell-shaped flowers open along the bottom midrib of each arching branch. 'Variegatum' is the most popular cultivar, with green leaves that have creamy white margins.

How to Plant & Grow—Plant in early spring in partial to full shade in moist soil. It doesn't like to be wet during winter, but requires moisture during the growing season. Leave 6 to 12 inches between plants. The variegated varieties with white leaf margins add some light to shady areas.

Care & Problems—This is a fairly trouble-free plant as long as soil is kept moist. Watch out for slugs; use diotamaceous earth around plants to prevent slugs from munching, if necessary. Cut back in late fall.

Bloom Color(s)—White, but primarily grown for green or variegated foliage

Bloom Period/Peak Season—Blooms in spring, foliage in summer

Mature Size (H x W)—2–3 feet x 1–2 feet

Hardiness—3–8

Water Needs—Medium

SPIDERWORT
Tradescantia 'Sweet Kate'

Why It's Special—Spiderwort is an often-overlooked perennial that performs well in the shade garden. 'Sweet Kate', with brightly colored chartreuse leaves, really lightens up the shade garden. The species is native to moist woodlands and is attractive too. Spiderwort tolerates poor soil, so it's a good choice for difficult areas.

How to Plant & Grow—Plant in part shade to shade in moist soil. Its foliage will start to decline and die back midsummer, so plant spiderwort in the middle of a garden bed where other plants can cover declining foliage. Water to establish.

Care & Problems—Keep the soil moist throughout the growing season. Cut back foliage in midsummer to renew the plant. It will grow back out and, possibly, rebloom in fall. Watch out for slugs and snails. Divide every three to four years in early spring. The species can spread fairly aggressively if happy with its garden location.

Bloom Color(s)—Purple flowers, chartreuse leaves

Bloom Period/Peak Season—Summer

Mature Size (H x W)—18 inches x 12–18 inches

Hardiness—5–8

Water Needs—Medium to high

SPOTTED DEAD NETTLE
Lamium maculatum

Why It's Special—This plant could as easily be classified as a groundcover. It is a fast grower. Spotted dead nettle's variegated leaves brighten up the shade garden. There are white- and pink-flowering varieties, but you'll grow spotted dead nettle primarily for its foliage. 'White Nancy' is named for the leaf color, which is white in the center with green edges. 'Pink Pewter' has larger, showier pink flowers and primarily white leaves with a thin margin of green.

How to Plant & Grow—Plant in full to partial shade in moist, well-drained soils. Water to establish. Leave 12 to 18 inches between plants because they do spread. Plant them where you can take advantage of their vigorous growth habit.

Care & Problems—You may have to divide or root prune to halt its aggressive spread. It's better to plant where that's an asset instead of an annoyance. Keep the soil moist through the growing season.

Bloom Color(s)—Pink or white (depending on variety)

Bloom Period/Peak Season—Blooms later summer

Mature Size (H x W)—6–12 inches x 2–3 feet

Hardiness—5–8

Water Needs—Medium

STOKES ASTER
Stokesia laevis

Why It's Special—Stokes aster is a perennial native to the Southeast, though it grows as far north as Zone 6. It has daisylike, frilly purple flowers that bloom in early summer. 'Blue Danube' has semi-double flowers. They aren't picky, once established, and will grow in almost any soil conditions. Stokes aster is just a hard-working plant with pretty flowers. Cut individual stems for long-lasting bouquets. What's not to love?

How to Plant & Grow—Plant in full sun to partial shade in moist, well-drained soil. These plants aren't big spreaders; space at 12 to 18 inches. Water to establish.

Care & Problems—Mulch during winter if you're growing it in Zones 6 or lower. Deadhead to encourage longer bloom periods. Cut back the entire plant in late fall when it is entirely dormant. Flower stalks will sometimes lay down after a heavy rain. Once they dry off, they'll pop back up. There's no need to stake.

Bloom Color(s)—Light purple

Bloom Period/Peak Season—Early summer

Mature Size (H x W)—1–2 feet x 1 foot

Hardiness—5–9

Water Needs—Medium

SWITCHGRASS
Panicum virgatum

Why It's Special—Switchgrass is another native that has been cultivated for ornamental use in the garden. 'Shenandoah' has burgundy and green leaves and absolutely glows when the sun shines through it. 'Dallas Blues' has a strongly upright habit and clouds of bluish/pinkish flowers in late summer.

How to Plant & Grow—Plant after frost in full sun in moist, well-drained soil. Water to establish. Spacing depends on the cultivar, but allow 2 to 4 feet between plants. Switchgrass is one of the larger ornamental grasses. Plant with native sun perennials such as coneflowers and coreopsis.

Care & Problems—These are easy-care plants provided they're growing in full sun and moist, well-drained soils. Allow the flowers and foliage to stay in the garden through winter to add height and color. The birds also enjoy eating the seeds. Shear it to 6 inches in late winter. You can divide it in spring if the clump starts to decline in the middle.

Bloom Color(s)—Pinkish

Bloom Period/Peak Season—Blooms in midsummer; garden interest in summer, fall, and winter

Mature Size (H x W)—3–6 feet x 2–4 feet

Hardiness—5–9

Water Needs—Medium

TIARELLA
Tiarella cordifolia

Why It's Special—These plants remind many of heuchera, and there are tiarella/heuchera hybrids called "heucherellas." This woodland wildflower is also called foamflower, because when grown in masses, its spring blooms looks like a carpet of foam on the forest floor.

How to Plant & Grow—Plant outside in early spring after the ground has thawed. Tiarella needs partial to full shade and continually moist, though well-drained, soil. It is a clumping perennial, and while a clump will slowly get larger, it doesn't really spread much. Water to establish. Combines well with some ferns, Solomon's seal, hosta, bleeding heart, and other shade perennials.

Care & Problems—It's fairly pest-free, but watch for slugs and snails. Sprinkle diatomaceous earth around plants to create a barrier. You can cut off the flowers after they are finished blooming. Divide in fall every three to four years. Keep the soil evenly moist throughout the growing season.

Bloom Color(s)—White, pinkish white

Bloom Period/Peak Season—Blooms in spring, foliage interest in summer

Mature Size (H x W)—6–12 inches x 12–18 inches

Hardiness—4–9

Water Needs—Medium

TOAD LILY
Tricyrtis hirta

Why It's Special—Toad lilies look like tropical orchids that should be growing on an island with softly blowing salt breezes. Instead, they are relatively tough, cold-hardy plants that thrive in the moist soils of shady perennial gardens. They're spectacular in the fall garden.

How to Plant & Grow—Plant in spring or fall in partial shade to full shade in moist soils. Toad lilies like it wet; keep watered to establish. (I plant mine next to my bird bath so that I know it always gets extra water.) Leave 1 to 3 feet between plants, depending on the eventual mature size of what you're growing.

Care & Problems—These are easy-care plants. They can sometimes flop open and flatten everything around them. If you're particular about them staying upright, use the star and single stake method to stake them or construct a lattice. Watch out for slugs. Keep the soil evenly moist throughout the growing season.

Bloom Color(s)—Shades of white, purple, pink; usually spotted bicolor

Bloom Period/Peak Season—Late summer to fall

Mature Size (H x W)—1–3 feet x 1–3 feet

Hardiness—5–8

Water Needs—High

VERONICA
Veronica spicata

Why It's Special—Veronica, also called speedwell, is sometimes mistaken for salvia. They have similar growth habits—spikes of purple or pink flowers—but they're not the same genus. Veronica blooms a little later than many perennial salvias and has a softer texture in the garden. 'Royal Candles' is a dwarf cultivar with purple flowers. 'Twilight' has tall, light purple bloom spikes and slightly larger leaves than the species.

How to Plant & Grow—Plant outside after the last frost in full sun in well-drained soil. Leave 12 to 18 inches between plants. Water to establish. Veronica makes a big splash when mass-planted, and it looks great with low-growing shrub roses.

Care & Problems—It's pest- and problem-free unless it sits in wet soil. It is, in fact, a good problem-solver plant for dry areas. If it's not happy, move it. Deadhead to encourage repeat bloom. It rarely needs staking, but cut it back in early spring before new foliage emerges.

Bloom Color(s)—Purple, pink, white

Bloom Period/Peak Season—Summer

Mature Size (H x W)—12 inches x 12 inches

Hardiness—3–8

Water Needs—Medium to low

YARROW
Achillea millefolium

Why It's Special—Yarrow is beloved by butterflies. That's reason enough to plant it. The blooms are unique composites of small, flat, daisy-shaped flowers on top of fernlike foliage. Yarrow does have a strong aroma, and as such is deer resistant. It makes a good cut flower, tolerates poor soils, and is easy to grow. There is a tall yellow variety that makes a good dried flower and shorter varieties that are good for cutting. Historically, this plant has been used for medicinal purposes, and you will often find it listed as an ingredient in herbal teas.

How to Plant & Grow—Plant in full sun in well-drained soil. Leave 12 to 18 inches between plants, as they will spread. Water to establish.

Care & Problems—Yarrow absolutely requires good drainage, particularly in winter, to thrive. Cut flowers back to the ground after bloom. Yarrow is a spreader. Divide clumps every three to four years to reinvigorate the plant clumps.

Bloom Color(s)—Pink, white, yellow

Bloom Period/Peak Season—Summer

Mature Size (H x W)—2–3 feet x 2–3 feet

Hardiness—3–9

Water Needs—Low

PERENNIALS MONTH-BY-MONTH

JANUARY

- Walk through the garden and look for signs of animal damage, winter damage, and frost heaving. Heucheras are notorious for this. Use your foot or the bottom of a hoe to push the plant back into the soil. If it looks like animals are chewing on the plants, spray repellants.

- Look through catalogs and online to order unusual and hard-to-find perennials.

- Order seeds for any perennials you want to try to grow from seed. I'm not a huge fan of starting perennials from seed because they can have some strange requirements. Foxglove (a biennial), penstemon, and columbine are relatively easy to start from seed, so try growing unusual varieties of those plants yourself.

FEBRUARY

- Shear ornamental grasses that have given up for the year. If there's been heavy snowfall, you've probably seen the last of their utility in the landscape.

- Start perennial seeds indoors. Before planting, sterilize any flats or pots that you are reusing. Plant in sterile seed-starting mix and keep the mix continuously damp, but not soggy, as seeds are sprouting.

- Visit a garden show. You can get good ideas for plant combinations from looking at the display gardens. The thing about garden shows is just that—they're shows. The plants combined in display gardens might or might not grow well together in the garden, but you can get some ideas for interesting colors and textures to put together—even if you have to find those in different plants.

MARCH

- Cut back perennials that have died back over winter. This is your last chance to clean up the garden before things grow like gangbusters. Do not cut back lavender until you see signs of new growth (which will probably be in May).

- Look for hellebores and other early-blooming perennials. You might need to gently rake leaves and winter debris away from the plants so that you can enjoy the blooms.

- Store any mail-ordered bare-root perennials until they can be planted outside. If they're still dormant, store them in a cool, dry location. If they're showing signs of growth, pot them up and keep them indoors in a cool location until they can be hardened off and planted outside.

APRIL

- Enjoy early-blooming perennials such as creeping phlox, candytuft, lungwort, and more. Deadhead candytuft after it blooms to keep the plant looking tidy and to encourage it to grow a healthy root system.

- Clear leaves and debris from the winter out of the garden so that emerging perennials don't rot before they have a chance to grow.

- Transplant perennial seedlings that you've started indoors into larger pots so they can get bigger before going out into the garden.

- Position peony cages so that the foliage can grow up through the supports.

- Plant bare-root perennials.

MAY

- Spray perennial foliage with deer and rabbit repellent if you have problems with those animals snacking on your garden plants.

- Divide perennials that have overgrown their spots in the garden or that have declined in vigor. Replant and gift extras to friends.

- Harden off and plant seedlings that you started indoors.

- Thin beebalm, garden phlox, and other plants susceptible to powdery mildew. Remove one-third to one-half of flower stalks, creating areas for airflow through the plants.

- Spread new mulch—shredded hardwood, shredded leaf compost, or compost. This is easiest to do before plants become huge.

- Plant new perennials.

- Cut back lavender when new growth appears.

JUNE

- Stake tall perennials that might be flopping over. It's better if you can catch them before they flop. Create a lattice of stakes and twine for perennials that grow in large clumps so that they can have some support while still maintaining a natural growth habit.

- Spread diatomaceous earth around perennials to prevent slugs and snails from chomping on the plants.

- Divide and move early spring-blooming perennials. Water to help the plants re-establish themselves.

- Deadhead Shasta daisies, false indigo, daylilies, peonies, and dianthus.

- Pinch or cut back fall-blooming perennials if you want to control size or delay bloom.

JULY

- Search for and destroy Japanese beetles. Knock them off your plants and into a bucket of soapy water.

- Look for leafminer damage. That will present as S-shaped patterns in leaves. Cut the infected areas to the ground and let them grow back out.

- Continue general summer garden maintenance. Water if there is drought. Deadhead perennials. Reapply deer, rabbit, and squirrel repellents. If plants are flopping open in the center, cut them back by half.

- Cut back daylilies to the ground if the foliage is looking ratty. It will regrow.

- Scout the garden for signs that plants need to be fertilized. If you've had heavy rains this summer or you garden on sandy, nutrient-depleted soil, plants might be showing signs of hunger, including yellow leaves. Feed with liquid organic fertilizer or spread a slow-release fertilizer around the garden. Water well.

AUGUST

- Sow seeds for biennials, such as foxglove, outside to allow them to grow a healthy basal rosette of leaves in the garden before winter.

- Pinch mums to delay flowering.

- Cut back heavy bloomers such as blanket flower and coreopsis to encourage more foliage growth and to give the plants a break from blooming.

- Visit garden centers for end-of-season sales. Cut plants back by half when planting so that they put energy into establishing good root systems, not into producing flashy flowers.

SEPTEMBER

- Plant mums in containers and in the landscape for fall blooms. Stop pinching mums that have perennialized and allow them to form flower buds.

- Change out container plantings and consider adding semi-evergreen or evergreen perennials to container gardens.

- Apply pre-emergent herbicide to the garden to keep cool-weather weeds at a minimum.

- Dig and divide any perennials that you didn't get a chance to move in spring.

OCTOBER

- Allow perennials to go to seed for the birds.

- Remove any infected or infested plant material from the garden and throw away (don't compost). Otherwise, you can allow plants to simply go dormant. Resist the urge to cut everything back. You don't want to stimulate new growth this late in the season.

- If you have any perennial seeds that didn't make it into seed flats during the spring, now is a good time to scatter them around the garden.

NOVEMBER

- Resist the urge to remove mums from the garden or cut down the foliage. If you want new mums to perennialize, leave this year's growth standing. It will protect any new growth that is stimulated near the bottom of the plant.

- Cut ornamental grass branches and perennial seedheads for use in fall decorations.

- Change out container gardens for fall/holiday plantings. Incorporate evergreen and semi-evergreen perennials such as heuchera and lenten roses for color all winter.

DECEMBER

- Cut back perennials and do some general garden cleanup. Plants should be dormant enough that you won't stimulate them to grow.

- Clean and sharpen garden tools and store them for winter. Spring will be here before you know it!

GROUNDCOVERS
for the Mid-Atlantic

True groundcovers should be used in the garden for their intended purpose—as groundcovers—not as individual perennials or shrubs, unless you want a very maintenance-intensive garden. One exception is to use them as border plants. I got tired of the empty spaces between the sidewalk and the seasonal annuals I plant in my front garden, so I planted *Lysimachia* along the walk. I still have to keep it inbounds on the sides of the plants that face the rest of the perennial bed, but at least it has a hard edge in the front.

Groundcovers have a wide range of uses:

- Plant them in the hell strip (the "grass" area between the sidewalk and the street) where nothing else will grow.
- Use them to fill in under trees where grass won't grow.
- Plant them on hills and embankments to control erosion or to eliminate the need to mow frequently.
- Replace part of your yard with groundcovers so you have less maintenance to do.
- Create living landscape bed edging (if you're willing to do the work to keep the plants out of the rest of the bed).

Most groundcovers are aggressive growers, even in less-than-ideal conditions, so put them to work for you, instead of fighting with them.

SELECTING GROUNDCOVERS

Select a groundcover that matches its intended purpose. Want to keep people out of a certain area? Creeping cotoneasters or creeping junipers are good choices. They're kind of prickly and not easy to walk on. Have an area that gets absolutely baked by the sun? Sedum is your go-to groundcover. What about under trees where grass won't grow? Lirope will give you a grasslike look with much less maintenance.

Other things to consider when selecting groundcovers:

- Does it need to be evergreen?
- How tall can it be, reasonably, before it interferes with whatever else is going on around it?
- How often do you want to or can you mow it or trim it?
- Will it be growing in a wet area or a dry area?
- Do you want a groundcover that will flower at some point?
- Is a groundcover that truly grows fast and takes over the area where it's growing desirably, or do you want to use perennials that aren't as aggressive as groundcover? (Heuchera, tiarellia, and some ornamental grass come to mind for this type of use.)

SOURCING GROUNDCOVERS

Garden centers and home-improvement stores are stocking more types of groundcovers, and in more sizes too. If you can swing it, pick up six-packs or 4-inch pots of your chosen groundcovers. Those will give you coverage the fastest. Sometimes when you order online you'll be given the option to purchase plugs or liners. These are small plants (usually with rootballs less than 1 inch in diameter) that are often purchased by growers, potted up to larger sizes, and grown larger so that you, the consumer, can purchase a more developed plant. These are a cost-effective option, when you can find them.

Most groundcovers are vegetatively propagated, or grown from cuttings, so they're not readily available as seeds.

DESIGNING WITH GROUNDCOVERS

Longwood Gardens in Pennsylvania used to have a section of the garden devoted to groundcovers, and I always thought it did an amazing job of showing how interesting a garden can be when only planted with groundcovers. There are so many textures, colors, and forms available.

Whether you're planting the hell strip or an area under a tree, let yourself branch out from growing just a single type of groundcover. Sure, that means you'll have to do a little bit of maintenance to keep the two or three types of plants from growing all over each other, but you can do that by cutting a hard edge between them a couple of times each year.

Contrast is key when working on this type of design. Pair a narrow-leafed, grass-type groundcover with lady's mantle or a hosta, a plant with larger leaves. Plant plants with chartreuse leaves next to plants with burgundy leaves. Without contrast, a groundcover garden will just look like a blob.

CARING FOR GROUNDCOVERS

Groundcover care is a cross between maintaining a lawn and maintaining a perennial garden, but on the low end of what it usually takes to maintain either.

WATERING

Part of the attraction of groundcovers is, once they are established, they need little extra input, including water. If you're experiencing a drought, groundcovers will need water, just as lawns or flowerbeds will need water. Water groundcovers until they're well established, and then leave them alone unless you have to water the rest of the garden.

WEEDING

Weeding the groundcover bed can be incredibly frustrating, especially when you're just getting the bed started. Whenever you disturb the soil, which you do when planting, you expose new weed seeds to light, encouraging germination. You can prevent some of this by planting, then mulching to cover the seeds back up.

Once the bed is established, you can use pre-emergent herbicides in the spring and fall to keep weeds that grow from seeds from sprouting. If a weed that spreads by stolons (horizontal stems) or rhizomes gets in the bed, you'll have to hand-pull or spray with weedkiller, taking care not to spray everything else around the weed.

The best plan of attack for weeds in the groundcover bed is to do everything you can to stay on top of them. With persistent attention to removal, the pressure from weeds will eventually decrease.

FERTILIZING

Most groundcovers grow just fine without extra fertilizer. If you are gardening on sandy soil with poor nutrient retention, fertilize once in spring and once in midsummer with a multipurpose liquid fertilizer. You can also apply a slow-release fertilizer in spring. Just make sure to water it in and wash it off the plant leaves so that they don't burn.

MOWING AND PRUNING

Some groundcovers need a yearly mowing in the spring. You can use a lawn mower set on the highest setting or a string trimmer. Be careful not to trim down to bare earth. Liriope is one that looks better if it gets a yearly trim. If the groundcover has grown to the point that it forms a thick mat, you can also mow and allow the plants to regrow fresh.

You might have to prune shrubby groundcovers. Junipers and cotoneasters can throw up a branch that grows vertically instead of horizontally. Just get out the hand pruners and snip off the branch. Cut it back to the nearest horizontal branch.

EDGING

Just as you'd edge the lawn to keep it neat and tidy along walkways and flower beds, you can edge groundcover areas. Use a power edger or a shovel to cut a clean edge in spring, midsummer, and in fall. If you're growing two types of groundcovers in close proximity, you'll probably have to edge between the two types to keep them separate.

Here are some of the best groundcover choices for mid-Atlantic gardeners. Not only are these plants functional, they add beauty and life to the garden where they're planted.

AJUGA
Ajuga reptans

Why It's Special—Ajuga is one of my favorite groundcovers. It has blue flowers and burgundy-purple leaves, so it looks great whether or not it is flowering. It is semi-evergreen too. Sometimes you'll see it referred to as bugleweed. In addition to the species, look for the cultivar 'Chocolate Chip', which has small leaves, about the size of your pinky nail. 'Burgundy Glow' has green, pink, and white leaves.

How to Plant & Grow—Plant in full sun to shade in moist, well-drained soil. It's a good one to plant under larger trees or in areas where grass doesn't grow. It's also deer resistant. Leave 12 inches between plants.

Care & Problems—This plant can experience crown rot if planted in wet, slow-draining soils. Divide every three to four years if the plants get overcrowded and die back in spots. Water to establish. After that, provide supplemental water only if you're experiencing drought.

Bloom Color(s)—Bluish purple

Bloom Period/Peak Season—Spring to early summer

Mature Size (H x W)—6–8 inches x 6–12 inches (spreads)

Hardiness—3–9

Water Needs—Medium

CREEPING COTONEASTER
Cotoneaster adpressus

Why It's Special—This creeping cotoneaster is at home in the rock garden, climbing over walls, or as a groundcover in landscape beds. It has small, pinkish white flowers in spring that mature into little red fruits in fall. It is highly adaptable to a wide range of soils and is rabbit resistant. 'Little Gem', sometimes sold as 'Tom Thumb', is more compact than the species.

How to Plant & Grow—Plant in full sun to partial shade in well-drained soils. If you're using it as a groundcover, leave 3 feet between plants. Water to establish.

Care & Problems—This plant can collect trash and leaves, depending on where it is planted. Use a shrub rake to remove them. If you're experiencing a drought, give it extra water. Fireblight can be a problem. Cut the infected areas 12 inches below the canker, sterilizing pruners before each cut. It has a compact growth habit and requires little pruning to maintain size and shape.

Bloom Color(s)—Pinkish white

Bloom Period/Peak Season—Early summer

Mature Size (H x W)—1 foot x 6 feet

Hardiness—4–8

Water Needs—Medium to low

CREEPING JENNY
Lysimachia nummularia 'Aurea'

Why It's Special—This groundcover is highly aggressive, but that comes in handy when you need something that will cover everything in sight. 'Aurea' has bright chartreuse-yellow leaves that develop their best color in full sun. This plant is semi-evergreen in warmer areas and develops a bronzy color during winter.

How to Plant & Grow—Plant in full sun to part shade (it can take more shade in warmer areas). Creeping Jenny thrives in moist soil and declines in dry soil. Can be used as a "spiller" in containers or in rock gardens or to trail over retaining walls. It truly shines when grown with plants that have burgundy-colored leaves or dark purple flowers.

Care & Problems—It's pretty hard to kill this plant, like it or not. Water if your area is not receiving regular rain. You can chop it back, dig it up and divide it, and use a power edger on it to keep it inbounds. There are few pest problems.

Bloom Color(s)—Grown for chartreuse foliage

Bloom Period/Peak Season—Year-round; semi-evergreen

Mature Size (H x W)—2–4 inches x 12–18 inches

Hardiness—4–8

Water Needs—Medium to wet; adaptable

CREEPING JUNIPER
Juniperus horizontalis

Why It's Special—Creeping juniper is a commonly planted groundcover shrub because it's so easy to grow. As an evergreen, it provides year-round interest. It looks really cool if planted along the edges of retaining walls and allowed to cascade down the side. It will sometimes develop a rusty burgundy color in winter. 'Blue Rug' is one of the most popular cultivars. 'Blue Chip' is slightly more compact (not as wide). 'Plumosa' has spiky, upward-facing branches.

How to Plant & Grow—Plant in full sun in well-drained soil. Leave 3 feet between plants to allow it to spread. Blue rug juniper looks really good when planted in a combination with miscanthus and shrub roses. (That's a fast way to fill up a landscape bed!) Water to establish.

Care & Problems—This plant is drought tolerant once established. It does best in dry soils. Cedar apple rust overwinters on junipers, creating orange galls. If you see those, cut them off and throw them away. Plants tolerate salt spray.

Bloom Color(s)—No bloom. Blue-gray foliage.

Bloom Period/Peak Season—Year-round, evergreen

Mature Size (H x W)—6–18 inches x 4–6 feet

Hardiness—3–9

Water Needs—Medium to low

CREEPING SEDUM
Sedum spp.

Why It's Special—Creeping sedums add a lot of variety to the garden, offering many different leaf colors, from burgundy to silver to chartreuse, and an equally diverse array of flower color. They are succulent plants and highly drought tolerant. Grow them along the edges of a perennial garden, in rock gardens, or cascading over walls. Some garden stores are even offering "sedum sod," which are square mats of a variety of sedum cultivars grown together.

How to Plant & Grow—Plant in full sun in well-drained soil after the last frost. They will rot if they sit in wet soils. Water to establish.

Care & Problems—Most sedums do not require extra water once established. If the leaves start to shrivel or take on a grayish cast, you'll know it's time to water. If the plants get leggy or ratty, cut them back in spring. You can divide and replant in spring or summer. Sedum has few pest problems.

Bloom Color(s)—Varies, but primarily grown for leaves

Bloom Period/Peak Season—Summer to fall

Mature Size (H x W)—Varies, between 3–6 inches x 12–18 inches

Hardiness—Varies by species and cultivar

Water Needs—Low

CREEPING ST. JOHN'S WORT
Hypericum calycinum

Why It's Special—St. John's wort is a woody, creeping groundcover shrub that's widely adaptable to a variety of soil and growing conditions. The leaves are bluish gray. Yellow flowers with hundreds of stamens (which give them a fluffy appearance) cover the plants in late summer. Traditionally, the plants are used medicinally, but that's not something you should engage in without proper training!

How to Plant & Grow—Plant outside in moist, well-drained soil in spring or fall. This is one shrub that will grow well under trees, creating a dense carpet of foliage. It's excellent for use along driveways or sidewalks to add interest in problem areas. Leave 2 feet between plants. Water to establish.

Care & Problems—This is an easy-care plant with few pest problems. May experience some winter dieback in cooler regions. Prune dead areas back in spring and shape the shrub, overall, after flowering. Water in winter if you experience high winds during sunny days that are also below freezing.

Bloom Color(s)—Yellow

Bloom Period/Peak Season—Late summer

Mature Size (H x W)—12–18 inches x 18–24 inches

Hardiness—5–9

Water Needs—Medium

CREEPING PHLOX
Phlox subulata

Why It's Special—This is an early-blooming perennial that can also be grown as a groundcover. It flowers after most woodland wildflowers but before many spring-blooming perennials. Its mossy foliage looks nice all summer. It grows well in rock gardens or over retaining walls. It's both deer resistant and semi-evergreen.

How to Plant & Grow—Plant in spring when the ground has thawed or in fall before the first frost. It does best in full sun but can take partial shade, particularly in warmer climates. Water to establish.

Care & Problems—This is a tough plant with few problems. Water during the growing season, particularly if there hasn't been much rain. You can shear the plant back by half after flowering to encourage a new flush of growth. If creeping phlox grows out of bounds, simply dig up part of the clump that's pushing the boundaries and plant it elsewhere, gift to a friend, or compost it.

Bloom Color(s)—Purple, pink, white

Bloom Period/Peak Season—Blooms early spring

Mature Size (H x W)—2–6 inches x 20 inches

Hardiness—3–8

Water Needs—Medium

EPIMEDIUM
Epimedium spp.

Why It's Special—Epimedium is just a cool plant. It has elongated, semi-evergreen (in Zones 7 to 8), heart-shaped leaves on wiry stems and delicate star-shaped flowers. The common name is "horny goat weed," also sometimes called "fairy wings." Leaves range in color from green to burgundy variegated and in size from thumbnail to 2 to 3 inches wide.

How to Plant & Grow—Epimedium is an excellent plant for dry shade. It does spread into larger clumps, but not aggressively, so it's best to plant in smaller areas for which you need groundcover, as opposed to a large area where you need quick coverage. The leaf size and texture contrasts well with hosta and other large-leafed, dry shade plants. Space 12 to 18 inches in the ground. Water to establish.

Care & Problems—It's fairly pest-free. Provide extra water if your area goes a month or more without rain. Cut back any foliage left in spring before new growth emerges.

Bloom Color(s)—Pink, white, rose, lavender (depends on cultivar)

Bloom Period/Peak Season—Flowers late spring

Mature Size (H x W)—12 inches x 12–18 inches

Hardiness—5–8

Water Needs—Medium to low

GOLDENSTAR
Chrysogonum virginianum

Why It's Special—This native groundcover blooms all summer with yellow daisylike flowers on top of bright green foliage. It's easy to care for and adapts well to moist soils, making it a true problem-solving plant. 'Pierre' is an improved fast-growing and long-blooming cultivar. 'Allen Bush' has shorter stems and is more compact in growth habit.

How to Plant & Grow—Plant outside after the last frost in part shade to full shade (it can take more sun if growing in a continuously moist location). Leave 12 inches between plants. Goldenstar is deer-esistant, so use it in outlying areas of the landscape if deer pressure is a problem. Propagate by digging clumps and transplanting them in bare areas. A few plants can populate an entire garden in a couple of years.

Care & Problems—This is an easy-care plant with few pest problems. Cut back foliage in early spring before new growth emerges. Water if your area is experiencing drought. No rain for two weeks or more is enough to push this plant toward decline.

Bloom Color(s)—Yellow

Bloom Period/Peak Season—Summer

Mature Size (H x W)—6 inches x 12 inches

Hardiness—5–9

Water Needs—High

HARDY VERBENA
Verbena 'Homestead Purple'

Why It's Special—Though not hardy in the entire Mid-Atlantic, hardy verbena is worth including because it can easily be grown as an annual. It's a fast grower. Butterflies *love* the purple flower clusters. Its dark green foliage is attractive. 'Homestead Purple' is a tough cultivar that will bloom from early summer through frost.

How to Plant & Grow—Plant just after frost in full sun in well-drained soil. Verbena will rot if it has wet feet. Leave 18 to 24 inches between plants. Water to establish.

Care & Problems—Verbena needs slightly moist soil, so if you aren't getting any rain, provide supplemental water every other week during summer. If the plant starts to look ratty during summer, cut it back. It will regrow and bloom. Fertilize once, midsummer, with liquid fertilizer. Leave the plant in the garden over winter and cut it back in spring. It might overwinter—you never know!

Bloom Color(s)—Purple

Bloom Period/Peak Season—Early summer, may rebloom in fall

Mature Size (H x W)—12–18 inches x 3 feet

Hardiness—7–10

Water Needs—Medium

LILY-OF-THE-VALLEY
Convallaria majalis

Why It's Special—The flowers of this native perennial groundcover are among some of the most fragrant you can grow. They are another one of the old-fashioned cottage garden flowers and seem like they should be much more fragile than they are. These flowers are excellent for little bouquets and nosegays. Lily-of-the-valley is an aggressive spreader if it is happy where it is growing, and it's deer resistant.

How to Plant & Grow—Plant in full sun to full shade in moist, well-drained soil. That being said, it will grow in dry shady areas where you have trouble getting other plants to thrive. Leave 12 inches between plants, as they do spread. Water to establish.

Care & Problems—If the plants threaten to take over, just dig up chunks and give them away to friends. You can cut the flower stalks back after the bloom, but you don't have to. Cut the foliage back in late fall or early spring before new growth appears.

Bloom Color(s)—White

Bloom Period/Peak Season—Spring

Mature Size (H x W)—6–12 inches x 6–12 inches

Hardiness—2–7

Water Needs—Medium to high

LIRIOPE
Liriope muscari

Why It's Special—Lirope is deer resistant, drought tolerant, will grow under trees, and adapts to almost any soil condition. If you have an area where grass won't grow, plant lirope for a grasslike look. It can be planted in perennial gardens to add a unique texture; use in place of ornamental grasses in areas with heavy shade. *Liriope muscari* is taller, has large purple flower spikes, and spreads in clumps, while its close relative, *L. spicata*, is shorter, has lighter lavender flowers, and spreads via runners.

How to Plant & Grow—Plant in full sun to full shade in moist, well-drained soils. Leave 12 inches between clumps as they do spread. Water to establish.

Care & Problems—This is a tough and relatively pest-free plant, not even appealing to deer. The biggest maintenance requirement is to shear it back in early spring before new growth emerges. You can divide it and move clumps to other areas of the garden or share with friends.

Bloom Color(s)—Lavender

Bloom Period/Peak Season—Late summer to fall

Mature Size (H x W)—12 inches x 12 inches

Hardiness—5–10

Water Needs—Medium

MONDO GRASS
Ophiopogon japonicus

Why It's Special—Mondo grass, sometimes called "monkey grass," is an excellent edging groundcover or lawn replacement for small patio spaces. It has short, dark green, grasslike leaves. You can plant it in between pavers for some color. It's best grown in protected areas. 'Nanus' is the dwarf variety and is half the size of the species. You'll frequently see this planted in Japanese gardens, providing a contrasting texture, and thus more interest, in what are traditionally almost fully green landscapes.

How to Plant & Grow—Plant in partial to full shade in moist, well-drained soils. In Zone 7, plant in a protected area, between pavers, or next to a south- or west-facing wall. Because of its thick and aggressive root system, this plant is excellent for erosion control. Water to establish.

Care & Problems—Mondo grass is easy to grow with few pest problems. If it gets too matted, dig up and divide in spring. If foliage gets ratty, cut back in spring before new growth appears.

Bloom Color(s)—Grown for foliage

Bloom Period/Peak Season—Summer to winter

Mature Size (H x W)—4 inches x 12 inches

Hardiness—7–10

Water Needs—Medium

PACHYSANDRA
Pachysandra terminalis

Why It's Special—Though pachysandra (also referred to as "Japanese spurge" is not the most interesting groundcover, it is one of the easiest to grow and that is worth something. It's deer resistant, adaptable to a wide range of soils and growing conditions, spreads rapidly, and is evergreen.

How to Plant & Grow—Plant outside in spring after last frost or in fall before the first frost. Grows best in partial to full shade in moist, well-drained, slightly acidic soils. It can develop chlorosis in alkaline soils. If the leaf color is off, get a soil test to check the pH and lower it with aluminum sulfate if it's above 6.5. Water to establish. Space plants 12 to 18 inches.

Care & Problems—This is a fairly trouble-free plant that's sometimes susceptible to fungal diseases. If those become a problem, take a sample to your County Extension for help finding a remedy. You can divide or mow this back in early spring if the center of the mat of plants starts to decline.

Bloom Color(s)—White

Bloom Period/Peak Season—Spring bloom; evergreen

Mature Size (H x W)—6–12 inches x 12–24 inches

Hardiness—5–9

Water Needs—Medium to low

SWEET WOODRUFF
Galium odoratum

Why It's Special—Sweet woodruff has small, fragrant, white flowers that emerge in spring and small, slightly hairy whorls of leaves that hold up well in shady areas throughout summer. The leaves are what give the plant such a unique look—arranged around the stem like spokes in a wheel. This groundcover should really be more popular than it is because it is so attractive throughout the entire growing season. It creates quite a unique texture in the garden when planted in masses.

How to Plant & Grow—Plant in part shade to full shade in moist, well-drained soils. It naturalizes well under trees and in shady landscape beds. It spreads through seed and underground runners. Water to establish.

Care & Problems—Provide supplemental water if you're experiencing a droughty summer. If plants get ragged, you can mow over them at the highest setting, midsummer or fall. This is a fairly pest-free plant. It may require power edging to keep in check.

Bloom Color(s)—White

Bloom Period/Peak Season—Spring

Mature Size (H x W)—6–12 inches x 12–18 inches

Hardiness—4–8

Water Needs—Medium to high

GROUNDCOVERS MONTH-BY-MONTH

JANUARY

- Water broadleaf groundcovers if you have windy, sunny days with temperatures above freezing. Broadleaf evergreens can dry out and be scorched by winter winds because they transpire water (soak it up and evaporate it through their leaves) faster than they can take it in when the ground is frozen.

- Keep an eye on groundcover shrubs. If they're getting munched on by animals, apply repellents. Netting works well on fruit trees to protect the harvest, but not as much for groundcovers. It's better to use repellants or select plants that pests do not find attractive.

FEBRUARY

- Take a walk through the garden. Are there any bare spots that you would consider planting with groundcovers? Take measurements and do some armchair shopping. Look for plants that will fill needs in the bare areas of the garden. While there will be an initial investment of plants, the cost will amortize over time because you won't have to keep applying mulch to bare areas year after year.

- Keep groundcover beds clean by raking, removing, and composting any leaves and debris that get stuck in the beds. Big leaves can trap moisture and cause rot.

MARCH

- Edge groundcover beds with a spade or power edger. It's easier to do this now than it is when plants are actively growing for the spring. If you have groundcover gardens where you're growing two or more groundcovers next to each other, this is a good time to establish a new edge between them as well.

- Prune groundcovers. Remove dead or declining plants or vines. Prune to control size in junipers and creeping cotoneasters.

- Apply pre-emergent herbicides in groundcover beds to keep weed seeds from sprouting. Water in well and wash off the foliage.

APRIL

- Plant new groundcover beds in warmer areas (Zones 7 to 8). Test the soil before planting and make adjustments if the pH is out of line. Spread compost and plant plugs or 4-inch pots. General spacing between plants is 12 to 18 inches, but check the growth habit and rate of the plants you're growing to determine the best distance between plants for an even, solid coverage in a reasonable amount of time (1 to 2 growing seasons). Mulch to suppress weeds. Three weeks after planting, you can apply pre-emergent herbicide to keep weeds from crowding out the new plants.

- Rake and remove any leftover winter debris from groundcover beds. Mow or use a string trimmer to cut back liriope. Cut back old growth on epimedium plants before new growth appears.

MAY

- Spray repellents on groundcovers as new foliage emerges. This is only necessary if you notice frequent deer or rabbit pressure. Nets are not practical for use with groundcovers.

- Plant new groundcover beds in cooler areas (Zones 5 to 6.) Follow instructions as listed for planting new beds in April.

- Prune dead or diseased growth from groundcovers. Now that plants are beginning to leaf out, you can tell if there are bald spots among the plant clusters.

JUNE

- Lightly shear flowering groundcovers after they have finished flowering. This will keep them tidy and encourage new growth.

- Water groundcovers if you're not experiencing regular rainy weather.

- Check for pests. If you see scale on euonymus, head to a garden center or home-improvement store for a treatment. Cut spotted leaves from lily of the valley and pachysandra. (Wipe pruners with rubbing alcohol between plants.)

- Renovate old groundcover beds. Dig up healthy plants and divide them up. Dig up rotten or declining plants and compost them. Add compost to the groundcover bed and replant healthy plants. Mulch to control weeds.

- Observe your plants for problems with soil pH. This is the time of year when leaves on plants sensitive to pH start turning yellow from chlorosis if the soil is alkaline (pH over 6.5 to 7.0). When the pH is too high, iron is unavailable to plants, causing the discoloration. If you get a soil test done and you need to lower the pH, apply aluminum sulfate according to package instructions.

JULY

- Water groundcovers if rainfall is not sufficient.

- Keep an eye out for pests including Japanese beetles (which you can pick off the plants) and munching mammals. Reapply repellents. (It is a good idea to switch up repellent varieties every couple of months. Alternating scents keeps animals from getting used to the control mechanism.)

AUGUST

- Edge groundcover beds. With the warm summer to grow, they're probably starting to get out of control in certain areas.

- Pull weeds from groundcover beds before they set seed. This is your best and fastest way to keep weeds from taking over the beds.

- Prune any groundcovers that have escaped their boundaries. This is the last time you should prune before plants are fully dormant during the winter. Pruning in August will allow any new growth to harden off before cold weather arrives, lessening the chance of winter damage to plants.

SEPTEMBER

- Plant new groundcover beds in areas where grass steadily declined this year. Now is also a good time to introduce new plantings into the garden. If you have a landscape bed without good edging, consider planting a live edging by incorporating groundcovers.

- Apply pre-emergent herbicide in groundcover beds to keep winter weeds from sprouting.

- Dig and divide groundcovers where they are crowded and give extra plants to friends or replant in bare areas of the garden.

OCTOBER

- Mulch groundcover beds for winter protection and to keep weed pressure to a minimum. Use a broom or shrub rake to get the mulch in contact with the soil and to knock it off plant stems.

- Use a shrub rake to remove leaves from groundcover beds. Large leaves can trap water, causing groundcovers to rot.

NOVEMBER

- Continue to remove fall leaves from groundcover beds to prevent groundcover stems from rotting.

- Apply repellents to keep animals from munching evergreen groundcovers after most other plants have gone dormant.

DECEMBER

- Be careful when applying snowmelt chemicals near groundcover beds. You might consider using sand instead of chemicals to improve traction in snowy areas.

SHRUBS
for the Mid-Atlantic

It seems like shrubs are sometimes an afterthought in garden design, but they definitely shouldn't be. Shrubs are integral parts of the garden and landscape. They're multi-functional, serving as hedges, screens, specimens, foundation plantings, and borders. They also fill out the middle level of the landscape. Shrubs connect ground-level perennials and annuals to trees at the top level, and they provide interest at eye-level. They offer important cover and food sources for wildlife. In addition to their aesthetic value, they add diversity to the landscape, and the more diverse your landscape, the fewer problems you'll have with pests.

SELECTING SHRUBS

Selecting shrubs works much like selecting trees or perennials. You need to think about where you're putting the shrubs, what you need them to "do" in the landscape—specimen or backdrop, how much space you have for them to grow, whether you want flowers or interesting foliage, or both. Do you care if the shrubs are deciduous or evergreen? Do you want them to be high maintenance or low maintenance? Integrate the features of the shrubs you're considering into your overall design plan. Remember, contrast is key.

If you want to get more out of shrub plantings, consider adding edibles to the landscape. Blueberries, elderberries, gooseberries, honeyberry, aronia, currants, and lingonberry are all attractive shrubs that produce edible berries and are hardy in our area. Blueberries and elderberries are my favorites, because they have beautiful foliage and fall color, in addition to their edible berries.

SOURCING SHRUBS

Garden and home-improvement centers are carrying a lot more varieties of shrubs these days, and there are a great many more to choose from. If you are looking for something unusual, there are also many reputable mail-order companies. (There are plenty of non-reputable mail-order companies, as well. There's a list in the back of the book of several that I have ordered from and had good luck with.) Here are a few terms to keep in mind when reading the plant descriptions or tags to make sure you end up with something you want.

Dwarf: True dwarf varieties are slow-growing, but not non-growing. They will stay small for a while, but not indefinitely. A dwarf Alberta spruce can still grow to be 8 feet tall instead of the 12 inches it is when you buy it.

Container-grown: Grown in the greenhouse or field in container. It's usually shipped in the container.

Bare root: Most likely field-grown. Before shipping, it is dug up, the soil removed, and shipped with "bare roots." These have special care and planting requirements. See page 104 for instructions about how to plant bare-root shrubs.

Compact: Usually smaller varieties of popular species. These often have a more full branching habit, if not pruned a lot. There are lots new compact flowering shrub varieties.

Reblooming: Has more than one sustained period of bloom during a single growing season.

Blooms on new wood: Blooms on this year's growth. This usually means you can prune it in the spring.

Blooms on old wood: Blooms on last year's (or previous) growth. This usually means you should prune in the summer after blooming.

PLANTING SHRUBS

The best time to plant shrubs is in the spring or fall, so they have the chance to establish good root systems before scorching heat or bitter cold. Water to establish and keep a close eye on plants as they root in. Shrubs generally don't need to be staked.

Plant shrubs that are container-grown or balled-and-burlapped the same way you'd plant trees. See page 104 for instructions.

HOW TO PLANT A BARE-ROOT FRUIT TREE OR SHRUB

Some shrubs, most frequently roses, but also edibles, are shipped bare root. Here's how to plant those.

1. Soak the bare-root shrub roots in water the night before you plan to plant.

2. Dig a hole twice as wide as the diameter of the root spread and just as deep as the length of the roots.

3. Build a mound of soil in the center of the hole that is as high as the hole is deep.

4. Place the plant on top of the soil mound and spread the roots over the mound.

5. Fill in the soil around the plant, taking care that the point where the roots meet the trunk is above the soil line.

6. Finish by mulching around the plant. Water deeply.

CARING FOR SHRUBS

Most shrubs are fairly easy-care, in comparison to herbaceous plants, but they have a few requirements for healthy growth.

DEADHEADING

Deadheading is different than pruning to control shape or size. You don't have to deadhead all flowering shrubs, but shrubs that have large flowers with inconspicuous or undesirable fruit benefit from deadheading. Deadheading also encourages repeat blooming. Deadhead shrub roses, hydrangeas, crape myrtles, and other shrubs as indicated by cutting back to a leaf.

WATERING

All shrubs need careful attention to watering while they establish new root systems. After establishment, some need more water than others. Hydrangeas are heavy drinkers, particularly during the summer, while most evergreens are not.

Broadleaf evergreens sometimes need water during windy, sunny days when the temperatures are below freezing.

FERTILIZING

Fertilize according to plant profiles. Some shrubs need it, while others don't. For example, azaleas benefit from a spring feeding with a fertilizer made for acid-loving plants while loropetalum rarely requires fertilizer.

PRUNING

Pruning stimulates compact, bushy growth; controls size; and reinvigorates older shrubs. Shrubs generally require more pruning than trees, but the techniques listed also work with trees, when needed.

Heading cuts control size and encourage bushy growth. When you cut off the end of a branch, that's called a heading cut. The response of the plant will be to produce more side shoots below where you made the heading cut.

Thinning cuts open up air flow within the shrub. When you remove some of the "bulk" or interior branches by cutting them all the way back to the main stem, you're making thinning cuts.

Renewal pruning encourages new growth. This is a process most often used with shrubs, but which can also be applied to fruit trees, whereby you remove at least one-third of the old growth on the plant each year, stimulating new growth.

Pruning stimulates fresh new growth that will produce fruit. Old orchards are brought back to life by careful pruning of the old trees. When you prune shrubs (or trees), it's like cutting hair—the plants will grow back.

TROUBLESHOOTING

I've selected most of these shrubs based on their easy-care nature, general lack of pest problems, and multi-functionality in the garden and landscape. However, it is inevitable you'll have issues from time to time. Here are some of the most common to affect shrubs.

DECLINE IN BLOOM

A decline in flowering or complete lack of flowering is most likely one of two issues:

- The plant is old and needs to be renewal pruned to stimulate new growth. (See renewal pruning, above.)

Thinning cuts involve removing some of the interior growth of the plant. (Before, left; after, right.)

- The plant was pruned at the wrong time and the flower buds were cut off. If a plant blooms on new season's growth, you can prune it in the spring. If it blooms on last year's growth, you have to prune it right after blooming. If a plant that blooms on old growth is killed back to the ground during the winter, it will not bloom because that has the same effect as pruning at the wrong time.

DIEBACK

Dieback of entire branches can be the result of age, an insect pest, mechanical damage, or weather. Oleander often experiences winterkill in growing Zones lower than 7. Flowering dogwood shrubs require renewal pruning, and individual branches can die back or decline. If the end of only one branch is affected, there is a good chance it's an insect pest. Look to where the dieback starts and you can sometimes see the chewing insect burrowing in. Cut off the affected part and take it to your County Extension Service for a diagnosis. If the outer branches of a shrub are affected, check to see if they were nicked with a string trimmer or lawn mower.

Heading cuts involve cutting off the ends of branches.

Renewal pruning is the process of removing one-third of a plant's growth each year.

STRANGE LEAF COLOR

When leaves turn yellow or purple, and they're supposed to be green, you probably have a nutrient deficiency. Get a soil test to check pH and the for presence of nutrients. Soil pH is important, because if the pH is off, it doesn't matter how much fertilizer you put in the soil, because the plants won't be able to access it.

Spots on the leaves are generally an indication of a bacterial or fungal disease.

Brown or tan leaves on broadleaf evergreens (boxwood, hollies) in the winter can be an indication of winterburn. If you get sustained winds during days under freezing, take a watering can (if the outdoor spigots are off for the winter) and water these shrubs.

WILTING LEAVES

Wilting leaves indicate a problem in the root zone—either not enough or too much water. Try pulling on the shrub. If it easily comes out of the ground, the roots are probably rotten. (If they're black and soft, that's the problem.) If it doesn't easily pull out, and the soil is dry, the plant needs water.

ABELIA
Abelia x grandiflora

Why It's Special—Abelia is a semi-evergreen, compact shrub with fragrant flowers in shades of pinks and whites that bloom throughout summer. It has glossy green or bicolor leaves. Birds and butterflies are attracted to it, and it is deer resistant. Because of its relatively compact growth, it's an excellent plant for smaller gardens or for use in perennial and landscape beds. It's low maintenance, so it will add interest without requiring a lot of attention.

How to Plant & Grow—Plant in full sun to part shade in moist, well-drained soil. Abelia can be planted as an informal hedge. Water to establish.

Care & Problems—This is a fairly pest-free plant. It is deciduous to 15 degrees Fahrenheit. It will die back to the ground at 0 degrees Fahrenheit, but will grow out again the next summer. Abelia blooms on new wood. You can renewal prune by removing one-third of the oldest branches back to the ground each year.

Seasonal Interest—Flowers, summer; foliage, summer and fall

Mature Size (H x W)—3–8 feet x 3–8 feet (depending on cultivar)

Hardiness—5–9

Water Needs—Medium

ARBORVITAE
Thuja occidentalis 'Polar Gold'

Why It's Special—Polar Gold arborvitae is an evergreen shrub to small tree with chartreuse leaves. The species tree is much larger, but for landscape use, smaller cultivars with interesting leaves work better. This plant tolerates shearing well, so use it as a living screen or fence. It can also be a medium-sized specimen tree to anchor a flowerbed.

How to Plant & Grow—It grows best in Zones 7 and colder. Plant in full sun to partial shade in moist, well-drained soil. Site it appropriately for its mature size. (If you're planning to trim and maintain as a smaller shrub, you need less room.) Polar Gold contrasts nicely with plants that have burgundy foliage or fuchsia flowers.

Care & Problems—Deer fully enjoy munching on arborvitae. Spray repellents, particularly during winter, to prevent this. When hedging, make sure to cut the plant in a slightly pyramidal shape so the bottom is wider than the top, ensuring that sunlight will reach all branches. Water during sunny, windy days with temperatures below freezing.

Seasonal Interest—Evergreen foliage

Mature Size (H x W)—5–15 feet x 4–6 feet

Hardiness—3–7

Water Needs—Medium

ARROWWOOD VIBURNUM
Viburnum dentatum

Why It's Special—This deciduous, medium-sized shrub has a nice overall rounded growth habit as it matures. The common name comes from the straight branches—legend has it that Native Americans used them for arrows. It blooms with tufts of white flowers in spring that turn into bright blue fruits in late summer. Use as a screen at the back of a landscape bed or as a loose hedge.

How to Plant & Grow—Plant in full sun to partial shade in moist, well-drained soil. Water to establish. For best fruiting, plant a pollinating cultivar. This native is attractive to birds and butterflies.

Care & Problems—Let this plant assume its natural habit. Starkly straight branches, when covered with leaves and flowers, create a rounded habit that can quickly look strange if pruned too much. It flowers on old wood, so prune after flowering, but cutting off the flowers eliminates some fruit.

Seasonal Interest—Early summer, flowers; late summer, fruits; fall, sometimes red or orange fall color foliage

Mature Size (H x W)—6–10 feet x 6–10 feet

Hardiness—2–8

Water Needs—Medium

AZALEA
Rhododendron spp.

Why It's Special—Azaleas are the flower of spring! Some cities have entire festivals dedicated to these shrubs. The most common azaleas are Formosa hybrids with small, hairy, evergreen leaves and bright pink, white, fuchsia, or bicolor flowers in spring. Encore® Azaleas are rebloomers with more cold tolerance (hardy to Zone 6). They have a slightly slower growth habit than Formosas. Once they're done flowering, these shrubs retreat to the background in the garden.

How to Plant & Grow—Plant as a hedge, screen, or background in the landscape. Azaleas need full sun to partial shade in moist, well-drained, acidic soil. Check the pH before planting, and add sulfur if needed to lower pH. Water to establish.

Care & Problems—Azaleas bloom on old wood, so prune after flowering. You can renewal prune Formosa types by cutting back hard after the bloom. Fertilize in early summer with fertilizer formulated for plants that like acidic soil.

Seasonal Interest—Spring, flowers; evergreen foliage

Mature Size (H x W)—3–8 feet x 3–8 feet

Hardiness—6–10, depending on cultivar

Water Needs—Medium

BARBERRY
Berberis thunbergii

Why It's Special—There are over 400 species of barberries, but the most commonly grown is the Japanese barberry, *Berberis thunbergii*. There are many cultivars available to introduce variable leaf colors and sizes into the landscape. 'Atropurpurea Nana', with burgundy leaves, is the most commonly planted cultivar. 'Pink Queen' has variegated pink-and-purple leaves. 'Aurea' has bright yellow leaves. Barberry is highly invasive. Although it is still widely sold, it is better to seek alternatives for hedging and small landscape shrubs.

How to Plant & Grow—Plant in full sun to partial shade in moist, well-drained soil. Water to establish. Barberry plants will tolerate shearing. If you plan to grow a hedge, space 2 feet between plants.

Care & Problems—When shearing for a hedge, train in a slightly pyramidal shape, with the bottom wider than the top so the sun can reach all branches; otherwise, the plant will die back from the bottom up. It makes the most sense to shear in spring after the first flush of new growth.

Seasonal Interest—Summer, foliage; fall and winter, fruits

Mature Size (H x W)—3–6 feet x 3–6 feet

Hardiness—5–8

Water Needs—Medium

BEAUTYBERRY
Callicarpa americana

Why It's Special—Beautyberries are some of my favorite shrubs. They're native, easy to grow, and have shockingly bright purple berries in late summer and early fall. It's so bizarre to see that color of berry on a shrub and know that they're real. They're a good food source for birds. Once established, they're fuss-free.

How to Plant & Grow—Plant in full sun to partial shade in moist, well-drained soil. This shrub can tolerate wet feet and grows best in full sun. Water to establish. It has a somewhat loose, vase-shaped growth habit and doesn't tolerate shearing. The mature size is also fairly large. Plant at the back of a landscape bed or border where they'll have room to grow.

Care & Problems—To control size and promote branching, you can prune individual limbs in winter or early spring. It flowers and blooms on new wood. Do not let the roots dry out. Mulch to aid moisture retention at the soil level.

Seasonal Interest—Late summer to fall, purple berries

Mature Size (H x W)—1–3 feet x 1–3 feet

Hardiness—6–12

Water Needs—Medium to high

BOTTLEBRUSH BUCKEYE
Aesculus parviflora

Why It's Special—I really love the bottlebrush buckeye. It gets its name from the flowers that open in June and July. They are white, feathery plumes—like a brush you'd use to clean a narrow-mouthed bottle. In fall the large palmate leaves turn a brilliant shade of yellow. This is a large, spreading shrub. Plant a mass of them at the back of the yard as a border, or use as a backdrop in landscape beds. Birds and butterflies love this shrub.

How to Plant & Grow—Plant in partial shade to full shade in an area where the shrub can reach its final mature width of 8 to 10 feet. Plants need to be in moderately moist to moist soil.

Care & Problems—Water during dry periods; it is not necessarily a drought tolerant shrub. Otherwise, it's relatively carefree. It blooms on old wood; prune in summer after flowering. If you plant it where it can spread out, you won't need to prune, other than to remove dead wood.

Seasonal Interest—Summer, flowers; fall, leaf color

Mature Size (H x W)—8–12 feet x 8–12 feet

Hardiness—5–9

Water Needs—Medium

BUTTERFLY BUSH
Buddleja davidii

Why It's Special—I'm going to be honest: I'm including information about this plant because it is widely sold at garden and home-improvement centers, so I want you to know how to grow it (or why not to grow it). Butterfly bush is listed as an invasive species in some areas of the Mid-Atlantic. It also attracts cabbage white butterflies, the larval form of which attacks cabbages and other cole crops. So it has some downsides.

How to Plant & Grow—If you're still interested, plant in full sun in moist, well-drained soils. Water to establish. (I would plant bluebeard, *Caryopteris*, instead of butterfly bush, but bluebeard blooms later in the summer. You have to go with butterfly bush for early summer bloom.)

Care & Problems—For best blooms and even, compact growth, cut the plant back to 3 to 4 inches above the ground in early spring. It does have some pest problems, but not bad enough to consider dealing with.

Seasonal Interest—Summer, flowers

Mature Size (H x W)—2–8 feet x 1–5 feet (depending on cultivar)

Hardiness—5–9

Water Needs—Medium

BOXWOOD
Buxus spp. and cultivars

Why It's Special—Boxwood is the quintessential hedge plant, bringing to mind clipped borders for knot gardens in England and parterres in France. It grows fairly slowly, but over time, can get big. Boxwood is used to create topiaries because it takes to shearing so well. Ladew Topiary Gardens in Monkton, Maryland, has some gorgeous specimens. There are many different cultivars available, some with variegated or gold leaves, some with dwarf growth habits. There's a boxwood for almost every garden situation.

How to Plant & Grow—Plant in full sun to partial shade in moist, well-drained soils. Protect from winter winds that can dry out or cause winterburn on this broadleaf evergreen.

Care & Problems—Water during winter if it's sunny, windy, and below freezing. Spray repellants if you have deer problems. Shear in the spring after the new growth emerges. There are some insect and pest problems that affect boxwood. If you see problems, clip a sample and visit your local Cooperative Extension for help.

Seasonal Interest—Evergreen leaves

Mature Size (H x W)—1–6 feet x 1–5 feet (depends on cultivar)

Hardiness—5–8 (depending on cultivar)

Water Needs—Medium

CARYOPTERIS
Caryopteris × clandonensis

Why It's Special—Caryopteris, also called "bluebeard," is one of my favorite shrubs, hands-down. There are some cultivars with chartreuse leaves that give you garden interest all summer, but the big star of the show are the bluish-purple flowers that cover these shrubs in fall. Caryopteris give one of the "last hurrahs" of the garden and are vastly underutilized, as far as I'm concerned. Plant these instead of butterfly bushes! To see what this plant can really do, visit Longwood Gardens when their caryopteris allée is in bloom.

How to Plant & Grow—Plant in full sun in loose, well-drained soil. Water to establish. This plant does not like wet feet. Spacing depends on cultivars and how large the mature plant will get.

Care & Problems—Top-growth is only hardy to Zone 7, so the plant will die back during winter in colder zones. It flowers on new wood, so this isn't a problem. Grow it as a woody perennial in Zones 5 to 6. Water during drought. It's deer resistant.

Seasonal Interest—Midsummer to fall, flowers

Mature Size (H x W)—1–2 feet x 1–2 feet

Hardiness—5–9

Water Needs—Medium

CORALBERRY
Symphoricarpos orbiculatus

Why It's Special—Coralberry gets its name from coral red-colored berries that line its branches in fall. It is native to the eastern United States and will grow wild in woodlands, forming colonies underneath the tree canopy. It has a mounding, fountainlike growth habit. Branches root where they touch the ground. Plant as a specimen or as a mass in a landscape bed. It's deer resistant and tolerant of clay soil. It's a host plant for hummingbird clearwing and sulphur moth larvae. Larger specimens have interesting shredding bark. Birds are attracted to the fruits.

How to Plant & Grow—Plant in full sun to partial shade in well-drained soil. This plant will naturally spread, so if you can, choose a spot where that is an asset, not an aggravation. Water to establish.

Care & Problems—This is a fairly problem-free shrub. It can grow out of bounds, so keep an eye on it and remove suckers to control spread. Water during dry periods. Prune after flowering.

Seasnal Interest—Summer, flowers; fall, fruits

Mature Size (H x W)—2–5 feet x 4–8 feet

Hardiness—2–7

Water Needs—Medium

CRANBERRY COTONEASTER
Cotoneaster apiculatus

Why It's Special—Cranberry cotoneaster is an easy-to-grow shrub that tolerates a wide variety of growing conditions. It has small, glossy, deciduous leaves. Small pink flowers in summer mature into bright red fruits in late summer and fall. The fruits persist on the shrubs through winter (until they are eaten by birds). It can be used as a groundcover or to tumble over walls. This species is taller than the true groundcover cotoneaster.

How to Plant & Grow—Plant in full sun in moist, well-drained soil. Water to establish. This is a good plant to use if you need to cover a large area, but instead want something shrubby and not just a groundcover vine. It's tolerant of salt-spray for those of you gardening near the ocean.

Care & Problems—It's fairly pest free, but needs extra water during hot, dry periods. Because of the sprawling habit, it can collect trash and leaves. Use a shrub rake to remove these. It can be sheared.

Seasonal Interest—Fall, fruits

Mature Size (H x W)—2–3 feet x 3–6 feet

Hardiness—4–8

Water Needs—Medium

DAPHNE
Daphne odora

Why It's Special—Daphne flowers have the loveliest fragrance of any flower other than, maybe, gardenias. You instantly know when you're around a shrub that's blooming because you can't miss their scent in the air. Perhaps that is why so many people have patience for these slow-growing, fussy shrubs. If you can get daphne situated where it is happy, it will grow and bloom forever. If you can't, it will die a short death. 'Aureomarginata' has yellow leaf margins.

How to Plant & Grow—Plant in partial to full shade in sharply well-drained soil. In colder areas, plant along the south side of the house; it's hardy to Zone 7. You can grow them in containers in colder areas, but they're so picky, I'm not sure it's worth the effort.

Care & Problems—Keep soil evenly moist during summer. They *cannot* sit in water during winter. Daphne are slow growing, so do not bother pruning. If you find that your plant is happy, try to leave it alone!

Seasonal Interest—Winter to early spring, flowers; evergreen leaves

Mature Size (H x W)—3–4 feet x 3–4 feet

Hardiness—7–9

Water Needs—Medium

DEUTZIA
Deutzia gracilis

Why It's Special—Deutzia is another compact-growing, spring-flowering shrub for the landscape. Cultivars vary widely in their size and best features. Most of them bloom in late spring to early summer. Some have been bred for a slightly extended blooming period. Creme Fraiche® is a low-growing cultivar with variegated leaves. Yuki Cherry Blossom™ has pink and white flowers and burgundy fall color. Chardonnay Pearls® has chartreuse green-yellow foliage that turns pink in fall—something different for the garden!

How to Plant & Grow—Plant in full sun in moist, well-drained soil. It grows well at the front of perennial borders, and it's deer resistant.

Care & Problems—Keep soil evenly moist during summer. Individual branches can be short-lived, so renewal prune this shrub by removing one-third of the branches back to the ground every year. Prune for size after blooming, but this has such a compact growth habit that you will likely not have to prune much for size.

Seasonal Interest—Early summer, flowers

Mature Size (H x W)—2–5 feet x 2–5 feet

Hardiness—5–8

Water Needs—Medium

DOGWOOD, REDOSIER
Cornus sericea

Why It's Special—The real attraction of this native shrub is not the fluffy white flowers or variegated foliage, though those are certainly attractive—it's the bright red or yellow twigs that shine during winter that really brighten the landscape. It's extremely cold-hardy, so plant it if you live in an area that gets a lot of snow, which will highlight the red branches. 'Flaviramia' has yellow stems.

How to Plant & Grow—Plant in full sun in moist to wet soils. (These plants natively grow in wetlands and bogs.) The red stems show up best during winter against a solid green or white background. Water to establish.

Care & Problems—Redosier dogwoods are susceptible to a variety of blights and diseases. You will get more out of them if you renewal prune by removing one-third of the branches back to the ground every year, or, alternatively, cut the entire plant back almost to the ground every three years or so.

Seasonal Interest—Red or yellow twigs in winter

Mature Size (H x W)—3–6 feet x 6–10 feet

Hardiness—3–8

Water Needs—Medium to high

ELDERBERRY
Sambucus nigra

Why It's Special—Elderberries are flowering shrubs with edible fruits and attractive, lacy leaves. The eventual size of your shrubs depends on the cultivar you grow, but they're all somewhat leggy, with mounding, spreading habits. Lemony Lace™ has finely dissected chartreuse leaves and looks more like a Japanese maple than anything else. Black Lace™ has similar leaves, but in shades of burgundy, with pink flowers. Grow these as specimen plants in the landscape. 'Gerda' has compound, but not lacey, burgundy leaves.

How to Plant & Grow—Plant in full sun to partial shade in moist soil. Because elderberries like to spread, plant in rain gardens, along low spots in the yard, and in areas where the plant can naturalize. Water to establish.

Care & Problems—Water consistently to help the plant get established. It blooms on old wood, so if you need to prune, do so after flowering. It's deer resistant. Use bird netting to protect fruits if you want to harvest them for cooking.

Seasonal Interest—Early summer, flowers; summer and fall, foliage

Mature Size (H x W)—8–15 feet x 6–10 feet (depends on cultivar)

Hardiness—6–8

Water Needs—Medium to high

EUONYMUS
Euonymus fortunei cultivars

Why It's Special—*Euonymus fortunei*, the species, can be invasive in certain areas. If you want to grow this plant, select one of the cultivars. They're more interesting anyway. 'Goldy' is a compact grower with chartreuse-yellow leaves and a maximum size of 2 x 2 feet. 'White Album' has green-and-white variegated leaves and a compact growth habit as well. These small shrubs add low-maintenance, year-round interest to the garden.

How to Plant & Grow—Plant in full sun to partial shade in moist, well-drained soil. Water to establish. These plants are adaptable to a wide range of growing conditions and are not fussy. Add color to perennial borders or landscape beds.

Care & Problems—Water during dry periods. Plants will tolerate shearing, but if you grow a cultivar with a compact growth habit, you probably won't need to shear. Scale can be a major problem with euonymus; use horticultural oil to treat. Always follow package label instructions when applying pest-control products.

Seasonal Interest—Evergreen, usually variegated foliage

Mature Size (H x W)—2–6 feet x 4–8 feet (depends on cultivar; varies widely)

Hardiness—5–9

Water Needs—Medium

FALSE CYPRESS
Chamaecyparis pisifera

Why It's Special—False cypress is a slow-growing evergreen shrub with lacy, somewhat drooping foliage. There are a few popular cultivars for the garden, each with distinct characteristics that will appeal to you, depending on where you plan to plant the shrub. 'Golden Mop' has yellow foliage and a weeping growth habit. 'Filifera' has long, flat, green needles and a weeping growth habit. 'Boulevard' has an upright growth habit and fluffy blue needles. Dwarf cultivars are popular for use in miniature and fairy gardens.

How to Plant & Grow—All false cypress grow best and exhibit their best color, whatever that may be, in full sun in medium moist, well-drained soils. Once established, they are drought tolerant.

Care & Problems—These are easy-care shrubs. Ensure good drainage, particularly in winter. They rarely need to be pruned, so long as you select a cultivar with a growth habit that matches your needs. Watch out for bagworms and, if they appear, immediately consult with your local Cooperative Extension for treatment instructions.

Seasonal Interest—Evergreen foliage

Mature Size (H x W)—2–8 feet x 2–6 feet (depending on the cultivar)

Hardiness—4–8

Water Needs—Medium

FLOWERING QUINCE
Chaenomeles speciosa

Why It's Special—Flowering quince are some of the earliest shrubs to bloom in spring. They usually start flowering right at the tail end of the forsythia bloom. The species has red flowers and a messy, sprawling growth habit. Newer cultivars have more compact habits and lengthened bloom times. You can cut branches to bring inside for forcing into bloom during winter.

How to Plant & Grow—Plant in full sun for best flowering. Plants are adaptable to a wide range of growing conditions except for wet soil. These can be used as background plants in the garden. Once they finish flowering in early spring, they provide a nice backdrop.

Care & Problems—These are easy-care plants. The most pressing issue is to control spreading, which you can do by removing suckers before they get a foothold. Flowers bloom on old wood, so prune directly after bloom if you need to control size. If the shrub gets rangy, renewal prune it.

Seasonal Interest—Early spring, flowers

Mature Size (H x W)—3–8 feet x 3–8 feet (depends on cultivar)

Hardiness—5–8

Water Needs—Medium

FORSYTHIA
Forsythia × intermedia

Why It's Special—Yellow forsythia flowers are a longtime symbol of spring. These tough shrubs bloom early, providing much-needed cheer when almost everything else in the landscape is sleeping. The species has an arching, vase-shaped growth habit, but can grow large and unwieldy. Newer cultivars have compact habits, making them much better behaved in the landscape, and even the perennial garden. Show Off™ series plants are stellar—compact and floriferous.

How to Plant & Grow—Plant in full sun in moist, well-drained soils. It will tolerate some shade, but blooms best in full sun. Water to establish.

Care & Problems—These plants bloom on old wood, so do any pruning right after they flower in spring. Prune to control size, or, better yet, plant cultivars that stay within bounds. Keep plants flowering heavily by renewal pruning. Remove one-third of the oldest branches back to the ground every year. Forsythias are deer resistant.

Seasonal Interest—Early spring, flowers

Mature Size (H x W)—2–10 feet x 2–10 feet (depends on which variety you're growing)

Hardiness—5–8

Water Needs—Medium to low

FOTHERGILLA
Fothergilla gardenii

Why It's Special—This species of fothergilla is also called "dwarf fothergilla" because it naturally stays fairly small and compact. It is a definite three-season shrub. Thumb-sized, plume-like white flowers appear in late spring. The leaves are an attractive bluish green during summer, turning yellow, red, or orange in fall. It's a native plant and host to many insect, butterfly, and moth species. Plant in masses or use as a specimen.

How to Plant & Grow—Plant in full sun to partial shade in moist, well-drained, acidic soil. These create quite the show when planted *en masse*, but they can also be used as specimens in the landscape. They will tolerate shearing, but it isn't their best look. Water to establish.

Care & Problems—It's a shame more people don't grow these shrubs because they're so easy to grow and have so much to offer in the landscape. They rarely need pruning. Water during drought, and let 'em grow!

Seasonal Interest—Spring, flowers; fall, leaf color

Mature Size (H x W)—2–4 feet x 2–4 feet

Water Needs—Medium

FRINGE FLOWER
Loropetalum chinense

Why It's Special—Distinctive fuchsia flowers cover this plant in early spring. They look like pink witchhazel flowers (they are related to native witchhazel plants), only flashier. The *Loropetalum chinense* species grows to enormous size in Zones 7 and higher. Recently some dwarf cultivars have been introduced. They have better leaf color and behave nicely in the landscape. Look for 'Purple Pixie', which reaches a max height of 2 feet and spread of 4 to 5 feet. Carolina Moonlight™ and Snow Muffin® are selections with white flowers.

How to Plant & Grow—Plant in moist, well-drained, acidic soil in full sun to partial shade. Select a site that matches the species or cultivar you're planting. If you plant the species in a small landscape bed, you'll have to prune multiple times per year.

Care & Problems—Dwarf cultivars are easy to maintain. The species requires frequent pruning to keep it inbounds. Water during dry periods.

Seasonal Interest—Spring, flowers; evergreen burgundy foliage

Mature Size (H x W)—2–20 feet x 2–10 feet (depends highly on cultivar)

Hardiness—7–9

Water Needs—Medium to low

HOLLY, BLUE
Ilex × meserveae

Why It's Special—Blue holly is an evergreen holly shrub or small tree with glaucous blue-green leaves and bright red fruits. These plants are male or female, with the females putting on the big fruit show. You need to plant at least one male nearby to get the most fruit. Blue hollies are usually sold as cultivars; for example, Blue Princess® is a female and Blue Prince® is a male. 'Blue Girl' is another female cultivar.

How to Plant & Grow—Plant blue holly in spring or early fall in full sun in moist, well-drained, acidic soil. Check the pH before planting and add aluminum sulfate if the pH is above 6.0. Water to establish.

Care & Problems—This is a mostly pest-free plant. If leaves turn yellow, check the soil pH and use aluminum sulfate to lower it if it is too high. Water during extremely cold, windy, sunny days, because plants will transpire water faster than they can take it up and will dry out.

Seasonal Interest—Evergreen leaves; fruits in fall and winter

Mature Size (H x W)—8–15 feet x 5–8 feet

Hardiness—5–9

Water Needs—Medium

HOLLY, JAPANESE
Ilex crenata 'Sky Pencil'

Why It's Special—This is another one of those shrubs that I think you need to know about because you'll see it available for purchase, and you need to know what to do, or not do, with it. The species of Japanese holly can be invasive and is rarely sold. You're most likely going to run into 'Sky Pencil', a strongly upright cultivar that stays relatively small in the grand scheme of things. This plant is popular among train gardeners. It can be used as a specimen in highly formal container plantings. Other cultivars are sometimes grown in place of boxwood.

How to Plant & Grow—Plant in containers, train gardens, or in formal gardens as an accent or specimen plant. Requires full sun and moist, well-drained soil. 'Sky Pencil' holly has specific uses in the landscape and looks a little ridiculous if plunked in the garden without thought to design.

Care & Problems—It can dry out during winter. Water when it's windy, sunny, and freezing (at the same time).

Seasonal Interest—Evergreen

Mature Size (H x W)—3–5 feet x 1–2 feet

Hardiness—5–8

Water Needs—Medium

HOLLY, WINTERBERRY
Ilex verticillata

Why It's Special—Winterberry is a deciduous holly with a spectacular display of red fruits from fall through winter, until they are eaten by birds. Because it's deciduous, all of the focus is on the fruits, not the leaves. It is an excellent plant for wet, sunny areas of the garden where other plants do not grow very well. For a big fruit display, plant at least one male plant as a pollinator. (Whether the plants are male or female will be indicated when you purchase.) You don't need an even balance of sexes; one male is enough.

How to Plant & Grow—Plant in full sun in moist to wet soils. These hollies can be used as massing plants or specimens. They must be grown in acidic soils or their leaves will turn yellow.

Care & Problems—Water during dry periods. This is a fairly pest-free plant. Prune in early spring to control shape or size. You can fertilize with an acid-specific fertilizer after plants bloom.

Seasonal Interest—Fall to winter, berries

Mature Size (H x W)—3–10 feet x 3–6 feet, depending on cultivar

Hardiness—3–9

Water Needs—Medium to high

HOLLY, YAUPON
Ilex vomitoria

Why It's Special—Yaupon holly grows well in Zones 7 to 10, not the entire Mid-Atlantic but enough to be useful. It is sometimes mistaken for boxwood as it has similarly shaped small, glossy, evergreen leaves. It does have showy red fruits in late summer to fall, unlike boxwood. Yaupon holly tolerates shearing well. It can be grown as a hedge, foundation plant, or background planting. You need to plant a male pollinator in order to get fruits. Yaupon holly is important, ecologically. It's the larval host plant for the Henry's elfin butterfly. There are several different cultivars with varying growth habits available.

How to Plant & Grow—Plant in full sun to partial shade in moist to wet soils. Leave less space between plants if you want to train them into a hedge.

Care & Problems—This plant will spread through suckers, so remove them if you want to keep it confined to a smaller area. It is largely pest and disease free.

Seasonal Interest—Evergreen foliage

Mature Size (H x W)—10–12 feet x 8–10 feet

Hardiness—7–9

Water Needs—Medium to high

HYDRANGEA, HARDY
Hydrangea paniculata

Why It's Special—Hardy hydrangeas, also called "panicle hydrangeas," are some of the most cold-hardy, floriferous hydrangea plants. 'Limelight' is a popular cultivar. It has cone-shaped groups of light green flowers in summer that gradually mature and dry to a speckled green-white-pink in fall. 'Little Lime' is a dwarf cultivar with many of the same characteristics. Plant as a specimen or mass this shrub in larger landscape beds. You can cut the flowers for fresh and dried arrangements.

How to Plant & Grow—Plant in full sun to partial shade. Water to establish. This hydrangea tolerates pruning, but looks best when allowed to assume its natural growth habit.

Care & Problems—These are easy-care plants with few pest problems. They bloom on new wood, so prune in late winter to early spring to control size and shape (if necessary). They can wilt during hot afternoon sun in summer. Keep the soil moist but not soggy.

Seasonal Interest—Summer, flowers; fall, drying flowers

Mature Size (H x W)—6–8 feet x 6–8 feet

Hardiness—4–8

Water Needs—Medium

HYDRANGEA, BIGLEAF
Hydrangea macrophylla

Why It's Special—Bigleaf hydrangeas are the shrub you think of when people think "hydrangea flowers for weddings." This species has the large mophead flowers—big balls of blue, purplish, or pink blooms. They flower on the previous season's growth, so sometimes they do not bloom because they're killed back to the ground in winter.

How to Plant & Grow—Hydrangeas need moist, fertile, deeply cultivated soil to grow well. Bigleaf hydrangea flower color is usually affected by soil pH. Acidic soil yields blue flowers and alkaline soil yields pink. (There are a few cultivars that are reliably pink.) Test the pH before planting to know what you're working with. They will grow in full sun to partial shade.

Care & Problems—Provide extra water in summer. These plants can wilt in harsh afternoon sun. That doesn't necessarily mean they need water immediately; only water more than usual if the plants are still wilted in the morning. Prune immediately after flowering, if needed, so that you don't cut off next year's flower buds.

Seasonal Interest—Summer, flowers; fall, leaves

Mature Size (H x W)—4–6 feet x 4–6 feet

Hardiness—6–9 (depending on cultivar)

Water Needs—Medium to high

HYDRANGEA, OAKLEAF
Hydrangea quercifolia

Why It's Special—Oakleaf hydrangea was a revolution when it first hit the market. It's an easy-to-grow, non-fussy native hydrangea that provides almost year-round interest, between its large cones of flowers, brilliant fall color, and shedding bark. There's a new group available, the Gatsby series, with some gorgeous selections. Gatsby's Star™ has white, star-shaped double flowers in the clusters; it's absolutely stunning. Gatsby's Pink ™ has pink blooms. 'Gatsby's Moon' can tolerate wetter soils and has jam-packed flower clusters.

How to Plant & Grow—Plant in full sun to partial shade in moist but well-drained soils. These plants are highly drought tolerant once established. They are fairly large shrubs and look best when allowed room to grow. Mass in the landscape or plant as specimens.

Care & Problems—These hydrangeas bloom on old wood, so prune immediately after flowering if necessary to control size. Plants will immediately begin setting flower buds for the following season after blooming. Mulch in summer to retain moisture. They have few pest problems.

Seasonal Interest—Summer, flowers; fall, foliage; winter, bark

Mature Size (H x W)—6–8 feet x 6–8 feet

Hardiness—5–9

Water Needs—Medium

HYDRANGEA, SMOOTH
Hydrangea arborescens

Why It's Special—Smooth hydrangea is a deciduous flowering shrub native to the eastern United States. In the wild, this plant grows along the forest margins, near wetlands, and on hillsides. It blooms in late summer to early fall with large pompoms of small white flowers. Invincibelle® Spirit is a popular cultivar with pink flowers. These are great shrubs to add to the garden for late summer and fall interest.

How to Plant & Grow—Grow in partial shade in moist, well-drained soil. Smooth hydrangeas do not like to dry out. They make the biggest impact when mass-planted. Consider creating a shrub border with them, planting as a foundation plant, or using as a background plant in the perennial garden. Clumps will slowly spread and naturalize, if allowed.

Care & Problems—They are easy care. Water during dry periods. Plants bloom on new growth, so prune in early spring after the shrub starts to leaf out, if necessary, to control size and rejuvenate it.

Seasonal Interest—Summer to fall, flowers

Mature Size (H x W)—4–6 feet x 4–6 feet

Hardiness—3–9

Water Needs—Medium

LEUCOTHOE
Leucothoe axillaris

Why It's Special—This little shrub is native to the eastern United States, growing along hillsides at the edge of wooded areas. It has an arching growth habit with narrow, oblong, glossy evergreen leaves and white flowers that look a little like lily-of-the-valley blooms. It is in the family *Ericaceae*, which includes blueberries and other acid-loving plants. Grow it instead of non-native broadleaf evergreens.

How to Plant & Grow—Plant in partial shade in moist but well-drained acidic soils. It's an excellent foundation plant for winter interest. It is most effective when planted in loose clumps of three plants or more, and it will appreciate protection provided by the house.

Care & Problems—Leucothoe needs acidic soil. Test the pH if the leaf color seems off and lower the pH if necessary (apply aluminum sulfate). Prune after flowering, if necessary, and use a fertilizer formulated for acid-loving plants. This plant looks best if allowed to just grow into its natural form. Mulch yearly to aid moisture retention.

Seasonal Interest—Spring, flowers; evergreen foliage

Mature Size (H x W)—2–4 feet x 3–5 feet

Hardiness—6–8

Water Needs—Medium

LILAC
Syringa vulgaris

Why It's Special—Lilacs are definitely old-fashioned garden shrubs that your grandma and your great grandma probably grew. In the landscape, these shrubs require a little bit of maintenance to look their best. The common lilac has clusters of purple flowers in spring. There are also white and pink cultivars. 'Sensation' has flower clusters with large showy purple flowers with white margins. Bloomerang® series plants are lilac hybrids that rebloom during the growing season. They're also a bit more compact than the species.

How to Plant & Grow—Plant in full sun to partial shade in moist, well-drained soils. Powdery mildew can be a problem, so try to plant where there is good airflow around plants. It's highly cold-hardy but doesn't grow well in Zones 8 and above.

Care & Problems—Lilacs bloom on old wood, so prune directly after flowering. This shrub does well with renewal pruning, cutting one-third of the oldest branches back to the ground each year. Check soil pH; these like slightly alkaline soil.

Seasonal Interest—Spring, flowers

Mature Size (H x W)—8–10 feet x 8–10 feet

Hardiness—3–7

Water Needs—Medium

MAHONIA
Mahonia aquifolium

Why It's Special—Mahonia, or "Oregon holly grape" is a unique evergreen shrub with cascading yellow flowers and dusky purple-blue fruits in the shape of grape clusters. Its foliage looks like holly leaves and unfurls with a reddish tinge in spring before turning a dark, glossy green.

How to Plant & Grow—Wear gloves when handling! This plant is spiny. Plant in partial to full shade in moist, acidic soils. It's a good idea to plant groups of three or more for the best effect and to get the most fruit. If planting next to a house, check the soil pH. You might have to lower it with aluminum sulfate.

Care & Problems—Mahonia spreads by underground suckers, so if you want to control the size of the clump, remove the suckers as they appear. It blooms on old wood, so if you have to prune, do it after flowering, but you'll miss out on the fruits. Feed it with holly-specific fertilizer after flowering.

Seasonal Interest—Spring, flowers; summer, fruit; evergreen foliage

Mature Size (H x W)—3–8 feet x 3–5 feet (depending on cultivar)

Hardiness—5–9

Water Needs—Medium

NINEBARK
Physocarpus opulifolius

Why It's Special—Ninebark is a native, deciduous flowering shrub with white to pink flower clusters and a delicately arching branching habit. Flowers look like spiraea blooms, and the plants are closely related. Ninebark has a slightly less messy habit and larger leaves. 'Diabolo' is one of the popular cultivars. It has burgundy leaves. 'Tiny Wine' is a compact grower, reaching heights and widths of 3 to 4 feet. It has a strong upright growth habit and densely packed light pink flowers along the branches.

How to Plant & Grow—Plant ninebark in full sun in moist, well-drained soils. It grows well in a wide variety of soil conditions. Smaller cultivars can be used near the front of a shrub bed or landscape. Water to establish.

Care & Problems—Ninebark blooms in spring to early summer on old wood, so prune directly after flowering. This shrub looks its best when allowed to assume its natural growth form; reserve pruning for renewal purposes.

Seasonal Interest—Summer, flowers and foliage; fall, foliage; winter, shredding bark

Mature Size (H x W)—3–8 feet x 3–6 feet (depends on cultivar)

Hardiness—3–7

Water Needs—Low to medium

OLEANDER
Nerium oleander

Why It's Special—Oleander is hardy in Zones 8 and higher, but can be grown as a container plant and overwintered indoors. Should you do that? It's up to you. If you live in an area where this is hardy, it's a useful plant because it's covered in beautiful pink flowers in mid- to late summer when almost everything else is suffering from the heat. It is drought tolerant once established. **Caution:** all parts of this plant are poisonous.

How to Plant & Grow—Plant in full sun in moist, well-drained soils. It doesn't like wet feet and is highly drought tolerant once established. If grown as a hedge or divider, leave 6 feet between plants— they'll fill in.

Care & Problems—Even in Zone 8, this plant can experience winterkill. It blooms on new growth, so just cut it back in spring and it will grow out and flower profusely. In warmer areas, you can train oleander as a small standard.

Seasonal Interest—Mid- to late summer, flowers

Mature Size (H x W)—4–8 feet x 3–6 feet

Hardiness—8–10

Water Needs—Medium

PEARL BUSH
Exochorda hybrids and cultivars

Why It's Special—Pearl bush is a deciduous shrub in the rose family that has cascades of white flowers in spring. The flowers look somewhat like apple blossoms, and they absolutely cover the plants. 'The Bride' is an older cultivar. Snow Day® is a newer variety with more and bigger flowers. Snow Day Surprise® is a compact grower with a more upright habit. It's a pretty spring specimen plant that somewhat recedes into the background during the rest of the year.

How to Plant & Grow—Plant in full sun to part shade in moist, well-drained soil. It benefits from protection from early spring frosts, so a microclimate near the house is a good spot. This grows best in slightly acidic soil.

Care & Problems—Keep the soil evenly moist. Check the pH and lower it with aluminum sulfate if it is above 6.5. This shrub blooms on old growth, so prune directly after flowering. It can be trimmed back hard to maintain size, if needed.

Seasonal Interest—Spring, flowers

Mature Size (H x W)—3–4 feet x 3–4 feet

Hardiness—4–8

Water Needs—Medium

POTENTILLA
Dasiphora fruticosa ssp. *floribunda*

Why It's Special—Potentilla is a tough, deciduous flowering shrub in the rose family. It is covered with yellow blooms from midsummer through fall. Once established, it's highly drought tolerant. This is a problem-solving shrub to plant in dry areas with poor soil where you have trouble getting anything else to grow. It can be used to control erosion in dry areas and on slopes.

How to Plant & Grow—Plant in full sun in well-drained soil. Attractive for massing, this plant also looks great planted with Russian sage, ornamental grasses, and shrub roses. Water to establish. It grows best in Zones 7 and colder.

Care & Problems—This is an easy-care plant. It blooms on new growth, so prune in spring, if necessary, but if sited properly in the landscape, it shouldn't need much pruning. Leave it alone! It will have more problems if coddled than if ignored. It's a great plant for tough spots in the landscape.

Seasonal Interest—Summer, flowers

Mature Size (H x W)—3–5 feet x 3–5 feet

Hardiness—2–7

Water Needs—Medium to low

RHODODENDRON
Rhododendron spp. and hybrids

Why It's Special—Rhododendrons have specific growth requirements to thrive, but if you can provide those, they'll reward you with stunning spring flowers and glossy evergreen foliage that serves as an excellent backdrop in the garden. Wild shrubs grow along the Appalachian Mountains, some getting as large as 20 x 20 feet. It's a treat, seeing them in bloom along the highway.

How to Plant & Grow—Plant in partial shade in moist, well-drained, acidic soils on the north or east side of the house where it will get afternoon sun protection. It also grows well as an understory plant under tall trees. Space according to predicted mature size.

Care & Problems—Rhododendrons bloom on old wood, so prune lightly after flowering if needed. Fertilize with an acid-specific fertilizer after bloom. Water in winter if it's windy, sunny, and below freezing at the same time for a prolonged period. If leaf color looks off, test the soil pH to see if it is above 6.5; lower it with aluminum sulfate.

Seasonal Interest—Spring, flowers; evergreen foliage

Mature Size (H x W)—3–15 feet x 3–15 feet (depending on which one you grow)

Hardiness—5–8

Water Needs—Medium

ROSE-OF-SHARON
Hibiscus syriacus

Why It's Special—I've had two-hour conversations about the Malvaceae family with one of my friends, because we both just love all of the plants in the family! Rose-of-Sharon is part of this family, the hibiscus family, and it fills an important spot in the garden—it blooms heavily in late summer when a lot of plants are hanging it up for the year. Grow it as a specimen or a shrub border. It blooms with single or double flowers in shades of white, pink, lavender, and bicolor from late summer through fall.

How to Plant & Grow—Plant in full sun (will tolerate some afternoon shade in warmer climates) in moist, well-drained soils. Rose-of-Sharon plants adapt to a wide range of growing conditions. Water to establish.

Care & Problems—It blooms on old wood, so prune, if necessary, in spring. Water during drought. It has few pest problems. Rose-of-Sharon has a nice vase-shaped growth habit, so try to avoid hedging.

Seasonal Interest—Late summer, flowers

Mature Size (H x W)—6–12 feet x 6–12 feet

Hardiness—5–9

Water Needs—Medium

SHRUB ROSE
Rosa cultivars

Why It's Special—Why plant a shrub without flowers when you can plant one with flowers? Shrub roses have been growing in popularity due to their easy-care nature and summer-long interest. The most well-known shrub rose right now is the Knock Out® rose and its variants. Easy Elegance® roses, and Oso Easy® roses are newer shrub rose series with more color and size choices, but the same disease resistance. Shrub roses are drought tolerant and more pest resistant than their hybrid tea relatives. These plants are real garden problem solvers.

How to Plant & Grow—Plant in full sun in moist, well-drained soils for best results. Roses cannot sit in wet soil, and they're drought tolerant once established. If massing, plant according to mature expected size.

Care & Problems—If you select from the varieties listed, you won't have a lot of problems. Prune roses in late winter to early spring, removing old, dead wood and thinning out the crown. Pruning stimulates new growth, so don't be afraid!

Seasonal Interest—Summer, flowers

Mature Size (H x W)—2–6 feet x 4–6 feet (depending on variety)

Hardiness—4–9 (depending on cultivar)

Water Needs—Medium to low

SPIREA
Spiraea spp.

Why It's Special—There are two types of spirea commonly grown. *Spiraea nipponica* 'Snowmound' has clusters of white flowers in spring borne on arching stems, highlighted by dark green leaves. *S. japonica* ('Little Princess' is a popular cultivar) has pink flowers that bloom in early summer on upright branches with light green to chartreuse leaves. Shrubs with lighter-colored leaves are excellent for contrast in the garden.

How to Plant & Grow—Plant in full sun in moist, well-drained soil. Space according to the expected size of the mature plant. Water to establish. Most often seen growing in masses, this plant is good for foundation plantings, filling large landscape beds, and as part of a mixed border.

Care & Problems—These are fairly easy-care plants, but their growth habits can be kind of messy. Prune after flowering. If the plants get too out of control, cut them back hard after blooming and let them grow back out.

Seasonal Interest—Spring to summer, flowers

Mature Size (H x W)—2–6 feet x 2–6 feet, depending on type

Hardiness—4–8

Water Needs—Medium

ST. JOHN'S WORT
Hypericum kalmianum 'Deppe'

Why It's Special—This is an upright, mounding form of St. John's wort, at home in the landscape. It is usually sold under the trade name Sunny Boulevard™. It has attractive bluish-green leaves in summer and blooms with buttery yellow flowers in late summer to early fall. It is deer resistant and native to North America. Birds and butterflies flock to the flowers. The foliage is evergreen.

How to Plant & Grow—Plant in full sun in moist, well-drained soil. It creates a spectacular look when mass-planted. Water to establish. Leave 2 to 3 feet between plants if massing. Group with other native shrubs to create a shrub border, or include in mixed borders. Pairs well with shrub roses, perennial salvia, purple coneflowers, and other drought tolerant, full-sun perennials. Because it is drought tolerant, it is also a good choice for rock gardens.

Care & Problems—This easy-care shrub blooms on old wood. Prune in spring if necessary to control shape. Water during dry periods.

Seasonal Interest—Late summer to fall, flowers

Mature Size (H x W)—2–3 feet x 3–4 feet

Hardiness—4–8

Water Needs—Medium

SUMMERSWEET
Clethra alnifolia

Why It's Special—Summersweet is definitely one of my favorites. It blooms with white to pink spikes composed of fluffy, fragrant flowers in mid- to late summer. In fall, the leaves turn golden yellow. Hummingbirds and butterflies love this plant. It's perfect to grow in moist areas of the garden where you have trouble finding other plants that thrive. It is sometimes confused with Virginia sweetspire, because the flowers look similar, but summersweet blooms later and has a more upright growth habit.

How to Plant & Grow—Plant in full sun to partial shade in moist, somewhat acidic soils. It can be grown as a specimen or a mass planting. Water to establish. It will tolerate some shade.

Care & Problems—Summersweet spreads by suckers, so if you want to maintain a neat-looking shrub, remove the suckers as they appear. Otherwise, you can let this shrub naturalize into a larger colony. It blooms on new growth, so prune in spring if necessary to control size. Do not let soil dry out.

Seasonal Interest—Summer, flowers; fall, foliage

Mature Size (H x W)—3–8 feet x 4–6 feet

Hardiness—3–9

Water Needs—Medium to wet

SWEETSHRUB
Calycanthus floridus

Why It's Special—Sweetshrub is a deciduous flowering shrub that blooms in late spring to early summer with multi-petaled, fragrant, burgundy flowers. The flowers look a little bit like small, red star magnolia flowers. The glossy green foliage is also fragrant and turns yellow in fall, giving this plant multiseason interest. 'Athens' is a cultivar with white flowers. 'Hartlage Wine' is a hybrid with large, showy flowers (3 inches across).

How to Plant & Grow—The flowers are pretty, but not in an "in your face" type of way. I would plant this shrub in full sun to partial shade somewhere that you can enjoy the fragrance when you walk by. Sweetshrub needs medium-moist soils, but will develop root rot if situated in soggy sites.

Care & Problems—They're no big pest and disease problems. Water during times of drought. Plants bloom on previous season's growth, so prune after flowering if you need to control size. It's just a nice, interesting, easy-care shrub.

Seasonal Interest—Early summer, flowers; fall, leaf color

Mature Size (H x W)—6–10 feet x 6–12 feet

Hardiness—4–9

Water Needs—Medium

VIBURNUM, CHINESE SNOWBALL
Viburnum macrocephalum

Why It's Special—This plant is affectionately called the "snowball bush." We had one of these along the lot line of my backyard when I was little, and I loved cutting the flowers and putting them in a little vase on my bedside table. Grow it as a background plant in the garden or as a loose hedge along the lot line. It can also be used as a foundation planting or as a background plant in large landscape beds. Its biggest season of interest is spring, though, and it adds little to the garden after that.

How to Plant & Grow—Plant in full sun to partial shade in moist, well-drained soil. Protect from windy exposure. It grows best in slightly acidic soil.

Care & Problems—This plant is relatively easy to grow with few problems. It blooms on old wood, so prune in early summer after the shrub finished flowering. You can renewal prune by removing one-third of the branches back to the ground every year. Water during drought.

Seasonal Interest—Late spring to early summer, flowers

Mature Size (H x W)—6–10 feet x 6–10 feet

Hardiness—7–9

Water Needs—Medium

VIBURNUM, DOUBLEFILE
Viburnum plicatum f. tomentosum 'Mariesii'

Why It's Special—This viburnum has horizontal layers of lacecap-type flowers that bloom in late spring to early summer. The ridged green leaves are almost corduroy-like. (The species name *plicatum* comes from the Latin for "pleated" or "folded.") They turn a brilliant red in fall. When growing doublefile viburnum, it's best to let the natural growth habit shine. It's strongly horizontal, and any attempt to prune it into a ball will be futile. You'll end up with a mess. Flowers give way to blue-black fruits enjoyed by birds in summer.

How to Plant & Grow—Plant in full sun to part shade in moist, well-drained soils. Water to establish. Plant this where it can spread out and grow naturally. It makes a spectacular specimen plant, but can also anchor a landscape bed in the center or edge of the yard.

Care & Problems—It's fairly easy to grow. If necessary, prune after flowers but maintain the horizontal branching pattern. Plants need to stay evenly moist throughout the growing season.

Seasonal Interest—Spring, flowers; fall, leaf color and purplish red berries

Mature Size (H x W)—10–12 feet x 10–12 feet

Hardiness—5–9

Water Needs—Medium

VIBURNUM, KOREANSPICE
Viburnum carlesii

Why It's Special—The best feature of Koreanspice viburnums are the pinkish white pompoms of fragrant flowers in early spring. They have a wonderful, warm fragrance and are so much easier to grow than a similarly fragrant shrub, daphne. These make great foundation plantings or background shrubs in landscape beds or gardens next to the house. Plant several to enjoy the fragrance and create a uniform look in the garden. 'Compactum' stays a small 2 to 4 feet in width and height.

How to Plant & Grow—Plant in full sun to partial shade in moist, well-drained, slightly acidic soil. These plants can benefit from growing in microclimates near brick walls that radiate heat in winter. They make attractive borders and hedges as well. Water to establish.

Care & Problems—Water during winter if it's windy, sunny, and freezing. These plants bloom on the previous season's growth, so prune right after flowering if necessary because plants will immediately start to set blooms for the next growing season.

Seasonal Interest—Spring, fragrant flowers

Mature Size (H x W)—4–6 feet x 4–6 feet

Hardiness—4–7

Water Needs—Medium

VIRGINIA SWEETSPIRE
Itea virginica

Why It's Special—Virginia sweetspire is sometimes confused with summersweet. Sweetspire blooms earlier than summersweet and has an arching, rather than upright growth habit. 'Henry's Garnet' is a popular cultivar. 'Little Henry' is a smaller version. This shrub blooms with fragrant creamy white flowers in spring. It has excellent fall color and distinctive red twigs that stand out during winter.

How to Plant & Grow—Plant in full sun to partial shade in moist soils. All cultivars and the species of this plant spread through suckers, so plant it where it can naturalize if that's something you're interested in.

Care & Problems—This blooms on new wood, so prune after flowering if necessary. The natural growth habit of sweetspire is fountainlike and gorgeous, so try to avoid pruning it into a ball. Remove suckers if you want to prevent the plant from spreading. Do not let the soil dry out. It's a fairly pest-free plant.

Seasonal Interest—Spring, flowers; fall, foliage; winter, bark

Mature Size (H x W)—3–6 feet x 3–6 feet

Hardiness—5–9

Water Needs—Medium to high

WEIGELA
Weigela cultivars

Why It's Special—Weigela are compact, spring- to summer-blooming shrubs with trumpet-shaped flowers in shades of white or pink and interesting, variably colored foliage. There are cultivars with green, burgundy, and bicolor foliage. The plants are as prized for their flowers as they are for the colorful leaves. Ghost™ has chartreuse leaves and fuchsia flowers. Midnight Wine® and Fine Wine® have burgundy foliage. My Monet® has pink, white, and green tricolor leaves. They have a big impact when mass-planted in the landscape. Hummingbirds and butterflies love drinking from the flowers.

How to Plant & Grow—Plant in full sun in moist, well-drained soil. Water to establish. Leave 2 to 3 feet between plants if massing. The species grows quite a bit larger than popular cultivars sold in the nursery trade, so space accordingly.

Care & Problems—This plant blooms on new growth, so prune after flowering. Keep the soil evenly moist during the growing season. Mulch to conserve moisture.

Seasonal Interest—Spring, flowers; summer, foliage

Mature Size (H x W)—3–5 feet x 3–5 feet

Hardiness—4–8

Water Needs—Medium

WITCHHAZEL
Hamamelis virginiana

Why It's Special—This is the native, fall-blooming species of witchhazel. It will naturalize in woodlands or underneath hardwood trees in your front or backyard. This is an interesting plant, having unique branch structure, flowering time, and attractive leaves throughout summer. It is a good plant to grow to boost the diversity of the native ecology, as it serves multiple purposes for wildlife. Chinese and Japanese witchhazels flower in late winter and are also good landscape plants. Look for cultivars that drop their leaves before they flower so that the flowers can be the stars of the show.

How to Plant & Grow—Plant in full sun to partial shade in moist, well-drained soil. You can plant under trees if some dappled sunlight will reach the shrubs. Allow 4 to 6 feet between plants if you're massing. Water to establish.

Care & Problems—These are extremely low-care plants. Water during droughty times and prune directly after flowering if needed to control size. Mulch to keep the roots cool. Otherwise, leave them alone!

Seasonal Interest—Fall, flowers

Mature Size (H x W)—5–20 feet x 5–20 feet

Hardiness—3–8

Water Needs—Medium

SHRUBS MONTH-BY-MONTH

JANUARY

- Take pictures of the garden now to identify areas that could benefit from additional deciduous or evergreen shrubs for winter interest.

- Lift snow-covered branches up to allow the snow to slide off without damaging the shrub. Never try to break ice off a shrub branch, as you can break the branch.

- Water broadleaf evergreen shrubs and coniferous evergreen shrubs if you have windy, dry, below-freezing conditions.

- Prune crape myrtle shrubs now. Remove any branches or twigs that are smaller than your pinky finger. Do not commit "crape murder." While you can cut these shrubs back hard, there's no need. They'll produce better flower displays if you just prune for general tidiness and size.

FEBRUARY

- Prune late summer-flowering shrubs now to control size. Do not prune spring-flowering shrubs because you will cut off their flower blooms.

- Renew deer and animal repellent on shrubs to prevent munching mammals.

- Spray horticultural oil on shrubs that have exhibited pest problems over the previous year.

- Cut branches of spring-flowering shrubs, such as flowering quince and forsythia, and bring inside to force into bloom. Keep them in a cool, dark location until the buds break, then bring them out into the light. Change the water so that it remains fresh.

MARCH

- Shop for unusual shrubs via catalog and websites. I've had varying success with mail-order plant shopping. There's a list of reputable online nurseries in the Resources section in the back of the book.

- Clean up tropical shrubs that you are overwintering indoors. Check for pests and remove dead leaves. Prune off any dead wood.

- Prune shrub roses to stimulate new growth. Remove at least one-third of the oldest canes back to the soil line.

- Check the soil pH around hydrangea plants. If you have hydrangeas with flowers that change colors depending on the acidity of the soil, you might need to amend the soil with sulfur (to lower the pH for blue blooms) or lime (to raise the pH for pink blooms).

- Fertilize blueberries.

APRIL

- Receive bare-root shrubs and keep them in a cool, dry location while it is still too cold to plant out. If the shrubs break dormancy while the ground is still too cold to plant, pot them up and keep them in the garage. When it's time to plant the shrubs, soak the roots in water overnight before planting.

- Scout for spring pests. If you have an infestation, take photos and a sample of the plant and pest in a clear plastic bag to your local Cooperative Extension office for diagnosis and a treatment plan.

- Shear evergreen hedges before spring growth begins.

MAY

- Move shrubs outside that were overwintered indoors, including hardy hibiscus, citrus, and gardenias. You will need to harden these off as you would for vegetables or annuals grown inside. Keep them in a sheltered location outside for a week or so before moving them to their permanent (for the summer) locations.

- Fertilize azaleas and rhododendrons after they finish blooming. There are fertilizers specifically formulated for these acid-loving plants. If you want to prune these shrubs, this is the time to do it.

- Mulch around shrubs to keep plant roots cool and the soil around them moist. This also creates a buffer around the plants so that you do not accidentally injure them while mowing or trimming the lawn. Do not let the mulch directly touch the plant stems.

- Prune late summer- and fall-blooming shrubs.

JUNE

- Plant new shrubs. There is still time for them to grow healthy root systems before the oppressive heat of summer descends.

- Water newly planted shrubs once a week for the first month and then every other week for the next three to four months.

- Take softwood cuttings of shrubs you want to propagate. Dip the ends in rooting power, stick in a pot of sterile seedling mix, and put a plastic bag over the pot to keep the cutting moist while it roots. Azaleas are especially easy to propagate this way.

- Shear deciduous hedges. Prune them so that the bottom of the hedge is slightly wider than the top. That allows light to reach every part of the shrub, and you won't have dieback from the bottom up.

JULY

- Continue watering newly planted shrubs. Keep an eye on mature shrubs, as well. If you experience droughty conditions, you'll need to water existing shrubs, as well.

- Deadhead shrub roses and/or cut them back by one-third after their first flush of bloom to encourage a big second flowering of the season.

- Look for Japanese beetle damage. If they're a problem, look up systemic insecticides that can be applied in the spring to control the pests. Traps are not an effective way of controlling these pests.

AUGUST

- Do not prune shrubs this month, as you can stimulate growth that will not have time to become hard enough to withstand frosts.

- Water shrubs that are under heat stress or drought stress. This is usually the hottest and driest month, and what you need to do, as the caretaker of the plants, is simply keep them alive.

- Deadhead hydrangeas to encourage continuous bloom in reblooming varieties. Deadhead crape myrtles to keep the plants looking tidy.

SEPTEMBER

- Plant new shrubs this month! September is one of the best months for planting. Water to encourage rooting, and mulch around the shrubs to conserve moisture and protect the roots.

- Transplant any shrubs that need to be moved this month. Water the shrubs deeply the day before you plan to transplant. When transplanting, dig up, replant, water, and mulch on the same day, if possible. If you are unable to replant the same day you dig them up, temporarily pot the shrubs in containers.

- Cut hydrangea flowers to bring inside to dry.

- Bring tropical or marginally hardy shrubs inside for winter.

OCTOBER

- Apply deer repellents to broadleaf and needleleaf evergreen shrubs. Periodically change the formula or scent of the repellent you use.

- Rake up leaves and debris from around shrubs. Leaving leaves over the winter can provide a climate that fosters pests and diseases.

- Continue planting new shrubs in the garden. When planting, always dig a planting hole that is twice as wide as it is deep. It's better to have the top of the rootball just barely above the soil line than it is to plant the shrub too deep. Backfill with the same soil that you removed from the hole. There is no need to amend the soil.

NOVEMBER

- Water newly planted shrubs until the ground freezes. Water evergreen shrubs on windy, cold, sunny days to prevent them from drying out.

DECEMBER

- Cut boughs from evergreens and make your own holiday gardens.

- Prepare porch pots with twigs from redosier dogwoods, holly branches, and other evergreens.

- Sharpen and clean pruning tools and put them away until after the holidays.

TREES
for the Mid-Atlantic

As part of your garden plan, please plant some trees. It seems like every time I drive around my neighborhood, I see more trees cut down without anything planted to replace them. If you live in a patio home or have a smaller lot, there are some small tree options so that you can still enjoy some height in the landscape. If you have space, there's nothing more majestic than a big oak or beech. Sure, those take a while to grow, but think of it as an investment in your property and in future generations. You'd also be surprised—within 10 or 15 years, even slow-growing trees can make a big impact on the landscape.

SELECTING TREES

There's more to selecting a tree than the eventual size, although that's an important factor. You don't want to plant a tree that will outgrow its spot in 10 or 15 years. Tree removal is expensive.

You also want to plant a tree where it can reach its mature size without growing into anything: the house, power lines, your neighbor's property. Recently, my local electric company's hired guns hacked off pieces of my sycamore tree (that were plenty far away from the 15-foot setback, thank you very much). I actually started to cry. Dramatic? Maybe, but that tree and the sweet gum next to it were part of the reasons my husband and I bought that house. There is a place for large trees in the residential landscape, and because many of them are removed when a new neighborhood is built, it is our job to put them back.

FACTORS TO CONSIDER DURING TREE SELECTION
- Purpose—shade, screening, visual interest?
- Growth rate and mature size
- Maintenance needs
- Interesting features—flowers, fruit, bark
- Evergreen or deciduous?

In general, if I'm planting a tree closer to the house, it will be one that tops out on the smaller size—20 to 30 feet instead of 60 to 70 feet. It will have shedding or multicolored bark or pretty flowers in spring. It might be a tree with interesting flowers that grow into striking fruits. I tend to plant shade trees a little further from the house and use evergreens for screening purposes.

TREE SIZES

SMALL
Small trees grow no taller than 20 feet. These trees are good to plant in foundation beds (landscape beds next to the house) or to provide height in an island bed (larger landscape bed in the lawn).
- Japanese maple
- Serviceberry
- Star magnolia
- Kousa dogwood
- Crape myrtle

MEDIUM
Medium-sized trees reach a mature height of 20 to 40 feet. They are great for landscape beds that extend away from the house at least 20 feet into the yard.
- Redbud
- Flowering plum
- Crabapple
- Carolina silverbell
- 'Little Gem' magnolia
- Golden raintree
- Zelkova
- Weeping cherry

LARGE

Large trees grow to heights of 50 feet or more and make great shade trees. Give these trees lots of room to grow.

- Tulip poplar
- Beech
- Princess tree
- Sugar maple
- Sweetgum
- 'Autumn Purple' ash
- Red oak
- Honey locust

PLANTING TREES

Fall is the best time to plant trees, with spring a close second. The middle of summer is the worst time to plant a tree because trees will lose water faster than they can take it back up, and in winter, well, the ground is frozen. In spring and fall, trees have the chance to grow and establish roots before harsher conditions—summer heat or winter cold—set in.

HOW TO PLANT A TREE

1. Use a shovel or marking paint to mark the area for the hole. The planting hole should be twice as wide as the tree's rootball.
2. Dig the planting hole. This hole should be just as deep as the rootball—no deeper. If you sharpen the spade before digging, this step will go faster.
3. Set the tree in the planting hole to check the depth. If the top of the rootball is lower than the soil line around the edge of the planting hole, add some soil back into the hole, pull the tree out of the pot, and replace the tree in the hole. You never want the crown of the tree (the point where the tree trunk meets the tree roots) to be below the soil line.
4. Fill in around the tree with the same soil that you removed from the planting hole. Do not add fertilizer or new topsoil. Water will move more easily and the tree will root properly if the soil in the planting hole and around the planting hole are the same.

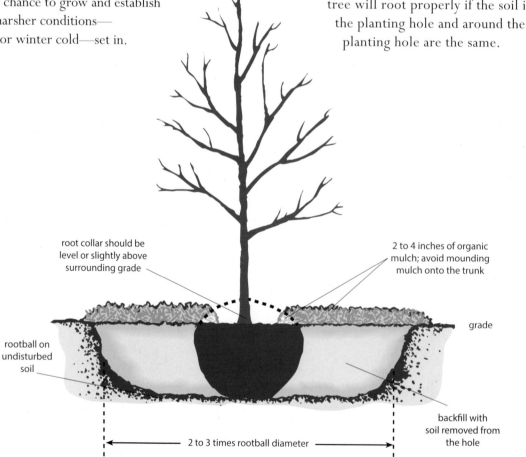

root collar should be level or slightly above surrounding grade

2 to 4 inches of organic mulch; avoid mounding mulch onto the trunk

grade

rootball on undisturbed soil

backfill with soil removed from the hole

2 to 3 times rootball diameter

5. Mulch around the tree, taking care to pull the mulch away from the tree trunk. Do not create a "mulch volcano" around the tree by piling mulch up high around the trunk. That just encourages insects and creatures that snack on tree bark to take up residence next to your delicious young tree.

6. Water the tree. Plan to water newly planted trees every three days (every other day if it is hot and dry). New trees don't need to be staked unless they're in areas prone to heavy rains and frequent winds. It can take a couple of years for newly planted trees to root all the way into the surrounding soil, so continue to monitor the tree for signs that it needs water.

TO STAKE OR NOT TO STAKE?

I lean on the side of *not* staking, unless you live in a really windy area. Most trees will root in just fine without being staked. If a new tree topples over before it roots in, it's easy to go back and stake it. If you do stake a tree, use soft, wide straps or foam-covered straps and remove them after a year. Check periodically to make sure that they aren't rubbing against the tree bark and that the bark isn't growing around the straps.

CARING FOR TREES

Trees require less care, overall, than most other landscape plants or edibles. They do require some care, though, with newer trees needing more than older trees.

WATERING

Water new trees a couple of times per week, gradually tapering off to once a week. During the second year, water deeply once per month. After that, water if your area is experiencing drought and the leaves look grayish or wilted.

FERTILIZING

If nutrients are available in the soil where the tree is planted and the pH of the soil is normal, making the nutrients available, the trees should not need extra fertilizer. Occasionally, trees will have problems with unavailable micronutrients, particularly iron. If the leaves of the tree are a strange color during the summer, take a sample of the tree and a nearby soil sample (from around the tree) to your Extension office for help identifying the problem.

PRUNING

Tree pruning is one of the most nerve-wracking aspects of gardening for most people. If you prune a perennial or shrub, it will grow back. When you prune older, larger trees, you're generally taking off sections of the tree that will not grow back. There is more risk of injuring an older tree. However, that is not a reason to avoid pruning. Here's why you prune:

YOUNG TREES
- For shape
- To control size
- To remove branches that might be rubbing or crossing each other
- To eliminate watersprouts (branches that grow straight up)

MATURE TREES
- To remove rubbing branches
- To eliminate dead wood that could be a safety hazard
- To keep branches away from the house, power lines, or other obstructions
- To open up the canopy for light penetration and air flow
- To limb up (raise the level of the lowest branch on the tree)

In general, the best time to prune is during the winter when trees are dormant. If a tree is a bleeder (maples, in particular have a big spring sap run), wait until after spring to prune.

Just like other plants, trees grow from the tips of their branches. There are a few types of trees that can be cut anywhere and they'll resprout from the middle of a branch. But, in general, if you make a cut and leave a big stub, the stub will be there for a long time and nothing will grow from or around it. When possible, cut back to another branch (even just a small branch) or to the trunk as described on page 30.

REMOVING LARGE BRANCHES

Use the three-cut pruning technique to remove large branches. This will keep you from accidentally stripping the bark below the branch you're cutting and harming the tree.

1. Make the first cut on the underside of the branch, about 6 inches from the tree trunk. You'll only cut one-fourth to one-third of the way through the branch.

2. Make the second cut farther out on the branch from the first cut. Cut the branch all the way off. The branch will probably break off while you're cutting it. That is why you made the first cut on the underside of the tree—to help the branch break in the direction you want without stripping the bark off the branch.

3. You can see the finished second cut here. At the very bottom of the cut edge, you can see where part of the branch ripped. Heavy branches will rip further, often down to the cut on the

underside of the tree. The cut on the underside of the limb keeps the branch from ripping all the way down the tree trunk and causing more damage. You never want to make a cut that strips the bark off of a tree branch, because all of the water and food in the tree travels up and down the tree right under the bark.

4. Cut off the branch stub remaining on the tree. Place the pruning saw just outside of the branch collar, which is the bark swelling between the branch and the main trunk. Saw all the way through to remove the stub. Do not cut the branch flush with the tree trunk, or you'll hurt the tree's chances of healing itself.

5. In this picture, you can see that there's still about one-fourth to one-half inch of branch left to allow the branch collar to heal. Never cover pruning cuts with tar, concrete, or sealant. The tree will heal itself if left alone. Sealant or tar creates a dark, moist environment that is perfect for bacteria to grow. If you follow this pruning technique, the tree will heal itself.

MULCHING

Spread mulch in a 2- to 4-foot diameter around a tree, no more than 4 inches deep at the time of planting, to help retain soil moisture. Pull the mulch away from the tree bark slightly. Do not make a mulch volcano. That can do more harm than good. The mulch also gives you a buffer so that you don't accidentally nick the bark of the young tree with a string trimmer.

PEST PROBLEMS

There are so many pest problems that can plague trees that it would be impossible to go into all of them in one paragraph. In general, I try to figure out whether the problem is affecting the entire tree. If not, I usually ignore it. If there are bagworms on one section of the tree, I might cut them off. If there's a big fungal problem, I take a piece to the Extension office to get recommendations.

For the most part, pest problems will either go away on their own or kill the entire tree, and there's not much you can do other than sit back and watch. The way pest populations in nature work is that they tend to rise over a period of years and then collapse. If you try to treat the problem, you can end up not eliminating it, but ensuring that you live with low-key issues indefinitely.

AMERICAN BEECH
Fagus grandifolia

Why It's Special—American beech is one of the most majestic native American shade trees. The tree provides garden interest year-round; between beautiful smooth gray bark, glossy toothed green leaves, and bright fall color, there's everything to love about this tree. The leaves persist on the tree throughout winter. They can live for up to 400 years.

How to Plant & Grow—Plant in full sun to partial shade in moist, well-drained soil. It grows best in loose soils. This isn't a great urban street tree, but grow this if you have lots of space.

Care & Problems—American beech is fairly pest-free. Squirrels and other small mammals like to snack on the fruits (beech nuts) but don't usually damage the tree. (The fruits are edible for humans, too, in small quantities.) The tree will sometimes produce suckers, eventually creating a grove if left alone. If you want to remove suckers, prune them; do not use systemic herbicide, as that will kill the entire plant.

Fall Color—Yellow

Peak Season—Summer to fall

Mature Size (H x W)—50–80 feet x 40–70 feet

Hardiness—3–9

Water Needs—Medium

AMERICAN HOLLY
Ilex opaca

Why It's Special—American holly is also known as the "Christmas holly," as its red berry-laden branches with glossy, thorny leaves are often the centerpieces for holiday decorations. This native tree grows best in areas with moist soil and can be found in the wild growing along rivers and lakes. Small white flowers in spring are an important source of food for pollinators.

How to Plant & Grow—Plant outside in acidic, moist, well-drained soil in full sun to partial shade. The warmer the area, the more shade the plants can take. Water to establish. For best fruiting, make sure to plant at least one male and one female plant in the same yard.

Care & Problems—Hollies need acidic soil. If the pH is high, you may have to amend the soil with aluminum sulfate before planting. You might also have to give the trees supplemental iron throughout their life. American holly requires little pruning and has a natural pyramidal form.

Fall Color—Evergreen

Peak Season—Fall to winter

Mature Size (H x W)—15–30 feet x 10–20 feet

Hardiness—5–9

Water Needs—Medium

ATLAS CEDAR
Cedrus atlantica

Why It's Special—The first time I saw an atlas cedar I was interning at the Washington Park Arboretum where there was a giant specimen near the front entrance. I asked the staff what it was before I even greeted them for the first time. These loosely pyramidal trees have soft, waxy blue needles. Branches droop slightly at the ends, giving the plants a bit of a Dr. Seuss appearance. They are unique specimen trees for the landscape if you live in an area where it is hardy. *Cedrus atlantica f. glauca* is what is most often sold in the nursery trade.

How to Plant & Grow—Plant in full sun in well-drained soil where the tree has room to spread. Part of its charm is in its natural growth habit.

Care & Problems—This is a fairly pest-free plant. If a heavy snow occurs, gently use a rake to lift branches up (not down) to allow snow to slide off. It's drought tolerant once established.

Fall Color—Bluish gray evergreen

Peak Season—Year-round

Mature Size (H x W)—40–60 feet x 30–40 feet

Hardiness—6–9

Water Needs—Low once established

BALD CYPRESS
Taxodium distichum

Why It's Special—Bald cypress is a deciduous conifer. It has soft, fernlike, needle leaves that turn a rusty golden brown in fall and then drop off, revealing reddish exfoliating bark and a striking pyramidal architecture. All of its attributes come together to make this a beautiful tree with four-season interest. The genus name means "taxus-like" referring to the fact that the flat leaves look like smaller, finer versions of yew leaves.

How to Plant & Grow—Bald cypress naturally grow in wetlands, sloughs, and swamps. They need moist soil and can grow in shallow water. You'll recognize knobby knees poking up all around the trees especially in wet areas. These help the tree roots breathe. It will grow in the home landscape despite its penchant for moist soils. Water regularly throughout its first growing season.

Care & Problems—This is a fairly easy-care, pest-free tree provided that it gets enough water. Spherical cones mature in fall, adding interest.

Fall Color—Golden brown

Peak Season—Year-round

Mature Size (H x W)—50–70 feet x 20–40 feet

Hardiness—5–10

Water Needs—High

BLACK GUM
Nyssa sylvatica

Why It's Special—Black gum is also called the tupelo tree. Bees collect pollen from the insignificant flowers in spring to make honey. (You've probably heard of tupelo honey, right?) This tree is woefully underutilized in the landscape. It grows well in poorly drained soils, but also tolerates drought when established. It has beautiful reddish-orange fall color, even in warmer climates, and a symmetrical, pagoda-like growth structure that's mostly apparent in winter. All of these attributes combine to give this tree year-round interest.

How to Plant & Grow—Plant in full sun to partial shade in moist, poorly to well-drained soils. Black gum tolerates a wide range of soil conditions. Water to establish.

Care & Problems—This tree is fairly pest-free. Ensure plenty of water while the tree is establishing roots. It is slow growing, but will eventually reach a height between 30 to 50 feet, so plant it where it will have room to grow if you don't want to remove it later.

Fall Color—Red-orange

Peak Season—Summer to fall

Mature Size (H x W)—30–50 feet x 20–40 feet

Hardiness—4–9

Water Needs—Medium to high

CHINESE FRINGETREE
Chionanthus retusus

Why It's Special—Fringetrees are some of the prettiest and most unusual spring-flowering trees. They have pendulous clusters of delicate white flowers that bloom in late spring, giving rise to clusters of blue-black berries in fall. The native species, *Chionanthus virginicus*, is also attractive, though Chinese fringetree has larger, denser flower clusters. It's a perfect specimen tree.

How to Plant & Grow—Plant fringetrees in groups for maximum impact or as specimens in a landscape bed near the house. These trees need consistently moist, well-drained soil. They will decline if planted in dry locations. Female trees produce dark blue-black fruits in fall if the flowers are pollinated. Plants are not always marked as male or female in the garden centers, though.

Care & Problems—Ensure the trees are watered throughout the growing season, particularly if you're having a dry summer. They rarely need pruning. This is a plant-it-and-forget-it tree, for the most part, except that you'll enjoy its profuse spring bloom and pretty fall color.

Fall Color—Yellow-orange

Peak Season—Spring

Mature Size (H x W)—15–30 feet x 15–30 feet

Hardiness—5–9

Water Needs—Medium

CRABAPPLE
Malus spp. and cultivars

Why It's Special—Crabapples have the prettiest pinkish-white flowers in spring. They are lightly scented. I always think they smell like pure, fresh spring water would smell if it were fragrant. There are hundreds of cultivars. 'Adams' has semi-double pink blooms. 'Manbeck Weeper' is a white-flowered weeping form with good disease resistance. 'Callaway' grows well during hot, humid summers and is disease resistant. The fruits are edible, but not for typical apple snacking; most people who cook with them make jelly.

How to Plant & Grow—Plant in acidic, moist, well-drained soil. Because they're relatively small for trees, you can grow them near the house.

Care & Problems—Crabapples are susceptible to a wide variety of plant disease, including fireblight, cedar-apple rust, and apple scab. The best way to deal with these is to plant resistant varieties, of which there are many. Do your research. Prune in winter to remove crossing branches and watersprouts. Prune in spring after flowering to control size and shape.

Fall Color—Red-orange

Bloom Period/Peak Season—Spring, fall

Mature Size (H x W)—Depends on cultivar. 15–25 feet x 10–15 feet

Hardiness—4–8

Water Needs—Medium

CRAPE MYRTLE
Lagerstroemia indica

Why It's Special—Crape myrtles bloom with abandon when few other trees or shrubs are in flower. During winter you can enjoy their exfoliating bark and vase-shaped architectural form. In cooler regions, plants can die back to the ground, but will resprout in spring. The US National Arboretum has released a series named for Native American tribes ('Cherokee', 'Seminole'). These have improved powdery mildew resistance.

How to Plant & Grow—Crape myrtles make gorgeous specimens, but their naturally arching, vase-shaped growth habit is also well suited for planting along driveways or as a hedgerow. They grow and bloom best in full sun only.

Care & Problems—Water regularly if you're experiencing a dry summer. They can sometimes have issues with powdery mildew. Prune during winter, removing all branches that are smaller in diameter than your pinky finger. You *can* cut crape myrtles back hard, but there is no need, and you'll miss out on their attractive natural shape if you do.

Fall Color—Yellow, orange, red

Peak Season—Summer, fall, and winter

Mature Size (H x W)—Depends on variety; there are tree and shrub forms. 5–20 feet x 5–20 feet

Hardiness—6–9

Water Needs—Medium

DOGWOOD, CHINESE
Cornus kousa

Why It's Special—Chinese dogwood, also called the Kousa dogwood, blooms later than the native flowering dogwood, with bright white flowers opening in early June. (The true flowers are actually a cluster of green in the center of the four showy white bracts that look like petals.) Flowers mature into red fruits in late summer. The trees have a mosaic-like bark that's attractive during winter, giving this tree true four-season interest.

How to Plant & Grow—Plant in full sun to part shade in moist, well-drained soil. It's fairly adaptable to a wide range of growing conditions.

Care & Problems—You can grow Kousa dogwood as a single-stemmed tree or a multistemmed shrub. If you want a traditional tree shape, prune off any suckers that emerge at its base. If you want a multistemmed shape, allow a few suckers to grow. Chinese dogwood is mostly resistant to anthracnose, unlike the native *Cornus florida*, so if you have issues with that in your garden, plant *C. kousa*.

Fall Color—Red

Bloom Period/Peak Season—Early summer

Mature Size (H x W)—15–30 feet x 15–30 feet

Hardiness—5–8

Water Needs—Medium

DOGWOOD, FLOWERING
Cornus florida

Why It's Special—Flowering dogwoods are native trees that grow along woodland margins in the Midwest, Northeast, and Mid-Atlantic. Plant it as a specimen in a landscape bed near the house or as an understory tree among larger hardwood trees. Dogwoods appear to bloom in layers, or platforms, with upward-facing flowers.

How to Plant & Grow—Plant flowering dogwoods in full sun to partial shade in moist, well-drained soil. Water to establish. Mulch to keep the tree's roots cool and moisture level consistent. Select cultivars that have demonstrated resistance to anthracnose, including 'Weaver's White'.

Care & Problems—The biggest problem that dogwoods have is anthracnose. In recent years, some cultivars have been introduced that exhibit resistance. Plant those when possible. Prevent plants from becoming stressed, as that helps with resistance as well. Keep the soil evenly moist during the growing season. Dogwoods have fairly uniform growth habits and should not need regular pruning other than to remove dead wood or crossing branches.

Fall Color—Red

Peak Season—Spring, blooms; fall, color

Mature Size (H x W)—15–20 feet x 15–20 feet

Hardiness—5–9

Water Needs—Medium

DOGWOOD, PAGODA
Cornus alternifolia

Why It's Special—The pagoda dogwood is an attractive, medium-sized dogwood with a pagoda-like, tiered branching habit (hence its common name). It can be grown as a multistemmed tree or large shrub, or pruned into a medium-sized tree with a central leader. The fluffy white flowers do not look like typical dogwood blooms, resembling spiraêa flowers instead. They mature into bluish-black fruits in late summer.

How to Plant & Grow—Plant the pagoda dogwood where it can be admired as a specimen plant, but where it has plenty of room to spread out. It does best in full sun to partial shade in acidic, consistently moist, well-drained soils.

Care & Problems—Keep the soil consistently moist, but not soggy. Prune early in a tree's life to establish the shape you want to keep—multistemmed or central leader. It's susceptible to dogwood blight and a range of insects and problems, so keep an eye out for pests.

Fall Color—Red

Peak Season—Early summer brings bloom; fall offers leaf color

Mature Size (H x W)—15–20 feet x 25–35 feet

Hardiness—3–7

Water Needs—Medium

EASTERN RED CEDAR
Juniperus virginiana

Why It's Special—Eastern red cedar (it's actually a juniper, not a cedar) is a native evergreen tree with a strong pyramidal growth habit. Females produce small bluish fruits that also attract birds, including the cedar waxwing (named after this shrub). These evergreens are mostly deer resistant. 'Globosa' is a small round cultivar well-suited for foundation plantings.

How to Plant & Grow—Plant in full sun in spring or fall in moist, well-drained soil. You can grow eastern red cedars as standalone specimen trees or as a hedge. If growing as a hedge, leave 5 to 8 feet between plants. For the best fruiting, plant a male in the vicinity.

Care & Problems—These trees are the winter host for cedar-apple rust. If you're growing apples or other fruits in the rose family, do not grow Eastern red cedars. Aside from that, these plants are fairly pest-free. They prefer moist soil, but will tolerate drier soil conditions once established.

Fall Color—Evergreen; may develop a brownish tinge in winter

Peak Season—Year-round

Mature Size (H x W)—30–60 feet x 8–15 feet

Hardiness—2–9

Water Needs—Low

EASTERN WHITE PINE
Pinus strobus

Why It's Special—Eastern white pines are fast-growing, tall, long-lived evergreens with clusters of long, soft needles. Their growth form is highly symmetrical, with a new whorl of branches growing each season from the growing tip at the top of the tree. These trees have a strong, straight central leader, unless the growing tip is cut off early in the tree's life, which causes the tree to spread out into a large, uneven blob. (Don't cut off the growing tip!) 'Fastigiata' is a strongly columnar form.

How to Plant & Grow—Plant in full sun in moist, well-drained soils. Eastern white pines can be grown as specimen trees or trained into deer resistant hedges.

Care & Problems—Eastern white pines are easy to grow, as they adapt to a wide range of soil conditions. Do your best to protect the top of the tree from damage, as it is what helps the tree maintain the strong upright form. If you need to clear space under the tree, prune off the lower branches.

Fall Color—Evergreen

Peak Season—Year-round

Mature Size (H x W)—50–80 feet x 20–40 feet

Hardiness—3–8

Water Needs—Medium

GINKGO
Ginkgo biloba

Why It's Special—Ginkgo trees were around during prehistoric times, making these trees true dinosaur food! They are deciduous conifers with light green fan-shaped leaves that turn a brilliant yellow in fall. Ginkgos have a striking architectural form—a strong central leader with neatly horizontal branches emerging at right angles to the trunk. There are some cultivars with weeping forms.

How to Plant & Grow—It is important to ensure that when you buy a ginkgo tree, you're getting a male plant, not a female. Females produce globular fruits in fall that drop to the ground and ferment, creating the most noxious, vomit-inducing scent I have ever had the displeasure to smell. Plant in full sun in moist, well-drained soils.

Care & Problems—These are slow-growing trees with few pest problems. You might want to stake the tree for the first year or two after planting, checking the straps seasonally to ensure they are not cutting into the bark.

Fall Color—Yellow

Peak Season—Summer, fall

Mature Size (H x W)—50–80 feet x 30–40 feet

Hardiness—5–9

Water Needs—Medium

HONEY LOCUST
Gleditsia triacanthos

Why It's Special—Honey locusts are native trees that add an interesting dimension to the landscape. They have compound, fernlike leaves that provide dappled shade where the trees are planted. The species has huge, long thorns, but the variety 'Inermis' is thornless. The name comes from long seedpods filled with a honeylike pulpy substance. Many cultivars available today are seedless, which is great because the pods are messy!

How to Plant & Grow—Trees adapt to a variety of growing conditions, but will grow best in full sun in moist, well-drained soil. They grow to be quite tall and wide, so plant them where they have room to spread out. They also make excellent street trees (or hell strip trees).

Care & Problems—Provided you purchased a cultivar that is thornless and seedless, you should have few problems. Honey locusts are nectar and host plants for many butterfly and moth species, so do not be alarmed if you see caterpillars munching the leaves.

Fall Color—Yellow

Peak Season—Summer, fall

Mature Size (H x W)—60–80 feet x 60–80 feet

Hardiness—3–8

Water Needs—Medium

JAPANESE CEDAR
Cryptomeria japonica

Why It's Special—Cryptomeria is another large, beautiful evergreen conifer. The species grows to be enormous, so only plant it if you have *lots* of room. The arrangement of needles on branches gives the plant an overall "fluffy" appearance. There are different cultivars, some with more widely spaced needles, different colored foliage, or dwarf sizes. If you like the look of the plant, but don't have the space, grow a dwarf cryptomeria.

How to Plant & Grow—Plant in full sun in moist, well-drained soil. Ideally, plant it on the south or west side of the house where it will be protected from winter winds. The species tree needs lots of space. It doesn't look particularly good when limbed up so only grow it where you have room for it to reach a mature spread of 20 to 30 feet.

Care & Problems—Provide extra water during prolonged periods of wind with below-freezing temperatures. Otherwise, this is an easy-care, pest-free tree.

Fall Color—Evergreen

Peak Season—Year-round interest

Mature Size (H x W)—50–60 feet x 20–30 feet

Hardiness—6–9

Water Needs—Medium

JAPANESE FLOWERING CHERRY
Prunus serrulata

Why It's Special—When you buy a Japanese flowering cherry, you're generally not purchasing the straight species; you're purchasing a cultivar. 'Kwanzan' is one of the most widely available varieties. These are some of the first trees to bloom in spring and have single and double flowers in shades of pink or white. They're spectacular in bloom, less interesting when they're not flowering though they have unique bark. Horizontal lines, called lenticels, wrap around the tree trunks, providing some winter interest. Trees sometimes exhibit a bronze-red fall color, but it's not a given.

How to Plant & Grow—Plant in full sun to partial shade in moist, well-drained soils. Purchase weeping forms for even more landscape interest.

Care & Problems—Flowering cherries are susceptible to a variety of pests and diseases. If something is amiss, take a sample to your Cooperative Extension for diagnosis and a treatment plan. Prune in winter to remove crossing or rubbing branches and watersprouts.

Fall Color—Red, yellow, or bronze. Check cultivar descriptions when purchasing.

Peak Season—Blooms in early spring

Mature Size (H x W)—15–20 feet x 15–20 feet

Hardiness—5–8

Water Needs—Medium

JAPANESE SNOWBELL
Styrax japonicus

Why It's Special—Japanese snowbell is a small flowering tree that grows as an understory plant in its native habitat. It blooms in late spring to early summer with white, bell-shaped flowers that hang from the undersides of branches. Young species trees are pyramid-shaped, though they mature into flat-topped trees. There are some cultivars, including one with a weeping growth habit.

How to Plant & Grow—Plant in moist, well-drained soil in full to part sun. This tree is definitely a specimen plant to be given pride of place in the landscape. Water to establish. Because of the dappled nature of the shade under the tree, it's a good plant to anchor landscape beds where you want to grow a shade perennial garden. Plant ferns, hellebores, compact-growing hydrangeas, and azaleas under Japanese snowbell.

Care & Problems—It has few landscape problems, provided that soil is kept evenly moist, because it is not at all drought tolerant. Japanese snowbells rarely need pruning.

Fall Color—Red-orange

Bloom Period/Peak Season—Late spring

Mature Size (H x W)—15–18 feet x 15–18 feet

Hardiness—5–8

Water Needs—Medium

137

KATSURA
Cercidiphyllum japonicum

Why It's Special—Katsura trees have a nearly perfect growth form. Branches angle upward from the trunk to create a vase-shaped canopy. Heart-shaped, medium green leaves turn brilliant shades of yellow, orange, and red in fall. In winter, their architectural form is on display, along with attractive gray bark. To really see what this tree can do, visit Dumbarton Oaks in Washington, D.C., where there's a beautiful mature tree near the front of the garden.

How to Plant & Grow—Plant in full sun to partial shade in moist, well-drained soil. These are medium-to-large shade and specimen trees, so plant where they'll have room to grow. Water to establish. *Cercidiphyllum forma pendulum* is a weeping form that takes up slightly less space and is a true specimen.

Care & Problems—Take care not to let the soil dry out during the first growing season. This tree has few pest and disease problems and does not need, nor respond well, to pruning. Leave it alone and let it grow!

Fall Color—Red, yellow, orange

Peak Season—Fall

Mature Size (H x W)—40–60 feet x 25–40 feet

Hardiness—4–8

Water Needs—Medium

LITTLELEAF LINDEN
Tilia cordata

Why It's Special—Littleleaf linden is another underutilized shade tree for the landscape. It is versatile, as it is adaptable to a wide variety of growing conditions and soils, tolerates shearing, and copes well with urban conditions. It blooms in summer with clusters of creamy white flowers hanging from showy light green leaflike bracts. Linden trees are a popular source of pollen for honey bees. The species name *cordata* refers to the heart-shaped leaves. 'Greenspire' is a popular cultivar; it has a tightly pyramidal growth habit.

How to Plant & Grow—Plant in full sun to partial shade where the tree will have the space to grow and mature into a large shade tree. It can also be planted as a street tree.

Care & Problems—Littleleaf linden tolerates heavy pruning, so it can be grown as a deciduous hedge. It has few pest problems unless it's under drought stress. Provide supplemental water in summer if rain is scarce.

Fall Color—Orangey yellow

Peak Season—Spring, summer, and fall

Mature Size (H x W)—50–70 feet x 30–50 feet

Hardiness—4–7

Water Needs—Medium

MAGNOLIA, SAUCER
Magnolia × soulangeana

Why It's Special—Saucer magnolias are another early-blooming flowering tree. They have large pinkish purple flowers that look somewhat like a teacup sitting in a saucer. Another common name for saucer magnolias is "tulip magnolia," again because of the flower shape. There are many cultivars available with different flower characteristics. The flowers are sometimes damaged in areas prone to late freezes.

How to Plant & Grow—Plant in a protected spot in full sun to partial shade. These make good specimen plants for their early blooms and attractive foliage during the summer. Keep the soil evenly moist—avoid extremes. Mulch to keep roots cool and water to establish.

Care & Problems—The biggest issue with these plants is flowers freezing in spring, but there's not much you can do about that. Do not plant in a warm microclimate of your garden, which could trigger early blooming and leave the plant susceptible to frost damage. These trees require little pruning to maintain shape.

Fall Color—Yellow-brown (not showy)

Peak Season—Early spring

Mature Size (H x W)—20–30 feet x 20–30 feet

Hardiness—4–9

Water Needs—Medium

MAGNOLIA, SOUTHERN
Magnolia grandiflora

Why It's Special—These large evergreen trees are more Southern than Mid-Atlantic, though there are some gorgeous specimens on the lawn of the US Capitol Building in Washington, D.C. Glossy evergreen leaves, dinner plate-sized flowers, and unusual fruits in fall give magnolias lots of seasonal interest. It is a handsome tree with a striking presence in the landscape where it is hardy. There are a few cultivars that are more cold-hardy and a smaller mature size.

How to Plant & Grow—Southern magnolias grow to be large trees that create dense shade under a canopy where nothing else will grow. Plant in full sun in medium-moist, well-drained soil where the trees will have room to spread out to a width of 40 to 50 feet.

Care & Problems—Keep the soil evenly moist around these trees. The main issue with Southern magnolias is that they are messy. They drop leaves year-round, and fruits in fall are heavy and have to be raked and shoveled up.

Fall Color—Evergreen

Peak Season—Flowers in summer; fruits in fall

Mature Size (H x W)—60–80 feet x 30–40 feet

Hardiness—7–9

Water Needs—Medium

MAGNOLIA, STAR
Magnolia stellata

Why It's Special—Star magnolias have gorgeous, white, star-shaped blooms in early spring before the leaves unfurl. This is a slow-growing, cold-hardy magnolia that is often grown as a multistemmed tree or shrub. It works well as a specimen plant. In late summer to early fall, it's covered in typical aggregate red magnolia fruits—several fruits on one cone-like structure.

How to Plant & Grow—Plant in full sun to partial shade in moist, well-drained soil. Do not plant in a warm microclimate, because that can trigger early bloom that's susceptible to frost damage. If you want a pretty specimen but have a small lot, this tree is for you. Water to establish and mulch around the base of these plants to keep the roots color and soil moist.

Care & Problems—Star magnolias are fairly easy-care trees. Do not prune except to remove dead or diseased growth. If you must prune, do so directly after flowering because plants will immediately begin to set flower buds for the next season.

Fall Color—Yellow

Peak Season—Early spring flowers

Mature Size (H x W)—15–20 feet x 15–20 feet

Hardiness—5–9

Water Needs—Medium

MAGNOLIA, SWEETBAY
Magnolia virginiana

Why It's Special—If you like the look of a Southern magnolia, but don't have space to grow it, the sweetbay magnolia is a good alternative. It is much smaller and less messy than its counterpart. Creamy white flowers bloom in early summer. The trees are covered in cone-like fruits with red berries late summer to fall. It's an excellent medium-sized specimen tree. MOONGLOW® is a cultivar with a strongly upright growing habit and better cold hardiness than the species. Sweetbay magnolias are the larval host for the sweetbay silkmoth, so don't be alarmed if you see large green caterpillars on this tree.

How to Plant & Grow—Plant in full sun to partial shade in moist, well-drained soil. It is more tolerant of wet soils than other magnolias. Water to establish. Mulch to conserve moisture.

Care & Problems—This is a fairly pest-free, medium-sized tree for the landscape. Plant it and enjoy! Prune only to remove dead or diseased wood.

Fall Color—Not showy

Peak Season—Flowers in early summer, fruits in fall

Mature Size (H x W)—20–40 feet x 15–30 feet

Hardiness—5–10

Water Needs—Medium to high

MAPLE, JAPANESE
Acer palmatum

Why It's Special—Japanese maples are a species of maples with palm-shaped leaves (hence the name "palmatum") that grow as multistemmed or single-stemmed trained trees. There are hundreds of cultivars available with varying growth habits, fall colors, and leaf shapes. Dumbarton Oaks in Georgetown (Washington, D.C.) has some amazing old specimens.

How to Plant & Grow—Plant in full sun to part shade in a location that is protected from wind and the worst of the elements. The amount of space needed around a tree depends on its eventual size and use. Weeping varieties are popular for specimen plantings. Plant larger, vase-shaped varieties near the house.

Care & Problems—You can prune Japanese maples during summer or midwinter to shape. The main trunk can be trained in a series of "S" curves for a sculptural specimen. These trees do best with evenly moist soil, and unless you are embarking on a big pruning and shaping project, they're fairly low-maintenance.

Fall Color—Burgundy, red, yellow, orange (depends on cultivar)

Peak Season—Year-round

Mature Size (H x W)—5–25 feet x 5–25 feet

Hardiness—6–8

Water Needs—Medium

MAPLE, RED
Acer rubrum

Why It's Special—Red maples, particularly specific cultivars, provide some of the most reliable fall color in the landscape. They are striking shade trees. Red maples are one of the first deciduous trees to flower in spring. While they don't produce showy, large-petaled flowers, they are a harbinger of warmer weather! The flowers give the trees an almost misty red glow. Autumn Blaze® is a popular hybrid that stays slightly smaller than the species and has reliably brilliant red fall color.

How to Plant & Grow—Plant in full sun to partial shade in moist, well-drained soils. Spring and fall are best times to plant. These trees grow to be large, so select a spot where they'll have room to grow.

Care & Problems—Red maples need pruning to establish solid branch architecture. Remove branches with narrow crotch angles (narrow angle between branch and trunk). Prune to remove crossing or rubbing branches. Keep the soil evenly moist during the growing season.

Fall Color—Red or yellow

Peak Season—Fall

Mature Size (H x W)—50–100 feet x 30–50 feet

Hardiness—3–9

Water Needs—Medium

MAPLE, SUGAR
Acer saccharum

Why It's Special—Sugar maples have the most reliably brilliant fall color of nearly all deciduous hardwood trees. These are the trees that make the hillsides in the Mid-Atlantic seem to burst into flame. They are large native trees that take up a lot of room in the landscape, but grow into amazing specimens. They are the trees that are tapped in spring for their sap, which is boiled down to make maple syrup and maple sugar. 'Commemoration' exhibits fall color earlier than the species and holds color well after a frost.

How to Plant & Grow—Plant in full sun to partial shade in medium-moist, well-drained soil. There won't be room for more than one of these in the yard unless you have a lot of acreage. Water to establish.

Care & Problems—Sugar maples are fairly easy to grow. Keep the soil evenly moist as the tree is establishing roots. It's mostly pest-free, but water during drought.

Fall Color—Red to orange

Bloom Period/Peak Season—Fall

Mature Size (H x W)—70–90 feet x 40–60 feet

Hardiness—4–8

Water Needs—Medium

NORWAY SPRUCE
Picea abies

Why It's Special—The species Norway spruce is a large evergreen tree that reaches mature heights of 60 feet. There are weeping and dwarf cultivars that are much smaller and more suited for use as a specimen plant in landscape beds. 'Pendula' is a weeping cultivar that reaches a maximum height of 15 feet.

How to Plant & Grow—Norway spruce grows best in cooler climates—below Zone 7. Plant outside in full sun. Spacing depends on whether you're growing the species or a cultivar. All varieties do best when grown in well-drained soil. This plant does not do well with wet feet. Use as a windbreak or screen in cooler climates, and it tolerates hedging.

Care & Problems—Water to establish. There are a few pest problems that affect this tree. Mites are the worst, when the weather is hot and dry. If needles on lower branches are yellow, clip a sample and take to your local Cooperative Extension for diagnosis. Shear hedges in spring after their first flush of growth.

Fall Color—Evergreen

Peak Season—Year-round

Mature Size (H x W)—40–60 feet x 20–30 feet

Hardiness—3–7

Water Needs—Low

OAK
Quercus spp.

Why It's Special—Many species of oak are native to the United States, so you have lots of variety to select from. No matter what your landscape has to offer, there is an oak that will thrive in it. According to Douglas Tallamy, chair of the University of Delaware Department of Entomology and Wildlife Ecology, a single oak tree can support 534 species of butterflies and moths, and their fruits (acorns) feed a variety of other animals. Planting an oak tree is a solid move for gardeners interested in supporting their local environment.

How to Plant & Grow—Plant oak trees in full sun in spring or fall. Select a site that will allow the tree plenty of room to grow and mature.

Care & Problems—Water needs differ depending on the species. Prune for shape during winter so that you can get a good look at the tree's architecture. Remove diseased or rubbing branches.

Fall Color—Usually red; sometimes orange or yellow

Peak Season—Summer, fall

Mature Size (H x W)—60–80 feet x 30–50 feet

Hardiness—3–10 (depending on species)

Water Needs—Depends on the species

RED BUCKEYE
Aesculus pavia

Why It's Special—Grow this small tree for its beautiful spikes of red flowers in the late spring to early summer. Depending on the specimen you acquire, you can grow this as a tree with a central leader or as a large shrub with multiple trunks. It attracts hummingbirds and butterflies. **Caution:** All parts of plant are poisonous.

How to Plant & Grow—Plant in full sun to partial shade in a location with moist, well-drained soil. The warmer your growing zone, the more shade it needs. Spring and fall are best times for planting. Give this tree some room to spread out—at least 20 to 25 feet. Water to establish.

Care & Problems—This is a fairly pest-free plant, as long as it is given adequate water. It doesn't like to sit in completely wet soils, but will need more water if planted in the sun or if your area is experiencing drought.

Fall Color—Yellow, but not showy

Bloom Period/Peak Season—Early summer, flowers

Mature Size (H x W)—15–20 feet x 15–20 feet

Hardiness—4–8

Water Needs—Medium

REDBUD
Cercis canadensis

Why It's Special—Eastern redbud, one of the earliest spring-bloomers, is one of my favorite trees. It's a small, native understory tree with purple flowers that emerge along its branches in spring. It grows in an almost perfect umbrella shape, giving it almost year-round interest, between its architecture, flowers, and leaf color.

How to Plant & Grow—Plant in full sun to partial shade in well-drained moist soils. Water to establish. Redbuds are good specimen trees for landscape beds close to the house. There are varieties with variegated leaves. 'Forest Pansy' is a popular cultivar with burgundy leaves. 'Lavender Twist®' is a weeping cultivar.

Care & Problems—Keep soil moderately moist. Prune in summer after bloom to remove dead or diseased wood. It is also a good idea to remove branches that are growing at a narrow (almost vertical) angle to the main trunk. Redbuds are susceptible to a variety of insect pests and diseases. Providing the plants with their preferred growing conditions can do a lot to prevent pest and disease problems.

Fall Color—Yellow; 'Forest Pansy' has burgundy foilage

Peak Season—Spring, flowers; fall, leaves

Mature Size (H x W)—20–30 feet x 25–35 feet

Hardiness—4–8

Water Needs—Medium

SERVICEBERRY
Amelanchier spp.

Why It's Special—Were I to choose one perfect tree, it would be the serviceberry. These smallish trees (they grow to a maximum of 40 feet) are interesting year-round. They have white flowers in spring, nice medium-green leaves and reddish (edible) fruits in summer, gorgeous color in fall, and uniform branching architecture in winter. There are several species, all with similar characteristics. This tree is sometimes called shadbush because its bloom coincides with shad spawning in spring.

How to Plant & Grow—Plant in full sun to partial shade as an understory tree or a specimen plant in the landscape. Water to establish.

Care & Problems—Usually serviceberries are grown as multistemmed trees. Prune to maintain their upright growth habit. As part of the rose family, serviceberries are susceptible to a number of pest and diseases issues, but few are serious enough to kill trees. This is an important food and shelter tree for wildlife, so it's worth growing for those reasons as well as aesthetic benefits.

Fall Color—Red

Peak Season—All seasons

Mature Size (H x W)—20–40 feet x 15–20 feet

Hardiness—4–9 (depending on species)

Water Needs—Medium

SWEETGUM
Liquidambar styraciflua

Why It's Special—Sweetgums have some of the most reliable and stunning fall color in the landscape. The trees have star-shaped leaves that turn shades of red, purple, yellow, orange, or multicolors in fall. They produce a sticky, hard fruit (sweetgum "balls") that can be messy. Birds love to eat the seeds, though, so that's a tradeoff. *Liquidambar styraciflua* 'Rotundiloba' is fruitless.

How to Plant & Grow—Plant in full sun to partial shade in moist, well-drained, slightly acidic soil. Sweetgums are tolerant of poor soil and are often used as street trees. They grow large, so make this your one big specimen shade tree in the yard. Do not plant near a driveway or sidewalk, as the roots can lift up the pavement.

Care & Problems—They're fairly easy to grow; you just have to clean up the fruits. When you can, leave them on the ground for animals. Goldfinches, in particular, love the seeds inside the sweetgum balls.

Fall Color—Green, yellow, purple, red, orange—it varies!

Bloom Period/Peak Season—Fall

Mature Size (H x W)—60–90 feet x 40–60 feet

Hardiness—5–9

Water Needs—Medium

TULIP POPLAR
Liriodendron tulipifera

Why It's Special—Tulip trees are native to North America. They're named for the showy green and orange flowers that bloom in late spring to early summer—and look like tulips. They have large, four-lobed leaves (that resemble sycamore leaves) with good fall color. The wood has historically been prized for carpentry projects and is still one of the top commercially grown trees for use in furniture making. It is the larval host for the Eastern tiger swallowtail butterfly—a beautiful black and yellow insect.

How to Plant & Grow—Plant in full sun to partial shade in moist, well-drained, loose soils. These are large shade trees and should be sited accordingly. Mature specimens can grow up to 150 feet tall. Water to establish and mulch around the roots to conserve moisture. It's not a good street tree; flowers are not often visible on a mature tree.

Care & Problems—These trees have few pest problems. They can be shallow-rooted, so it can be difficult to grow things under them. Water during drought.

Fall Color—Yellow

Peak Season—Early summer, flowers fall, leaf color

Mature Size (H x W)—60–90 feet x 30–50 feet

Hardiness—5–10

Water Needs—Medium

TWO-WINGED SILVERBELL
Halesia diptera

Why It's Special—Two-winged silverbell is a small flowering tree that puts on a spectacular show in spring when white, thumb-sized, pendulous, bell-shaped flowers open. Grow this as a small multistemmed or single trunk specimen tree. It's great for smaller lawns and landscapes. Carolina silverbells, *Halesia carolina*, grows well in colder zones (4–9) but it has a similar growth habit. *H. diptera* var. *magniflora* has larger flowers than the species. The common name "two-winged" describes the fruit shape. Its fruits are an important food source for wildlife.

How to Plant & Grow—Plant in full sun to partial shade in moist, well-drained soil. Water to establish and mulch to conserve moisture. This is an absolutely stunning specimen tree. If you can find one, definitely make room in the garden. You may have to search mail-order catalogs and websites, but it's worth the effort!

Care & Problems—This is an easy-care tree with few problems. Prune to establish your preferred growth habit (multi- or single-stemmed tree).

Fall Color—Yellow

Peak Season—Spring, flowers; fall, leaves

Mature Size (H x W)—20–30 feet x 15–25 feet

Hardiness—6–9

Water Needs—Medium

ZELKOVA
Zelkova serrata

Why It's Special—Zelkova trees are definitely underutilized in the landscape, which is a shame. You can remedy that, though. Zelkova trees have a lovely, upright, vase-shaped growth habit and a dense, bright green canopy of serrated leaves (hence its species name). These trees tolerate poor soil conditions and will grow in the landscape, hell strip, or as street trees. They have nice fall color too. It is sometimes planted in place of elm trees because it is resistant to Dutch elm disease.

How to Plant & Grow—Plant in full sun in moist, well-drained soil. Water to establish. Mulch to conserve moisture. It's a nice shade tree if you have limited space.

Care & Problems—Zelkovas have a relatively tight branching pattern. Prune to remove rubbing or crossing branches, which can sometimes be a problem. The wounds caused by rubbing can leave the trees susceptible to disease. Water during drought. Otherwise, it's relatively pest- and problem-free.

Fall Color—Yellow

Bloom Period/Peak Season—Summer and fall

Mature Size (H x W)—50–80 feet x 50–80 feet

Water Needs—Medium

TREES MONTH-BY-MONTH

JANUARY

- Prune dormant fruit trees this month. Use bypass pruners or loppers to ensure a clean cut. Remove crossing branches, watersprouts that are growing straight up, branches that are growing in toward the center of the canopy instead of out, and small, non-fruit bearing twigs.

- Shape shade trees and ornamental trees. Do not top your trees! Who knows how this "technique" got started, but all you'll get is weak, poorly structured growth.

- Prune crape myrtles. Remove all branches that are smaller in diameter than your pinky. Do not cut back crape myrtles hard, as you will lose their architectural interest.

FEBRUARY

- Spray dormant oil or horticultural oil on trees that have had insect problems during previous years. Read the labels and follow instructions when applying.

- Water broadleaf evergreen trees deeply if your area is experiencing bright sun combined with freezing temperatures and windy weather, which can produce leaf scorch from dehydration.

MARCH

- Order hard-to-find fruit trees online and from catalogs this month. If you already ordered trees, some might arrive bare root. If they're dormant, keep them in a cool, dark location. If they're showing signs of growth, pot them up until the ground is not frozen and you can plant them outside.

- Prune newly planted trees to establish shape—whether it's a central leader, an open vase shape, or a multistemmed tree.

- Mulch around trees, taking care to keep the mulch from touching the actual tree trunk.

APRIL

- Get a soil test done to determine whether you should fertilize established trees. When you receive the results, fertilize according to instructions. April is a good time to fertilize hollies and other acid-loving trees with fertilizers specifically labeled for those plants.

- Check for pests. Eastern tent caterpillars, leafminers, stem cankers, and apple scab symptoms all start showing up this month. If you think your tree has a pest problem, take pictures and a sample to your local Cooperative Extension for a diagnosis and treatment plan.

- Plant bare-root and container-grown trees. Soak the roots of bare-root trees overnight before planting. See page 104 for instructions about how to plant bare-root plants. The technique is the same for trees as it is for shrubs.

- Check straps from trees staked the previous year. If the tree appears to be rooting in well (doesn't move when you tug on it), remove the straps. If you decide the stakes need to stay in for another year, relocate the straps to another part of the tree trunk and retighten.

MAY

- Water newly planted trees and shrubs regularly to encourage good rooting.

- Prune evergreen trees. The specific technique is called "candle pruning." You will pinch the soft new growth at the tips of branches back by half.

- Plant new trees. There's still time for them to establish roots before the heat of summer. Some fruit tree vendors will have spring sales, so now is the time to snap up extra inventory at lower prices.

- Check plants for pests. Phomopsis tip blight affects junipers and causes dieback at the ends of branches. Cut off affected branches. Fireblight starts to rear its head on apples, crabapples, and plants in the rose family. Look for a sunken section of the stem, which is where the canker is. Prune 6 inches below that and disinfect pruning tools between plants.

JUNE

- Prune to clean up storm-damaged trees. Otherwise, now is not the best time to prune trees.

- Check for suckers at the base of multistemmed trees and remove them with hand pruners. Do not use systemic herbicides to kill suckers, as you can kill the entire tree.

JULY

- Water newly planted trees, as the heat of summer can be quite stressful. Monitor older trees as well. If any tree leaves look wilted during windy, hot days, let a hose run in the root zone for 10 to 15 minutes to give the area a good soaking.

- Prune out water sprouts from flowering ornamental and fruit trees. These are non-fruiting branches that grow straight up. Cut back to the nearest horizontal branch.

- Complete any summer pruning this month. You don't want to prune after July as you could trigger new growth that doesn't have time to harden off before winter. Pruning now can disrupt the natural cycle of dormancy, which gets underway in August.

AUGUST

- Clean up around fruit trees. Leaving fruits that have droped around the trees can encourage pests and diseases to flourish, not to mention the fact that the fruit can encourage visiting wildlife, which might also take a shine to your other plants.

- Mulch around trees that have surface roots emerging from the soil. You do not want to remove these roots because you risk damaging the trees. It's easier to mulch or plant groundcovers around them.

SEPTEMBER

- Go shopping for trees. Now is a good time to plant spring-flowering trees. Cherries, crabapples, flowering plums, and magnolias all grow well in our area. Look into unusual spring-flowering trees such as the Chinese fringetree and Japanese snowbell, as well. You might have to order these online, as they are not always common in nurseries.

- Deadhead crape myrtles to improve appearance. These small trees have nice fall color, and seedheads only take away from the show these plants put on in the fall.

- Rake leaves, shred them, and compost them. Leaf compost is one of the best mulches and soil amendments you can get. Better yet—it's free!

OCTOBER

- Continue planting new trees through mid-month. When planting a new tree, always dig the hole twice as wide as it is deep. Plant the tree so that the crown (where the trunk meets the roots) is just slightly above ground level, as the tree will settle slightly after planting. It's better to plant slightly high than too deep. Mulch around the newly planted tree, but do not mound mulch around the trunk. Deeply soak the soil around the tree a couple of times per week after planting.

- Apply repellents to broadleaf evergreens and needle-leafed evergreens to prevent deer and other mammals from munching on them.

- Continue raking leaves and composting them. Leaving large, soggy leaves on the lawn can cause fungal problems later.

NOVEMBER

- Refresh mulch around newly planted trees to protect roots from winter damage.

- Clean and sharpen pruning tools.

- Check straps and wires on staked trees to make sure they aren't rubbing the tree bark raw.

- Enclose newly planted evergreen trees in chicken wire cages to prevent damage if repellents aren't working.

DECEMBER

- Cut evergreen tree branches to use in decorations. You can create "porch pots," which are a combination container garden and flower arrangement made from evergreen boughs and sculptural sticks from deciduous trees.

- Water broadleaf evergreens if it's sunny, windy, and cold outside. Deeply soak the soil around the trees. These conditions make the trees lose water quickly—quicker than they can replace it by taking it up through the roots, particularly if the ground is frozen solid.

- Check trees after a large snowfall. If they are in danger of breaking branches, use a shop broom to gently lift the branches to a steeper angle that will allow snow to slide off. Never bend down branches with a snow load on them.

TURFGRASSES
for the Mid-Atlantic

A tidy lawn is like the frame to a picture. If it looks good, you won't notice it. If it's weedy and scraggly, you won't see anything *but* the lawn. You can choose to grow a high-maintenance lawn, but the truth is that you don't have to. And while there *has* been a movement to replace lawns with groundcovers or other plants, that is not practical, nor desirable, for everyone.

First, select the right type of grass for your area and your needs (high traffic versus low traffic areas, sun versus shade, warm-season versus cool-season). Then provide it with the care that the species you're growing requires, and you won't have a lot of problems.

Cool-season turfgrass grows actively during cool weather. It may go dormant in summer.

Warm-season turfgrass grows actively during warm weather. It goes dormant in winter and may or may not be cold hardy.

The areas that can be tricky are areas with hot summers and mild winters. These transition areas are not necessarily entirely favorable for cool-season or warm-season grasses. Often, warm-season grasses are planted and then overseeded with annual cool-season grasses.

Root growth

HOW TO FIX BALD SPOTS

1. Spread topsoil over the bald spot, evening it out with a hard rake.

2. Overseed using a rotary spreader—either hand-held or walk-behind.

3. Cover with straw to keep the grass seed moist as it germinates.

4. Water at least three times daily for 10 minutes at a time until grass germinates. Then cut back to twice daily, once daily, and finally every other day or so.

CARING FOR TURFGRASS

Individual instructions are noted within the plant profiles, but there are some general rules of thumb that apply to all aspects of lawn care.

MOWING

Mow frequently enough that you only remove one-third of the grass blade at a time, and set your lawn mower blade for the highest setting recommended for the grass type you're growing. This allows the grass to grow taller and shade weed seeds, which prevents them from sprouting.

Grass roots grow in proportion to the leaf blades aboveground, so the shorter you mow, the less of a root system the plants will have. You want a nice, deep root system in order for the plants to stay healthy and withstand droughty conditions.

WATERING

Water the lawn deeply and infrequently. In other words, give the lawn 2 inches of water twice a week instead of ½ inch of water every day.

FERTILIZING

Grass is a "hungry" plant. It needs quite a bit of nitrogen to grow well. However, before you can fertilize, check the soil pH. If it is lower than 5.5, add lime according to package instructions. If the pH of the soil is off, it doesn't matter how much fertilizer you add, it will not be available to the plants. Additionally, fertilize only according to recommendations for the type of grass you have. Extra fertilizer can cause grass to be weak and more susceptible to pests. Fertilizer requirements are noted in individual plant profiles.

KILLING OR PREVENTING WEEDS

Good lawn care goes a long way toward preventing weed problems. Taller mowing heights, infrequent irrigation, and avoiding overfertilizing will prevent some weed issues. Use pre-emergent herbicide or corn gluten at the beginning of spring and fall to prevent lawn weeds from sprouting. This only gets the weeds that grow from seed, though. You can individually spray, hand-dig, or pull weeds with a taproot.

Check herbicide labels carefully to make sure that you're using the right product to treat weeds. If broadleaf weeds are a problem, use a weed killer specifically labeled to work on broadleaf weeds. (Don't use a general herbicide that kills everything, or you'll kill both the lawn and weeds.)

Compaction can be problematic in lawns, especially those with high foot traffic. This can cause declining turf vigor, leading to weed issues. Rent a core aerator and aerate the lawn once yearly in fall to prevent the soil from becoming compacted.

TROUBLESHOOTING

When you take good care of the lawn, you'll have few problems. There are some fairly common issues that affect lawns, though. Here's how to deal with those.

Weeds

DOG SPOTS

To fix dog spots, first flush the soil by watering the area twice a day for three or four days. Then, dig out the top 2 inches of soil and replace it with new garden soil. Next, sprinkle grass seed on top and water the grass seed twice daily until it sprouts.

MOLES, VOLES, AND GRUBS

These three problems are related. People mistake voles for moles, and moles show up in lawns with grubs. If you have small holes all over your yard, voles are your problem. Voles eat plant roots, which can hurt plants. They also enjoy snacking on flower bulbs. The only way to get rid of voles is to get a cat. If you have tunnels on top of your lawn, you have moles, and the moles are there because there are lots of tasty Japanese beetle grubs in the lawn. Use milky spore powder (according to package instructions) to get rid of grubs, which will, in turn, help you get rid of moles.

MOSS

Moss is not necessarily a bad thing. In shady, damp areas, moss can serve as a stand-in for grass. After all, it is green! Several different conditions cause moss to thrive, and whether you can get rid of moss depends on whether you can control the conditions. Moss thrives in compacted, acidic soil (pH lower than 5.0) with low organic matter (generally very clay-heavy or sandy soils). Damp conditions encourage moss, as do low air movement and shade. To eliminate moss, raise the soil pH by adding lime, prune the tree branches so that more light reaches the ground, and rake compost into the area.

FAIRY RING

Fairy ring is a fungus growing in the lawn. Most of the fungus is underground, but you can see symptoms of the disease in the lawn. Sometimes, you'll see a large green ring with brownish grass in the center. Other times, you'll see a perfect circle of mushrooms. It's hard to get rid of fairy rings, but you can help your grass survive it. The main problem is that the soil in the center of the circle becomes so full of fungi that it won't hold any water,

Dog spots

Moss

and the grass dies. Fix this by renting a core aerator to aerate the center of the circle. Then rake compost into the aeration holes and water the lawn.

BROWN PATCH

Brown patch is another fungal disease. The damage can sometimes look like dog spot damage, but the patches are usually larger, and all of the grass in the affected areas isn't dead the way it would be in a dog spot. Brown patch is most often a problem in the summer when temperatures are above 70 degrees, and the grass stays moist for several hours at a time. (Lawns in the humid South suffer widely from brown patch.) Adjust the lawn watering schedule to water the lawn twice a week in the morning so that the grass has time to dry. Don't leave clippings on a lawn if brown patch is a problem.

Fairy ring

SCALPING

Scalping is a lawn problem caused by people and looks like a problem caused by bacteria or fungi. Scalping is when the mower blade is set so low that it doesn't just cut the top of the grass, it actually either rips the grass plant out of the lawn or cuts the plant so low that the grass stops growing. Scalping scars look like uneven strips of dead grass. The pattern could be irregular, depending on the mower pattern. You can avoid scalping by setting the mower blade on a higher setting. Watch out for scalping problems with riding mowers. Once you sit on the mower, your weight will move the blade down slightly.

Healthy turfgrass starts with planting the right variety in the right place. Here's what grows best in the Mid-Atlantic.

Scalping

BERMUDAGRASS
Cynodon dactylon

Why It's Special—Bermudagrass is a spreading warm-season grass that you'll commonly find on golf course fairways and lawns. It has an aggressive growth habit, spreading via rhizomes and stolons, and produces a finely textured, greenish gray carpet that's second to none in looks—if it's maintained well. It's good for high-traffic areas. 'Quickstand' is one of the most cold-hardy cultivars. 'Midway', 'Midiron', 'Midlawn', and 'Midfield' are also more cold-hardy than other varieties.

How to Plant & Grow—This grass grows best when grown from sod in late spring so that it can grow and establish during warm weather. You can also plant plugs, but that is a labor-intensive project best left to landscapers or for small areas.

Care & Problems—Practice good cultural maintenance and you'll have few problems with Bermudagrass. Water deeply and infrequently, mow to the correct height, and treat for grubs if they're a problem. Fertilize with 1 pound of nitrogen per 1,000 square feet when the grass is fully green and growing in spring.

Type—Warm-season

Texture—Fine

Mowing Height—¾ inch–2 inches (depends on cultivar)

Hardiness—7–10

Water Needs—1 inch per week

CARPET GRASS
Axonopus fissifolius

Why It's Special—Carpet grass is at its most useful when planted in soggy, shady areas with an acidic pH. It's a warm-season turf that spreads via stolons; it can be weedy. It does not tolerate foot traffic. Use it in lower areas of the yard where you need green coverage, don't want a groundcover, and have issues getting other turf to establish. Sometimes it's sold mixed with centipede grass.

How to Plant & Grow—Sow seed in early summer. This grass establishes best when it's warm out. It's a true warm-season grass. Keep irrigated, especially during droughty times.

Care & Problems—Mow carpet grass frequently during summer to keep it looking tidy. (It produces tall seedheads that can be somewhat messy.) Do not let it dry out. It's best to plant this in naturally wet areas, because it isn't so lovely that it should demand attention, but it does solve a specific problem for homeowners that have the conditions in which this grass thrives. Apply slow-release fertilizer in June.

Type—Warm-season

Texture—Medium-coarse

Mowing Height—2–3 inches

Hardiness—7–10

Water Needs—High

CENTIPEDE GRASS
Eremochloa ophiuroides

Why It's Special—Centipede grass is sometimes called the "lazy man's grass" because it isn't fussy and, because of a slow growth habit, requires less frequent mowing. It is, in some ways, a counterpart to carpet grass in that it grows well in moist, sandy, acidic, infertile soils (once established), except centipede grass prefers full sun where carpet grass does best in the shade. Centipede grass does not stand up well to foot traffic. Do not use where kids or pets frequent.

How to Plant & Grow—Centipede grass establishes best from sod, but can also be seeded in late spring or early summer. Whether seeded or sodded, it needs to be kept constantly moist while establishing.

Care & Problems—Fertilize with ½ to 1 pound of nitrogen per 1,000 square feet when the grass fully greens up in spring. Fertilize with 1 pound of potash (0-0-60 fertilizer) per 1,000 square feet in fall to encourage cold-hardiness. Water during times of drought. This grass type will decline in dry conditions.

Type—Warm season/transition

Texture—Medium

Mowing Height—1½–2 inches

Hardiness—7–10

Water Needs—Medium to high

KENTUCKY BLUEGRASS
Poa pratensis

Why It's Special—Kentucky bluegrass is the most widely grown cool-season lawn grass in the northern US. It can be grown as a blended lawn with other grass species, or as a mixture of bluegrass cultivars. Kentucky bluegrass grows and spreads through rhizomes and stolons, forming a dense turf cover.

How to Plant & Grow—Establish new sod and seed lawns in fall or mid-spring. (It's fairly easy to establish anytime other than the worst heat of summer.) Plant with other faster-growing varieties, including fescues and perennial ryegrass, that will fill in while the bluegrass becomes established.

Care & Problems—Your best bet is to keep this grass from being stressed, which will help it resist pest and disease problems. Fertilize in May and September. Treat grubs with Bt if they become a problem. During hot, dry periods, this grass can go dormant. You don't have to water enough to keep it green, but water once a week or so to keep it alive. It still won't green up. Don't worry.

Type—Cool season

Texture—Fine

Mowing Height—3 inches in summer, 2 inches in spring/fall

Hardiness—3–7

Water Needs—Medium, 1 inch per week

RYEGRASS
Lolium perenne

Why It's Special—Perennial ryegrass is a clumping cool-weather turfgrass that is often used in seed mixes to provide fast cover while other grasses germinate. It's not quite robust enough to use for establishing an entire lawn on its own. Ryegrass tolerates foot traffic and can be used to overseed Bermudagrass lawns in winter for green color and weed control. It also helps with erosion control in bare areas.

How to Plant & Grow—Sow seed for this grass in fall (September is ideal) to establish new lawns or overseed existing lawns for winter color. Ryegrass does not tolerate hot weather and will die out during summer. Water to establish.

Care & Problems—Water regularly during fall and winter. Ryegrass is not drought-tolerant in overseeded areas; in spring, gradually reduce watering and lower the mower blade height to encourage ryegrass to decline and warm-season turf to grow. Fertilize in October and February with 2 pounds nitrogen per 1,000 square feet.

Type—Cool season

Texture—Fine

Mowing Height—2 inches

Hardiness—3–8

Water Needs—Medium

ST. AUGUSTINE GRASS
Stenotaphrum secundatum

Why It's Special—This grass is useful because it grows fast and has high shade tolerance. It will not grow everywhere in the Mid-Atlantic, though—only the warmest areas. 'Raleigh' is the most cold-hardy cultivar. This is another problem-solver grass for specific areas of the Mid-Atlantic.

How to Plant & Grow—Plant a new St. Augustine grass lawn from sod in late spring. It's difficult, if not impossible, to establish from seed. This is a warm-season grass that grows best when the weather is warm. It won't have time to establish if planted in fall.

Care & Problems—Mow St. Augustine grass frequently during the summer. (If you mow sporadically, you can end up scalping the lawn, even if the mower blade is set high.) Chinch bugs and brown patch are the two most common problems. Use a power rake when the grass is actively growing to deal with thatch problems. Sometimes St. Augustine grass lawns need an iron treatment. Feed a slow-release fertilizer with ½ to 1 pound of nitrogen per 1,000 square feet every four to eight weeks.

Type—Warm season

Texture—Coarse

Mowing Height—2–3 inches

Hardiness—7–10

Water Needs—Medium; 1 inch per week

TALL FESCUE
Festuca arundinacea

Why It's Special—Tall fescue grass types are often grown as part of a blend with other cool-season grasses because it is a clumping, rather than spreading, grass. It has deep roots and is drought-tolerant. Of all of the turfgrasses, this one is best suited for growth in transition areas with hot summers and mild winters, a combination of conditions that can be problematic for establishing a healthy lawn. 'Jaguar' is one of the most drought-tolerant cultivars.

How to Plant & Grow—Tall fescue establishes best from seed on well-cultivated, deep, rich soils with a neutral pH (5.5–6.5). The best time to plant new lawns is early fall or, secondly, late spring. Water to establish.

Care & Problems—Once established, this turf is highly drought-tolerant. Water only when the grass shows signs of stress, and when watering, make sure that the top 4 to 6 inches of soil are thoroughly soaked. Fertilize in September and May with 1 pound nitrogen per 1,000 square feet. Reseed or overseed to thicken thin or patchy lawns.

Type—Cool season

Texture—Medium-coarse

Mowing Height—1½–3 inches

Hardiness—3–6

Water Needs—Medium

ZOYSIA
Zoysia japonica

Why It's Special—Zoysia is a great multipurpose warm-season grass with good cold hardiness. It only grows during the warmer months, but can be overseeded in winter if you want a green lawn year-round. If it's well cared-for (and not overseeded) it will turn into a nice golden carpet during winter. There are many cultivars. It is tolerant of foot traffic and somewhat shade tolerant.

How to Plant & Grow—Plant new lawns from sod in late spring to early summer. 'Zenith' is a cultivar available as seed, if you'd rather establish a new lawn from seed than sod. It's best to let the grass establish during warmer months when it is actively growing. Water to establish.

Care & Problems—Once established, zoysia is fairly drought tolerant and cold tolerant. Fertilize in spring when the grass has greened up and is actively growing. Dethatch in the early summer every three years or so. This is a tough grass that requires less care than many turfgrasses.

Type—Warm season

Texture—Fine to coarse (depends on cultivar)

Mowing Height—1–2 inches (depending on cultivar)

Hardiness—5–10

Water Needs—Low to medium

TURFGRASS MONTH-BY-MONTH

JANUARY

- Stay off the lawn this month. Walking on wet soil (if the ground is not frozen) will compact it. Walking on ice-covered grass will break it.

- Be careful with deicing agents. Use sand for traction or chemicals that won't kill plants. Some chemicals to look for that meet these criteria include potassium chloride, urea, and magnesium chloride.

FEBRUARY

- Take the lawn mower for its annual service this month before everyone else decides to do the same thing! You'll want them to sharpen or replace the blades, replace the air filter, test the spark plugs, and add new oil and fuel.

- If you live in Zones 7 or 8 and overseeded the lawn for winter, you can mow once this month.

- Water overseeded lawns if the temperature routinely climbs above 60 degrees Fahrenheit.

MARCH

- Mow overseeded lawns and water if the temperature is routinely above 60 degrees Fahrenheit and your area hasn't received rain for over a week.

- Lightly rake the grass after snow melts to prevent snow mold.

- Apply pre-emergent herbicides according to package instructions to prevent summer weeds from sprouting.

APRIL

- Repair damaged areas of the lawn. Overseed where possible, and purchase and cut sod patches where necessary.

- Overseed areas where the turf has thinned.

- Install a new lawn from seed or sod if you did not do this in the fall.

- Give the lawn its spring feeding (depending on the grass type).

MAY

- Start mowing regularly. Your mowing schedule should be set so that you never remove more than one-third of the grass blade at a time.

- Set the irrigation system or sprinklers to water newly planted or patched lawn areas, which will need more water than established turf.

- Aerate and dethatch. Before aerating, mow the lawn once on the lowest setting (without scalping the lawn). Irrigate the night before aerating. Run the core aerator and then irrigate again to break up the clods. You can top-dress with finely sifted compost to improve the soil.

- Check for grub problems. Brown patches can be an indicator of grubs, as can spongy turf. Visit a garden center or home-improvement store for a treatment. There are chemical treatments; you can also apply Bt. It can take a couple of growing seasons for Bt to build up enough in the soil to make a difference, though.

- Hand-dig or spot treat large broadleaf weeds before they flower and set seed.

JUNE

- Water the lawn deeply and infrequently. It is better to water twice a week for 15 or 20 minutes than to water every other day for five minutes. Watering deeply and infrequently ensures a healthy root system.

- Mow when the lawn is dry so that you don't end up with clods of cut grass spread throughout the lawn. If possible, leave the grass clippings on the lawn. Contrary to popular belief, clippings left on the lawn do not cause thatch buildup.

JULY

- Check regularly for pest and disease problems. Now is the time that brown patch, fairy ring, and other turf diseases will start to show up. If you have problems with the lawn, take pictures and consult with your local Cooperative Extension agency for treatment options.

- Decide what you want to do if the weather is extremely dry. You might elect to let the lawn go dormant. Both cool-season and warm-season lawns can be allowed to go dormant during the summer. Dormant does not mean dead. While you will cut back on watering, you will still want to water once every week or every other week to keep the turf alive. It might not be green, but it won't be dead.

AUGUST

- Set the mower blade as high as possible this month. Letting the lawn stay long encourages deep root growth, which will help the lawn make it through summer stress. Don't stop mowing, though. Doing that can cause even more stress once you restart.

- Check feeding schedules for the type of turf you are growing. It is time to feed some actively growing warm-weather turf varieties now.

- Treat for sod webworms, chinch bugs, and Japanese beetles.

- Apply pre-emergent herbicides to prevent cool-weather weeds from sprouting. Do not apply when temperatures are over 85 degrees Fahrenheit and make sure to water in any treatments thoroughly according to package instructions. Keep children and pets off the lawn for the length of time specified by the treatment label.

SEPTEMBER

- Install new or renovate existing cool-weather lawns this month. Now is the time to plant new lawns from seed or sod so that they can establish before cold winter temperatures. It is not the right time to install warm-season lawns.

- Rake leaves from the lawn, shred, and compost them. Large, wet leaves can foster fungal and bacterial diseases.

- Use a broadleaf herbicide to kill persistent non-grassy lawn weeds this month. Only do this when the forecast predicts a couple of dry days in a row. You need the herbicide to be absorbed by the plants, not washed away by the rain.

- Feed cool-season lawns according to the maintenance schedule suggested for the type of grass growing in your lawn. Nitrogen amounts vary by grass type.

OCTOBER

- Continue watering newly established or overseeded lawns.

- Overseed warm-season turf with cool-season annual grasses. Stay off the areas that you overseeded for at least a month.

NOVEMBER

- Set the mower blade lower. Warm-season grasses should be going dormant now. Mow them as low as you can without scalping them. Mow cool-season grasses one-third lower than you would during the summer.

- Continue to water new lawns and overseeded lawns as long as the temperature is above freezing.

- Do not mow warm-season turf overseeded with annual grass just yet.

DECEMBER

- Winterize the lawn mower. Drain the oil and gas and install a stabilizer. Disconnect the spark plugs. Clean and dry the lower deck.

- Stay off the grass! Walking on it when it is frozen or damp can cause easily preventable damage.

VEGETABLES & HERBS
for the Mid-Atlantic

othing beats the taste of a juicy tomato picked and eaten warm off the vine, and you simply haven't lived until you've tried carrots that you grew yourself. Plus, why pay six dollars a bunch for basil when you can grow 20 times that much for half the price?

It's definitely worth the time and energy to grow your own vegetables and herbs. In the long run, you'll save money and you'll eat well too.

Vegetable gardening is much easier than television commercials would lead you to believe. You're probably already versed in the basics, but just to cover those, here are the high points of vegetable care.

PLANNING

If you're starting a new garden, you'll have to choose a location, and sunlight is the biggest limiting factor in where you can site vegetable beds. Keep in mind that the sun's location during winter and summer are two different things. Sun hits areas in winter that it doesn't reach in summer because deciduous trees have lost their leaves, so be mindful if you're installing a new bed during winter. In addition to considering sunlight, try to site your garden near a hose hookup.

Once you select the location, allocate space. Plan to grow what you like to eat, and consider how often you eat it. If you're canning or freezing, plan to plant extra beyond what you'll eat fresh. This usually leads me to plant about four eggplant plants and 20 tomatoes!

COOL-SEASON VS. WARM-SEASON GARDENING

Most edible plants that we grow fall into two categories: cool-season plants that grow best when temperatures are cool (usually below 70 degrees Fahrenheit) and warm-season plants that grow best when temperatures are warmer (usually above 65 degrees Fahrenheit). In the Mid-Atlantic cool-season, plants thrive from March through May and again in September through November. (Dates vary depending on where you live.) The warm season runs from May (in the warmest areas) or June

through September. Allocate garden space according to plant temperature preferences.

COOL-SEASON STAPLES

These vegetables and herbs grow best before daytime temperatures are in the 80s. You can grow them from March through May or June and again in August through October.

- Beet
- Broccoli
- Cabbage
- Carrot
- Cauliflower
- Cilantro
- Dill
- Kale
- Leek
- Parsley
- Parsnip
- Spinach

TROPICAL ANNUAL EDIBLES LIKE IT HOT

These favorite summer vegetables are native to tropical areas and grow only when soil temperatures are warm enough (at least 65 degrees Fahrenheit). Don't plant these too early:

- Bean
- Corn
- Cucumber
- Eggplant
- Pepper
- Potato
- Pumpkin
- Summer squash
- Sweet potato
- Tomatillo
- Tomato
- Watermelon

PLANTING

Knowing *when* to plant, not just *how* to plant is crucial for vegetable gardening. Planting vegetables isn't terribly different than planting flowers, but timing is critical. You absolutely must plant at the right time, and a big part of that is soil temperature.

Harden off plants by setting them on your porch or patio.

You can buy an inexpensive soil thermometer to help you gauge when to plant different edibles. Most cool-season vegetables will sprout when soil temperatures are 50 to 70 degrees Fahrenheit. Warm-season vegetables grow best when soil temperatures are at least 65 degrees Fahrenheit. You can plant these when soil temperatures are lower, but the plants won't grow.

Diseases are also more of a problem in cool, wet soils. Sweet corn seeds will rot in the ground if planted too early while the soil is still cold. Damping off, pythium, and root rot diseases can strike seeds that are planted too early in the year when the soil hasn't warmed up yet.

It doesn't matter whether you're planting seeds or transplants—take the soil temperature before planting.

PLANTING TRANSPLANTS OUTDOORS
When it's time to plant transplants, harden them off before planting.

- Place plants in a sheltered location such as a porch or patio for the day, and bring them in at night. Do this for three or four days.
- Next, leave them outside all day in the protected location. Do this for about a week.
- Finally, move the plants from the sheltered location (the porch or patio) to a more exposed location (the front sidewalk or driveway). Leave them there for three or four days.
- Wait for a cloudy day (if possible) and plant your plants in the garden. Planting out on a cloudy day will lower the stress that the plants experience.

Use a trowel to dig a shallow trench for planting seeds.

Cover seeds with seed-starting mix. This lightweight soilless mix will not form a hard crust. It will also help you keep track of where you planted the seeds.

PLANTING SEEDS OUTDOORS

I prefer to direct-sow vegetables when I can. The key to success for direct-sowing seeds outdoors is to keep them moist. If they dry out, they'll die. My trick is to use seedling mix to cover them. The mix stays loose and resists soil crusting, making it easier for the seeds to sprout.

Sow according to finished spacing and germination rates. Seed packets will have instructions to sow "thickly" (lettuce) or "thinly" (carrots, radishes). Usually these instructions correspond to germination rates. The more closely you can plant according to the finished spacing requirements, the fewer seeds you'll waste and the less time you'll spend thinning.

Seedlings are fragile when they first sprout. Keep them moist, but not soaking wet, as they sprout and grow.

CARE

Once plants are in the ground, it's time to give them the best care possible to get the biggest yield.

WATERING

Watering is crucial with edibles. These plants never really become drought tolerant. Most edibles grow best when the soil is kept evenly moist. Soaker hoses are a great help if you have loose, fast-draining soil. When hand watering, use a watering wand and direct the stream at the plant roots, not the leaves. Overhead watering can spread fungal diseases. Individual plant needs are noted in the plant profiles.

FERTILIZING

Before fertilizing can be effective, the soil has to have the right properties to retain the nutrients from fertilizers and make them available to plants. If you read a lot of gardening books, you're almost guaranteed to see the phrase "Feed the soil, not the plants." Time spent getting the soil where it needs to be in order to support healthy plant growth is time saved trying to fix problems later.

START BY ADDING ORGANIC MATTER

Why would you add more compost to the soil before testing it? You can *always* add compost. Compost is the duct tape of the garden. It fixes everything! Compost improves soil structure by loosening tough clay soil and adding water- and nutrient-holding capacity to loose, depleted sandy soils.

TESTING THE SOIL

After you've added compost, manure, or topsoil to create the garden bed in which you'll grow your plants, it's time to test the soil. Testing now gives you a more accurate picture of the conditions

It's important to continually add compost to your raised beds and vegetable gardens. If you don't make your own compost, you can buy bagged compost.

159

PH RANGES FOR COMMON VEGETABLES

Asparagus	6.0–8.0
Beet	6.0–7.5
Broccoli	6.0–7.0
Cabbage	6.0–7.5
Carrot	5.5–7.0
Cauliflower	5.5–7.5
Celery	5.8–7.0
Cucumber	5.5–7.0
Lettuce	6.0–7.0
Muskmelon	6.0–7.0
Onion	5.8–7.0
Potato	4.8–6.5
Spinach	6.0–7.5
Tomato	5.5–7.5

the plants will have to deal with while they're growing and any additional adjustments you need to make.

You can pick up soil test kits from your County Extension Service. Follow the instructions included with the test. The results of the test will let you know if there are any nutrient deficiencies in the soil, as well as whether the soil pH is correct.

Soil pH and Fertilizing

The pH scale runs from 0 to 14. Most plants grow best in the range of 5.5 to 7.0, because nutrients in the soil are most available to plants at those soil pH levels. Landscape plants will usually struggle along if the soil pH is off, but edibles won't produce roots, leaves, and fruits for you to harvest if an off pH prevents them from getting the nutrients they need.

Changing pH

To lower the pH of alkaline soils so that the pH is in the neutral range of 5.5 to 7.0, add aluminum sulfate according to package instructions. To raise the pH of the soil, you will have to add lime, which

is also available at garden centers and home-improvement stores.

PEST CONTROL

Edibles are, unfortunately, susceptible to a fairly wide range of pest problems. Insects, bacterial infections, viruses, and munching mammals all plague edibles. These plants were bred to produce large and delicious fruit—not to defend themselves. Planting a variety of vegetables helps, as it can confuse insects. So does planting flowers and trap crops. There isn't room in this book to do an exhaustive pest-control section. First, though, decide what your threshold is. Can you live with a few holes here and there? If you have a severe problem, contact your Cooperative Extension or consult one of the reference books listed under Resources for a more detailed diagnosis and treatment plan.

Selecting for Disease Resistance

You can get ahead of viruses and diseases by planting resistant varieties. Look for these types of abbreviations on plant tags, labels, and catalog descriptions to help you select plants. These are some of the most common abbreviations for the most common diseases, but it's not an exhaustive list.

BCMW: Resistance to bean curly mosaic virus
CMW: Resistance to cucumber mosaic virus
Foc, Foc 1: Resistance to fusarium yellows
PM: Resistance to powdery mildew
PVY: Resistance to potato virus Y
TMV: Resistance to tobacco mosaic virus
ToMV: Resistance to tomato mosaic virus
TSWV: Resistance to tomato spotted wilt virus
V: Resistance to verticillium wilt

HARVESTING

A big question with vegetable gardening is, "When is it ready to pick?" It's easier to know with some plants than others. Summer squash and green beans are better when they're smaller, just after flowering. Tomatoes are ripe when they are easily removed from the vine without too much yanking. Notes about specific harvest times are in each individual profile.

SUCCESS WITH TOMATOES

Tomatoes are some of the most beloved vegetables. Everyone would rather eat a homegrown, fresh-picked tomato than one from the grocery store, but success with these vegetables depends on selecting the right plant for your garden space and for conditions in the Mid-Atlantic.

SELECTING FOR SIZE

There are three different types of tomato plants, each with hundreds of cultivars available.

Patio tomatoes are small, basically dwarf tomatoes that grow in raised beds or containers. Most patio tomatoes have small cherry- or grape-sized fruits.

Determinate tomatoes are still large vines, but they eventually stop growing taller and just grow more fruits.

Indeterminate tomatoes are vining plants that will grow forever if not cut back. These require sturdy support to grow and produce in the home garden.

SELECTING FOR DISEASE RESISTANCE

Most varieties that grow well here are resistant to some or most of the common diseases that plague tomatoes. Read the seed packets and plant labels to determine disease resistance. Growing plants with at least some resistance will put you ahead of the curve.

Plants resistant to fusarium wilt will have F, FF, or FFF after the cultivar name. VFN on the label indicates that the plants are resistant to verticillium wilt, fusarium wilt, and root-knot nematodes; VFNT indicates resistance to these three diseases, plus tobacco mosaic virus. Plants resistant to tomato spotted wilt virus have TSWV on the plant tags.

ASPARAGUS
Asparagus officinalis

Why It's Special—Asparagus is a long-lived perennial vegetable that tastes 100 percent better when you can grow and harvest it yourself than when you buy it at the grocery store. You do have to wait at least three years from planting to when you can harvest, but your appetite can grow in the meantime.

How to Plant & Grow—Plant asparagus crowns in full sun, in loose, well-drained soil when the soil has warmed at least to 50 degrees Fahrenheit to avoid crown rot. Check the soil pH and amend so that it is between 6.5 and 7.5. Dig a furrow or trench that is 6 inches deep. Space crowns 12 inches apart. Space rows 12 inches apart. Water to establish.

Care & Problems—Asparagus has few pest problems. Let the tops of the plants grow throughout summer. Do not cut back the tops until the following spring when you see new shoots. Only water during drought.

Harvest & Best Selections—Plant all-male varieties Jersey Giant, 'Jersey Prince', and Jersey Knight. You'll buy asparagus crowns, which are the roots of one-year-old plants. Harvest during the third season of growth (after the plant is two years old). Harvest 6-inch spears by snapping them off at the base of the soil. Harvest two to four times a week. Once the spears start to be less than ⅜ inch in diameter, stop harvesting and let the spears grow into ferns. This will allow the plant to replenish its reserves for next year's growth.

BASIL
Ocimum basilicum

Why It's Special—Basil is an easy-to-grow, almost essential herb. Two plants will give you everything you need to use fresh. Plant additional plants if you want to make your own pesto or can spaghetti sauce. Fresh basil is also delicious in salads and is a staple of Thai cuisine.

How to Plant & Grow—Plant transplants outside in full sun when the soil temperature is at least 60 degrees. Water to establish, but once established you can cut back sharply on the water.

Care & Problems—Japanese beetles and slugs are the most problematic pests for basil. There's not much you can do about Japanese beetles, but you can spread diatomaceous earth around the base of each plant to keep slugs from munching. Grow this plant lean—without extra fertilizer. To keep the plant producing fragrant leaves, chop the flowers off as they form.

Harvest & Best Selections—Snip leaves off the top of the plant in the morning. Basil is a forgiving and fast-growing plant. You can chop off any piece of the plant and it will grow back. Grow lemon basil for a different flavor in cocktails and lemonade. Sweet basil is the classic pesto basil variety. Large leaf Italian basil is a good all-around variety. 'African Blue' is a fairly cold-tolerant basil that you can grow on a sunny windowsill in the garage during winter. 'Greek Columnar' is a nonflowering variety of basil.

BEAN
Phaseolus vulgaris

Why It's Special—There are over 2,000 different cultivars of beans available to grow and enjoy fresh or dry. In the garden they pull double-duty and also fix nitrogen, adding to the soil quality where they're growing.

How to Plant & Grow—Plant in full sun when the soil temperature is at least 60 degrees. Place supports for pole types at the time of planting. Leave 12 to 18 inches of space between bush types (three seeds to a hill) and 6 inches between pole types (plant seeds in a circle around the wigwam, cage, or in a line along the trellis).

Care & Problems—Keep soil evenly moist, but not wet. Once beans start flowering, fertilize with a 0-5-5 or 0-10-10. Use row covers to keep beetles, stinkbugs, and corn earworms away from plants. Use insecticidal soap to control thrips and aphids.

Harvest & Best Selections—Snap beans, bush type: 'Provider', 'Bush Kentucky Wonder', 'Sequoia', 'Greencrop', 'Derby', 'Royal Burgundy', 'Roma II', 'Jade'. Snap beans, pole type: 'Emerite', 'Blue Lake', 'Kentucky Blue', 'Kentucky Wonder Green', 'Gold Rush', 'Indy Gold', 'Golden Rod', 'Scarlet runner'. Pick fresh beans shortly after pods begin to form. To harvest dry beans, allow the pods to dry on the plant. Then pull up the entire plant and hang it upside down to dry over a clean sheet. Thresh the pods in order to remove the dried bits of pod from the dried beans.

BEET
Beta vulgaris

Why It's Special—You can eat an entire beet plant! Eat young greens in salads and braise the tops of harvested beetroots. Boil them, pickle them, roast them, or grate them raw on salads.

How to Plant & Grow—Plant beets in deep, loose, fertile soils with a pH of 5.8 to 7.0 in spring when soil temperatures are between 55 and 75 degrees Fahrenheit. Sow seeds 2 inches apart and ½ inch deep.

Care & Problems—Water regularly to ensure even soil moisture levels to avoid scab, a condition in which brown, raised patches form on the outsides of the roots. Use a balanced fertilizer when planting, and follow up with a low-nitrogen, high-phosphorus fertilizer when the tops are 4 inches tall. Beets will develop internal blackspot if boron isn't available in the soil. If this is a problem in your garden, apply borax at a rate of ⅓ pound per 1,000 square feet at least seven days prior to planting.

Harvest & Best Selections—To harvest beet greens for salads while keeping the roots growing, use scissors to cut no more than one-quarter of the leaves at any time. Once beets reach their indicated maturity (usually after 60 growing days), it's best to harvest. Otherwise they'll become woody. Try 'Kestrel', 'Red Cloud', 'Red Ace', 'Ruby Queen', 'Frono', 'Detroit Dark Red' strains, and 'Rodina'. 'Golden' is a yellow variety. 'Chioggia' is a red-and-white striped variety.

BROCCOLI
Brassica oleracea, Italica Group

Why It's Special—Broccoli is one of the most nutritious vegetables you can grow, packed with vitamins and minerals. It's also versatile! Pack it for a picnic or enjoy it steamed with a traditional meat-and-potatoes dinner.

How to Plant & Grow—Plant broccoli in spring or fall when soil temperatures are 50 to 85 degrees Fahrenheit. It grows best when air temperatures are in the 60s. You can direct-sow fall broccoli if you plan for it to grow and mature when the temperatures cool down but spring crops do better if they're grown from transplants. Test the soil pH before planting. If it tests lower than 6.0, mix lime into the soil.

Care & Problems—Broccoli is susceptible to a variety of pests. Plant resistant varieties when possible and use floating row covers when flying insects are active. Use Bt for caterpillar control or Neem oil to control a wide range of pests. Keep soil evenly moist and fertilize mid-season by side-dressing with a balanced fertilizer.

Harvest & Best Selections—'Packman' and 'Southern Comet' grow best during the early-spring season. Both of these varieties produce side shoots. Cut the center flower head when it is still dark green and tight (about 60 days for most varieties—it will say so on the seed packet). If you're growing a variety that produces side shoots, leave the rest of the plant in the garden for up to two months.

BRUSSELS SPROUTS
Brassica oleracea var. gemmifera

Why It's Special—Brussels sprouts are highly nutritious and an excellent vegetable to help you squeeze the most out of a fall garden.

How to Plant & Grow—Before planting, test the soil pH. Add lime if it is below 6.0. You can plant Brussels sprouts in summer, but they need cold weather to mature. Plant transplants outside, 16 to 18 inches apart, or direct-sow at 6 inches spacing in midsummer. Thin seedlings to 16-inch spacing after plants are 6 inches tall.

Care & Problems—To protect young plants from cutworms, wrap the bottom 3 to 4 inches of stem with newspaper or foil. Control cabbageworms on plant leaves, control with *Bacillus thuringiensis* (Bt). Stake the taller varieties. You can cut off the top of the plant to trigger it to put more energy into producing the sprouts. Keep soil evenly moist. Apply 10-10-10 fertilizer three weeks after planting at 3 pounds per 100 square feet.

Harvest & Best Selections—Start harvesting the sprouts from the bottom, up about three months after planting. As a sprout begins to form, clip off the leaf below the sprout and let it grow to be ¾ to 1 inch in diameter. Then use clippers to harvest the sprouts as they mature (rather than yanking on them—you don't want to pull out the plant). (You can take enough at a time to eat!) 'Oliver' is tall. 'Jade Cross' hybrids are dwarf varieties less likely to fall over in the garden.

163

CABBAGE

Brassica oleracea var. *capitata*

Why It's Special—Cabbage is a classic cool-season vegetable. You can't beat it for utility—it is easy to store and can be added to soups, stir-fries, and cold salads. It's also one of the most nutritious vegetables you can eat.

How to Plant & Grow—Plant outside, 24 inches apart, in full sun in moist, well-drained soil with a pH of 6.5 to 7.0. (Add lime if the pH is too low.) Plant transplants outside in spring when soil temperatures are 50 degrees. Direct-sow seeds outside in all areas in mid-July for fall harvests or plant transplants in mid-August. Water to establish.

Care & Problems—Water regularly to keep soil evenly moist, but not soggy. Side-dress with organic slow-release fertilizer at the time of planting. One month after planting, make another application. Treat caterpillars with *Bacillus thuringiensis* (Bt). Rotate the cabbage planting areas in your garden. Cabbage plants and other cruciferous vegetables are highly susceptible to diseases that linger in the soil. Do not grow near butterfly bushes.

Harvest & Best Selections—Grow varieties that are resistant to common cabbage diseases such as fusarium wilt, yellows, and black rot. 'Resistant Golden Acre', 'Early Jersey Wakefield', 'Savoy Ace', 'Ruby Ball', 'Red Express', and 'Red Rookie' are good choices. Harvest once the head feels firm. Use pruners or a knife to cut off the head just below the base. Leave the stem in the ground because you might get a few smaller heads to form.

CARROT

Daucus carota

Why It's Special—You can't beat a carrot that you grew yourself. Grocery store carrots are completely flavorless, but homegrown carrots . . . now *they're* delicious!

How to Plant & Grow—Carrots germinate when the soil temperature is 45 to 85 degrees Fahrenheit. They'll grow best at temperatures of 60 to 65 degrees Fahrenheit. In the Mid-Atlantic, you can plant them in early spring and early fall in loose soil that's free of rocks. Sow seeds thickly and cover lightly with seed-starting mix. Keep the soil moist while the plants are germinating and thin to 3 inches between plants. Throw the babies into your spring salads.

Care & Problems—Keep the soil evenly moist and cover any root tops that might become exposed. Carrots are fairly pest-free. Rake up leaf debris to keep carrot weevils away.

Harvest & Best Selections—Carrots take 60 to 75 days to maturity. You can start to harvest them as soon as the roots turn orange (or red or yellow, depending on the variety). Don't let any carrots grow to be larger than 1½ inches wide—they'll start to taste like turpentine at that point. To harvest, just grasp the leafy top and pull. For carrots that look like typical carrots, grow 'Danvers Half Long', 'Spartan Bonus', 'Scarlet Nantes', 'Nevis' (heat tolerant), 'Apache', 'Camden', or 'Chantenay'. 'Orlando Gold' is a yellow variety. 'Little Finger' carrots are true "baby carrots," growing to 4 inches or less.

CAULIFLOWER

Brassica oleracea var. *botrytis*

Why It's Special—It's fun to grow your own cauliflower in the garden. It always seems like one day you see nothing but leaves, and you come back the next day to see a cauliflower. These plants are picky, though.

How to Plant & Grow—Plant in full sun in moist, well-drained soil with a pH of 6.0 to 6.5. For best growth, daytime temperatures should be 60 to 70 degrees Fahrenheit and nighttime temperatures 50 to 60 degrees Fahrenheit. For spring crops plant transplants outside in March in Zones 7 to 8 and, in April in Zones 5 to 6. Space transplants 12 to 18 inches apart and plant them 2 to 3 inches deeper than the soil line.

Care & Problems—Keep plants evenly moist throughout the growing season. Side-dress with a balanced fertilizer once a month. Protect young plants from cutworms by wrapping their stems with newspaper. Use *Bacillus thuringiensis* (Bt) as an organic remedy to treat cabbage loopers and cabbageworms. When the small cauliflower curds begin to form use twine to tie the top leaves of the plants together to blanch the heads. Cover if temperatures are predicted to be less than 50 degrees.

Harvest & Best Selections—'Amazing', 'Snow Crown', 'Fremont', and 'Graffiti' are good varieties. Check the seed packet or plant tag to determine when your cauliflower plants will be ready for harvest (the number of days from planting to maturity). Once they're ready, pull up the entire plant.

CHIVES
Allium schoenoprasum

Why It's Special—Chives are perennial herbs. This robust plant forms large clumps that can be divided and shared with friends. You can use chives in pastas, fresh salsas, and roasted or grilled dishes. The flowers are also edible!

How to Plant & Grow—Start seeds indoors one month before planting outside. When planting outside, leave 18 inches between each plant. The clumps will grow and spread out to be around 12 inches wide throughout the growing season. Chives are also easy to grow from direct-seeding in the garden. Sow seeds outdoors after the last frost and cover with seed-starting mix. Keep seeds moist while germinating.

Care & Problems—Chives are a relatively pest- and problem-free plant. Keep the soil a little on the dry side and maintain the plant to keep it producing leaves. You can divide the clumps after a few years in the ground. The flowers are edible too, but to keep plants focused on leaf production, cut off the flowers when they appear.

Harvest & Best Selections—There are not a lot of different varieties of chives. Plant and grow what you can find. Harvest chives before the flowers open by snipping the leaves off at the base of the plant. You can keep chives producing leaves by cutting sections of the plant back to 3 inches tall once the whole plant is 6 to 8 inches tall. (Don't cut the entire plant back all the way to the ground.)

CILANTRO
Coriandrum sativum

Why It's Special—Cilantro is an annual cool-season herb prized for its fragrant leaves. Either you love cilantro or you hate it. I love it. This parsley family plant grows best in the Mid-Atlantic in spring and early summer. Once the days get longer and hotter, it bolts, sending up a flower stalk that produces seeds. Cilantro seeds are the herb that we call coriander.

How to Plant & Grow—Cilantro grows best in temperatures of 50 to 85 degrees Fahrenheit. Sow seeds outside once the soil temperature is at least 50 degrees. The herb grows well in soils that are slightly alkaline, with a pH of 7.0 or above.

Care & Problems—Keep seeds moist while sprouting and avoid wet/dry/wet/dry periods while growing. Fertilize with a balanced fertilizer two weeks after germination. Cilantro has few pest problems, but is susceptible to some fungal diseases spread through splashing water. Try to water the plants at the root zone and avoid splashing the water.

Harvest & Best Selections—There aren't many varieties of cilantro. Grow what you can find. To harvest leaves, snip the top off the plant. The smallest, most immature leaves have the best flavor. If you want to save coriander seeds, pull up the whole plant once seeds have formed and the plant has turned yellow. Hang upside down to dry over newspaper to collect the seeds. Pair fresh cilantro with tomatoes and avocado for a delicious cold salad.

COLLARDS
Brassica oleracea var. *acephala*

Why It's Special—You might think of collards as a southern vegetable, but they grow just fine during cool fall or spring weather in the Mid-Atlantic. For healthy and tasty collards, braise leaves with garlic, onions, and lemon juice. For traditional Southern collards, cook in a crockpot for eight hours on low with one part white vinegar to two parts water, a chili pepper, and a ham hock. While that's nutritious, it is also delicious!

How to Plant & Grow—Direct-sow in full sun to partial shade in July for a fall crop and plant transplants in April for a spring/early summer crop. Prior to planting add generous amounts of compost or composted manure to the garden. Test the pH and add lime if necessary to raise it to 6.0 to 6.5. Space plants 24 inches apart. Water to establish.

Care & Problems—Keep plants evenly moist, never allowing the soil to completely dry out. Fertilize every four weeks during the growing season. Use floating row covers when you see white butterflies (cabbagewhites) around the plants. If you see cabbageworms, you can use *Bacillus thuringiensis* (Bt) to control them.

Harvest & Best Selections—Grow 'Top Bunch', 'Flash', 'Champion', and 'Blue Max'. Harvest individual leaves starting by cutting the outermost leaves first, which will keep the plant growing. After 60 to 70 days pull up the whole plant. They will keep in the refrigerator for a few weeks, but taste better if you consume them fresh.

CORN
Zea mays

Why It's Special—Even if you have a small garden, you can grow sweet corn. Corn is wind pollinated, so it is more important to plant corn close together in 4 x 4-foot or 6 x 6-foot blocks than it is to plant a big field.

How to Plant & Grow—Wait until soil temperatures are at least 60 degrees Fahrenheit before planting—between April and June in the Mid-Atlantic. If you have space to plant 10 x 10-foot blocks, sow seeds 6 inches apart in rows that are 18 inches apart. If you are growing corn in raised beds, make sure to plant at least twelve stalks spaced 8 inches apart, in a square. You will have to assist with pollination of these plants by shaking the plants once you see pollen forming.

Care & Problems—Keep the soil consistently moist. Feed once a month with a balanced fertilizer. To avoid issues with corn earworm, treat ears with a combination of Bt and mineral oil (ratio 1:20) five days after silks emerge. Place five drops on the silks at the end of each ear.

Harvest & Best Selections—Harvest when the juice that squirts from a kernel pierced by a fingernail is milky white. Start checking the corn after the silks start to turn brown.

Bicolor: 'Trinity', 'Temptation', 'Breeder's Bicolor', 'Mystique', 'Providence', 'Serendipity', 'Delectable', 'Seneca Dancer'

White: 'Spring Snow', 'Silver Princess', 'Silverado', 'Avalon', 'Argent'

Yellow: 'Seneca Horizon', 'Early Choice', 'Sundance', 'Sugar Buns', 'Legend', 'Bodacious'

CUCUMBER
Cucumis sativus

Why It's Special—Cucumbers are warm-season vining vegetables that are part of the squash family. They are related to pumpkins and melons. It's easy to make quick refrigerator pickles if you have extra cukes.

How to Plant & Grow—Plant cucumbers in full sun in moist, well-drained soil when the soil temperature is between 65 to 70 degrees Fahrenheit. Plant seeds in hills spaced 24 inches apart, three seeds per hill.

Care & Problems—Keep soil evenly moist during the growing season. Place soaker hoses along the base of cucumber plants to help deliver a steady stream of water at their roots. Side-dress cucumbers every two weeks during the growing season with a balanced fertilizer. Place floating row covers over young plants to protect plants from cucumber beetles and squash vine borers and remove the covers when the plants start flowering. Neem oil and pyrethrum are two organic pesticides that can help control the pests.

Harvest & Best Selections—There are several types. Slicers are larger and longer cucumbers best for slicing and eating fresh. Picklers are shorter and smaller. Burpless varieties have thinner skin. There are also vining types and bush types. Bush types are better if you have limited space. Look at disease resistance indicators on seed packets and try to find varieties with CMV, DM, and PM on the seed packet. Harvest pickling cucumbers when they are 2 to 6 inches long and slicing cucumbers when they are 6 to 12 inches long.

DILL
Anethum graveolens

Why It's Special—I love to pick dill at the same time I'm harvesting greens. I wash and keep the dill in the same salad spinner as the lettuce for an extra flavorful salad. Dill is an important addition to the vegetable garden, as it serves as a host plant for native butterfly caterpillars and a nectar source (the flowers) for beneficial insects and pollinators.

How to Plant & Grow—Plant in full sun after the last frost. Like its relative the carrot, dill needs well-drained, loose soil. Water to establish.

Care & Problems—Keep the soil evenly moist. No extra fertilizer is needed. Dill is susceptible to the same pests that eat carrots and parsnips. Keep an eye out for aphids and flea beetles. Don't be alarmed if you see caterpillars on the plants. The native black swallowtail butterfly loves dill and will munch some of your plants to the ground.

Harvest & Best Selections—There are not really a lot of notable varieties. Plant whatever seeds or plants you can find. The leaves are most fragrant and delicious before the plants start to flower. Use kitchen scissors to snip off leaves. If you want to harvest seeds, allow the plant to flower. (Flowers are also important nectar sources for pollinators.) As the seeds are forming, keep a close eye on the plants. Pull up the plants and hang them upside down to dry over newspaper to collect the seeds.

EGGPLANT
Solanum melongena

Why It's Special—Eggplants are members of the nightshade family, along with tomatoes, peppers, and tomatillos. Are you at a loss for what to do with eggplants? Two easy ways to eat them are rubbed with olive oil and grilled, and in a ratatouille (summer sauté of tomatoes, squash, and eggplant).

How to Plant & Grow—Plant transplants outside in full sun when nighttime temperatures are at least 70 degrees. Leave 12 inches between plants. Water to establish. Mulch at the time of planting to aid moisture retention.

Care & Problems—Keep the soil consistently moist. Feed eggplants every two weeks with a balanced fertilizer. Use floating row covers to control flea beetles, keeping plants under row covers until they have three sets of leaves. Keep an eye out for tomato hornworms and handpick them (gross, but effective). Look for the orange eggs of the Colorado potato beetle on the undersides of the leaves and wash the leaves with water or crush the eggs to control them. *Bacillus thuringiensis* (Bt) is effective on adult beetles.

Harvest & Best Selections—Try 'Black Magic', 'Purple Rain', 'Early Bird', 'Little Fingers', 'Longtom', 'Ichiban', and 'Pintung Long'. The biggest question with eggplants is, "When are they ready to harvest?" The best thing to do is pay close attention to the days to maturity on the label and harvest around that time. Use a knife or pruners to pick the fruits, leaving at least ½ inch of stem.

GARLIC
Allium sativum

Why It's Special—Selecting the right variety of garlic is paramount to success. It needs 40 days of weather less than 40 degrees Fahrenheit for the planted cloves to split into a bulb with multiple cloves. For this reason, garlic is a fall- and winter-grown vegetable in the Mid-Atlantic. If you can purchase garlic bulbs locally, all the better—you're more likely to be successful.

How to Plant & Grow—Plant garlic cloves in full sun in well-drained soil during fall, 1 inch deep and 4 inches apart.

Care & Problems—Keep the soil moist during the first four weeks after planting—this is when the garlic cloves are growing roots. After that, they do not need extra water until spring. Resume watering once you see leaves start to appear. At the end of the life cycle, decrease watering to allow the bulbs to dry out. Top-dress the area where garlic is planted with an organic fertilizer in spring. Garlic has few pest problems.

Harvest & Best Selections—Garlic is ready to harvest when the tops start dying back. When you see the leaves start to turn yellow, stop watering the bulbs. Once the tops have died back, use a trowel or soil knife to gently dig up the bulbs. There are two types of garlic: softneck (for Zones 7 to 8) and hardneck (for Zones 4 to 6).

Softneck: 'Burgundy', 'Ajo Rojo', 'Silverskin'

Hardneck: 'Rocambole', 'German Extra Hardy'

KALE
Brassica oleracea acephala

Why It's Special—Kale has become an "it" vegetable. Everyone is drinking kale smoothies, eating kale chips, and generally espousing the benefits of this leafy green vegetable. It's for good reason, though; kale is the most nutrient-dense vegetable per calorie you can eat.

How to Plant & Grow—Add compost to the soil before planting. Test the soil to make sure that the pH is 6.0 to 7.0 and add lime if you need to raise the pH. Sow seeds in full sun in all regions in July for a fall (and winter in some areas) harvest. Plant transplants outside in March and April for growing during spring and summer.

Care & Problems—Keep kale growing, thriving, and producing tender (not bitter and fibrous) leaves by watering consistently when the plants are actively growing. Fertilize by side-dressing with an organic slow-release fertilizer every three to four weeks during the growing season. Control aphids with insecticidal soap. Cabbageworms and cabbage loopers can also munch on kale. If you see the worms, treat with *Bacillus thuringiensis* (Bt).

Harvest & Best Selections—Recommended varieties include 'Green Curled Scotch', 'Early Siberian', 'Vates', 'Dwarf Blue Curled Scotch', 'Blue Knight', 'Red Russian', and 'Toscano'. Cut small young leaves (1 inch long or less) to use in fresh salads. Harvest the larger leaves from the bottom of the plant up. Wash leaves, tear them up (removing midrib) and scrunch with flavored vinegar for a great salad!)

167

LEEK
Allium porrum

Why It's Special—Leeks are so easy to grow, and they're fun to cook with. You can throw young, tender leeks on the grill. Or you can cut up larger leeks to make potato and leek soup.

How to Plant & Grow—Start seeds indoors eight to ten weeks before you plan to plant leeks outdoors. You can grow leeks in the garden all winter in Zones 7 to 8. Plant in March in Zones 4 to 6. Harden off before transplanting. Leave 4 to 6 inches between plants when transplanting in the garden. Add compost to the soil before planting. Leeks grow best in loose soils full of organic matter. Test the soil to ensure a pH of 6.5 to 7.0.

Care & Problems—Keep leeks evenly moist throughout the growing season. Do not let them dry out. Leeks are not heavy feeders. Side-dress with a balanced fertilizer every two months during the growing season. Leeks are fairly pest-free.

Harvest & Best Selections—'Lancelot' is a good variety to plant in for a fall and winter harvest. It is one of the most cold-tolerant types. 'Leefall' is very cold-hardy and will overwinter in all but the coldest areas of the Mid-Atlantic. Grow 'Jolant' and 'Dawn Giant' through summer for summer and early fall harvests. Leeks mature in 100 to 120 days, depending on the variety. Once the stalks reach ½ inch in diameter, you can start harvesting them. Harvest leeks by pulling up the entire plant.

LETTUCE
Lactuca sativa

Why It's Special—Lettuce is the quintessential cool-season crop. It isn't just the cool weather that lettuce likes though. Lettuce needs the short days (and long nights) associated with fall, winter, and early spring to stay in a vegetative state—producing leaves, not flowers. Once the weather starts to heat up, lettuce leaves get tough and bitter and plants will send up a flower stalk.

How to Plant & Grow—Sow seeds outdoors and cover with seed-starting mix. Sow head lettuce seeds with 1 inch between seeds. Thin to 4 inches after the plants have three sets of leaves. Thin to 12-inch spacing as the plants start to mature. Sow cut-and-come-again lettuces and leaf lettuces thickly—three seeds per inch.

Care & Problems—Keep the soil evenly moist. Feed with high-nitrogen fertilizers every two weeks during the growing season. Slugs are a major problem. Spread diatomaceous earth around lettuce plants to create a barrier against slugs.

Harvest & Best Selections—'Black-Seeded Simpson' and 'Simpson Elite' are two good green-leaf varieties that grow well here. 'Red Sails' and 'Lolla Rosa' are easy-to-grow red-leaf varieties. You can find a variety of mesclun and cut-and-come-again seed mixes at garden centers and home-improvement stores. Harvest head lettuce by pulling up the entire plant. Harvest leaf lettuce by using scissors to snip off leaves about ½ to 1 inch above the soil line. Wash and store in a salad spinner. Leaf lettuce will grow back after cutting.

MELON
Cucumis spp.

Why It's Special—Melons are annual vines related to cucumbers and squash. They have many insect pest issues. If you're limited on space in the vegetable garden, skip the melons and buy them at the farmers' market.

How to Plant & Grow—Direct-sow melon seeds in the garden when soil temperatures are at least 65 degrees Fahrenheit. Plant seeds in hills at least 4 feet apart, three seeds per hill. Thin plants to one plant every 4 feet after they grow three sets of leaves.

Care & Problems—Use soaker hoses to water plants every other day during the growing season. Sidedress with calcium nitrate when the vines are 3 feet long. Cucumber beetles, flea beetles, squash bugs, and squash vine borers are some of the worst pests. Use row covers to prevent flying insects from landing on the plants. Lift the row covers for two hours in the morning twice a week to encourage pollination, or hand-pollinate. Powdery mildew is sometimes a problem, but it's usually just more of a cosmetic issue than a life-ending disease.

Harvest & Best Selections—Harvest honeydews when they've turned pale green. Cantaloupes should smell sweet at harvest time. You can tell if watermelons are ripe by looking at the tendril closest to the fruit. When that turns brown, watermelons are ready to pick.

Watermelon: 'Charleston Gray', 'Crimson Sweet', 'Golden Crown', 'Royal Sweet', 'Tiger Baby'

Cantaloupe: Burpee Hybrid, 'Ambrosia', 'Park's Whopper', 'Scoop II'

Honeydew: 'Earlidew'

MINT
Mentha spp.

Why It's Special—Mint is a perennial herb that spreads like crazy. I remember picking handfuls of it from underneath my neighbor's porch when I was little. It is possibly the first edible plant I recollect eating straight from the garden. Use it in savory Middle Eastern dishes and to add sparkle to drinks.

How to Plant & Grow—Plant mint in full sun to partial shade in moist soil. Water well to establish. If you're planting more than one plant, space at 12 to 18 inches. A lot of people grow mint in a pot so that they can enjoy it without worrying that the plant will take over the garden.

Care & Problems—Mint is easy to grow. Give it plenty of water and let it run. Or, don't. The biggest problem with mint is keeping it under control. Cut plants back to the ground in spring. Do not fertilize.

Harvest & Best Selections—There several different species of mints, each with cultivars. Mint tea and mint juleps are made with spearmint, *Mentha spicata*. It is easy to grow to the point where it is almost weedy. Peppermint, *M. × piperita*, is used for candy flavoring and baking. Pineapple mint, *M. suaveolens*, is popular for use in herbal teas. Harvest mint in the morning when the leaves are at their most turgid. Simply cut off the tops of the plant. Harvesting also triggers more branching, which gives you more mint!

MUSTARD GREENS
Brassica juncea

Why It's Special—Mustard greens are spicy, nutritious, easy-to-grow greens that thrive during cool weather. You can grow them throughout winter in Zones 7 to 8 and in spring and fall in Zones 5 to 6. They are in the cabbage family, and eating them gives you many of the same health benefits as do the rest of the plants in that family. In addition to being grown as edibles, mustard greens, particularly the red varieties, are also excellent additions to the cool-season flower garden or winter container gardens.

How to Plant & Grow—Sow seeds in full sun to partial shade in moist, well-drained soils. Plant in March and April and again in August to September in Zones 7 to 8. Sow seeds in May and June in Zones 5 to 6. You can sow successive crops for a longer harvest period. Water to establish.

Care & Problems—Mustard greens are one of the toughest plants in the cabbage family and have few pests. Just keep the plants watered through the growing season. Once they bolt (send up a flower stalk), pull up the plant and compost.

Harvest & Best Selections—'Green Wave' and 'Red Giant' are two good varieties. You can really grow whatever you can find, though. Pick young mustard greens to add spicy crunch to salads. (Pick when leaves are 1 to 2 inches in length.) Larger leaves taste best when steamed or braised. A quick sauce of diced garlic sautéed in olive oil and tossed with lemon juice makes braised greens delicious.

OKRA
Abelmoschus esculentus

Why It's Special—Okra is a hot-weather vegetable known for its pointy pods that have a somewhat slimy texture when cooked. Although that may not sound very appetizing, okra is actually really delicious if prepared correctly. It makes excellent pickles!

How to Plant & Grow—Okra likes it hot. Don't bother planting until the soil temperature is at least 65 to 70 degrees Fahrenheit at a depth of 4 inches. Soak the seeds for 12 hours before planting outside to ensure good germination rates. Space transplants at 9 to 12 inches between plants. Sow seeds at a rate of one every 4 inches and thin to 9- to 12-inch spacing as plants grow.

Care & Problems—Allow the soil to dry out between plantings. Water deeply so that the soil is wet to a depth of 6 to 8 inches, but infrequently. Fertilize once during the growing season with a balanced fertilizer. It's fairly pest-free.

Harvest & Best Selections—'Clemson Spineless', 'Lee', 'Annie Oakley', and 'Cajun Delight' are all spineless varieties that grow well in the Mid-Atlantic. Harvest okra when the pods are 2 to 3 inches long. The larger the pod, the tougher it will be and the less tasty. Once an okra plant starts producing pods big enough to harvest, it will keep going until frost occurs or it wears itself out. Plan to pick new pods daily. Pick off large pods and compost them.

ONION
Allium cepa

Why It's Special—There are short-, long-, and intermediate-day onions. Your local garden center should carry onion types that are right for your area. Bunching onions, also called green onions, can grow anywhere.

How to Plant & Grow—Plant onions in full sun in loose, well-drained soil, April 1 to 15 in Zones 4 to 6, and in March in Zones 7 to 8. Space bunching onions close together (2 inches) and bulbing onions 6 inches apart.

Care & Problems—Water regularly during the growing season. Decrease watering the last two weeks before harvesting. Side-dress with a balanced organic fertilizer every four weeks during growing season only.

Harvest & Best Selections—Harvest bunching onions when they are at least ⅓ inch in diameter. Pull up the entire plant. A month before you want to harvest bulbing onions, start gradually pulling the soil away from the bulbs. By harvest time, the bulbs should be one-third uncovered. Pull up the onions when one-third of the tops have fallen over. Allow them to cure for three to five days on top of the soil. Cover the plants if rain is forecast. Before bringing the onions inside, cut the tops off, leaving 1 inch of stalk to dry on the plants. Store short-day onions for three months in a low humidity, cool environment.

Bunching: White Sweet Spanish, Long White Summer Bunching

Bulbing Plants: Mars, Giant Red Hamburger, Super Star, Candy, Prince, Copra, Alisa Craig, Sweet Sandwich, Walla Walla

Bulbing Sets: These are good for storage: Ebenezer, Southport Red Globe, Stuttgart type

OREGANO
Origanum vulgare

Why It's Special—Oregano a perennial herb that's so easy to grow, it's almost a weed. Thankfully, though part of the mint family, it doesn't spread as crazily as mint. Oregano grows in large clumps. Make a flavorful salad dressing by muddling fresh oregano with lemon juice and combining with olive oil.

How to Plant & Grow—Plant oregano outside after danger of frost has passed. Oregano grows best in soil with a pH of 6.5 to 7.5. You can start seeds indoors by sprinkling them on top of potting soil, watering, and covering the seedling flat with plastic wrap to keep the seeds moist as they germinate. You can also sow seeds outside directly on top of the soil and use plastic wrap to keep them moist.

Care & Problems—No extra water is needed after plants are established, nor is extra fertilizer needed. Aphids and spider mites can attack oregano when it's exceptionally dry outside. Water oregano if your region is experiencing drought; the insects will eventually go away. It's almost impossible to kill oregano. The primary objective is to prevent oregano from taking over the garden. Even though it is a clumping perennial herb, its stems will form roots and spread if allowed. Periodically cut the entire plant back. It will grow out amazingly fast.

Harvest & Best Selections—Leaves are most fragrant just before the flowers open, but you can snip leaves off to use anytime.

PARSLEY
Petroselinum crispum

Why It's Special—Parsley is a cool-season biennial herb grown for its leaves, which are high in vitamins and minerals. Parsley is a biennial that sometimes overwinters in the Mid-Atlantic, but sometimes it doesn't. Certain varieties are more cold tolerant than others. Parsley is a great addition to cold salads, soups, and sandwiches. The greens add a nutrient boost, along with a fresh flavor.

How to Plant & Grow—Start seeds indoors at least one month before you want to transplant outside. Parsley can be tricky to start from seed; soak seeds for 12 hours before planting. Sow seeds outside at one seed per inch. It can take two to three weeks for parsley seeds to germinate. Thin plants to 4-inch spacing once they've germinated.

Care & Problems—Parsley won't need extra water unless your area is experiencing a drought. Side-dress with a balanced fertilizer every four weeks during the growing season. The main pest you'll see on parsley is the larval form of the black swallowtail butterfly. These caterpillars will feed on parsley for a few weeks and then disappear, so leave them alone. The plants will regrow.

Harvest & Best Selections—If you want to overwinter parsley, plant the 'Banquet' variety. Keep parsley growing by frequently cutting its outermost leaves for use in the kitchen. You can prolong leaf growth by cutting back the flower stalks for a time. Eventually, though, parsley will flower, set seed, and die.

PARSNIP
Pastinaca sativa

Why It's Special—Parsnips are relatives of carrots, but they're sweeter with a buttery, smooth flavor. These cold-hardy vegetables require many of the same growing conditions as carrots but they're easier to grow.

How to Plant & Grow—Plant parsnips in Zones 4 to 6 in full sun in loose, deep soil April 1 to May 1. Plant parsnips in Zones 7 to 8 in September to grow through winter. Soak seeds for 24 hours before planting. Sow thickly, at a rate of three or four seeds per inch, and water. Keep the soil moist. Thin seedlings to 4 inches apart once they germinate and have two sets of leaves.

Care & Problems—Water deeply to wet the soil to 6 inches and side-dress monthly with a balanced fertilizer. Parsnips are fairly pest-free. If rabbits and squirrels are a problem in your area, use a floating row cover for young plants. Black swallowtail caterpillars will sometimes feast on the plant leaves. Let them eat; they'll go away eventually.

Harvest & Best Selections—There are not a lot of parsnip varieties. Grow what you can find. Parsnips are ready to harvest when the root tops are 1½ to 2 inches in diameter. Use a garden fork to loosen the soil around the parsnips and help dig them up. It takes 120 to 150 days for parsnips to grow from seed to maturity. Parsnips always taste better once they've been exposed to cool weather.

PEA
Pisum sativum

Why It's Special—Everyone can grow peas. They are, hands down, the easiest vegetable to grow. Fresh peas are delicious, but expensive. Save a lot of money by growing your own!

How to Plant & Grow—Plant peas outside mid-February to mid-March in Zones 7 to 8, and from mid-March to mid-April in Zones 5 to 6. If you sow twice, two weeks apart, you'll enjoy a longer harvest. Plant peas 1 inch deep, 2 inches apart in rows 8 inches apart in raised beds and 18 inches apart in regular garden beds.

Care & Problems—Keep the soil evenly moist, but not soaking wet. Do not allow the bed to completely dry out. Side-dress with a phosphorus and potassium fertilizer when plants are in bloom. Aphids are the biggest pest problem for peas. Use insecticidal soap according to package instructions to control these pests.

Harvest & Best Selections—Grow sugar snaps for fresh eating: try 'Sugar Snap', 'Mammoth Melting Sugar', 'Snowbird', and 'Sugar Bon'. For shelling peas, grow 'Wando', 'Green Arrow', 'Freezonian', and 'Tall Telephone'. Harvest snap peas when the pods are plump, but still dark green. Harvest snow peas when the pods are still relatively flat. The flowers might still be hanging onto the ends of the pods of both types when you harvest the pods. Harvest shelling peas when the pods are plump, but still dark green. You can eat shoot tips (the young plants) like you'd eat other greens—braised or in salads.

PEPPER
Capsicum annuum

Why It's Special—There are hundreds of varieties of peppers you can grow—from bell peppers to banana peppers, from hot to sweet. They're expensive to buy at the grocery store, so growing your own will definitely save money!

How to Plant & Grow—Plant in full sun when the soil is 65 to 75 degrees Fahrenheit at a depth of 4 inches. (That's around mid-May to mid-June in the Mid-Atlantic.) Plant transplants 12 inches apart.

Care & Problems—Keep the soil evenly moist to avoid problems with blossom end rot (which can also be caused by a low soil pH). Feed peppers with a balanced fertilizer when they start blooming, and again four weeks later. Peppers have many virus and pest problems. Planting resistant varieties helps keep some pests under control. Growing the plants under floating row covers until they start flowering can control other pests.

Harvest & Best Selections—Look for disease resistance when selecting plant types. This will be indicated on the plant tag or seed packet. The seed packet will also help you determine when it's time to harvest. Look at the picture, description, and days to maturity for information.

Bell pepper: 'Keystone Resistant Giant Strain 3', 'Yolo Wonder', 'King Arthur'

Banana pepper: 'Banana Supreme', 'Hy-Fry', 'Biscayne', 'Key Largo', 'Cubanelle', 'Gypsy', 'Hungarian Sweet Wax'

Hot pepper: Red Cherry (Small), Red Cherry (Large), 'Anaheim Chili TMR 23', 'AnchoVilla', 'Early Jalopeno', 'Mitla', 'Hungarian Yellow Wax', 'Habanero'

POTATO
Solanum tuberosum

Why It's Special—Potatoes are a kitchen staple, and they're just so easy to grow! You practically just plant them, periodically pile on some more soil to hill them as they grow, and wait until they're ready for harvest.

How to Plant & Grow—Plant certified disease-free seed potatoes in full sun 2 to 3 inches deep and 12 inches apart three to four weeks before the last frost. Potatoes grow well in slightly acidic soil; if the pH is above 6.5; consider amending with aluminum sulfate before planting. As the plants grow, hill them up by piling soil, compost, straw, or a mixture to keep new tubers covered. Stop hilling when the plants flower, and keep watering.

Care & Problems—Potatoes have several pest and disease problems, but you can avoid much of that by planting disease-free stock and promptly removing any debris from the garden.

Harvest & Best Selections—The individual potato variety is not as important as finding one that will grow well in your area and is certified disease-free. Check your local garden centers, home-improvement centers, and farmer's supply-type stores for seed potatoes. You can also order online. Dig new potatoes to use in shrimp and crab boils or serve in cold salads when the tops start flowering. Gently push the dirt away from the tubers and snap off the small potatoes. The mature potatoes are ready to dig when the tops (leaves) die back.

RADISH
Raphanus sativus

Why It's Special—Radishes are cool-season root vegetables. Spring radishes are fast to germinate and mature. You can get several radish crops from one package of seeds, so don't plant the whole thing at once. Radishes are beneficial plants for the vegetable garden too, because they deter pests and, when allowed to flower, attract beneficial insects and pollinators.

How to Plant & Grow—Sow seeds outside ½ inch deep and 2 inches apart in full sun when the soil temperature is at least 50 degrees Fahrenheit, usually between early April and late May depending on where you live. The more you space between the seeds, the less thinning you'll have to do. Sow successive crops every two seeks for a steady harvest.

Care & Problems—Radishes aren't fussy, but they do need even moisture levels to avoid cracking. Use row covers to prevent flea beetles and aphids from attacking the plants. You can also spray with insecticidal soap. For the most part, radishes are so fast-growing, it's not worth the trouble to try to control any pests on them.

Harvest & Best Selections—You can find infinite varieties of radishes. 'Cherry Belle' is the typical round, red-on-the-outside, white-on-the-inside variety that most people think of when they think "radish." 'French Breakfast' radishes have longer roots. You can purchase seed mixes with red, white, purple, and yellow radishes in them. Harvest radishes after three to four weeks of growth for the best taste and texture.

RHUBARB
Rheum rhabarbarum

Why It's Special—Though rhubarb is really a vegetable, it is used in the kitchen as a fruit. It makes delicious pies. Be careful with rhubarb; *only* the stems are edible after cooking. The rest of the plant is poisonous.

How to Plant & Grow—Not all regions can grow rhubarb. It requires temperatures below 40 degrees Fahrenheit in winter to break dormancy and temperatures below 75 degrees Fahrenheit to grow well during summer to replenish its stores for winter growth. Plant crowns 24 inches apart in spring or fall while the crowns are still dormant. Cover with just 1 to 2 inches of soil. Water well.

Care & Problems—Water rhubarb with the same frequency you'd water sugar snap peas, which is to say regularly, but don't let the soil stay soggy. Fertilize after harvest with liquid fish emulsion. Rhubarb has few pest problems. Once it's sited in an area to which it is well-suited, it will persist for years.

Harvest & Best Selections—Plant whatever you can find. It's easier to grow from crowns than seeds. Harvest during the third season of growth. Use a knife to cut off the stalks at the base of the plant. Never remove more than one-third of the plant at any given time. Stop cutting stalks when they are less than ½-inch wide. Let the plant keep growing to produce reserves to allow it to sprout next year.

ROSEMARY
Rosmarinus officinalis

Why It's Special—Rosemary is a woody, evergreen perennial herb native to the Mediterranean. It thrives in well-drained soil. It's easy to grow once established, and it's so fun to cook with. You can use fresh rosemary when roasting meats and vegetables. Rosemary twigs make excellent kebab sticks for grilling. Save a corner of the garden for this tasty herb.

How to Plant & Grow—Plant transplants outside after danger of frost has passed for best establishment. Rosemary is widely adaptable to many different soil types. Leave rosemary alone; if you baby it, you're more likely to kill it. Once it is established, don't water unless your area is experiencing a severe drought. Don't feed it as that promotes weak growth that's susceptible to pests.

Care & Problems—Mealybugs and scale are the two pests that afflict rosemary. Use horticultural oil to treat the plant for these pests.

Harvest & Best Selections—Cut pieces of rosemary anytime for cooking. The young tips are best for mixing into fresh salads. The rest of the plant is good for use in soups, stews, or roasting. To keep rosemary growing in your Mid-Atlantic garden, plant cold-hardy varieties. While rosemary topiaries are often sold as houseplants, they do not fare well indoors. The US National Arboretum recommends these varieties for excellent cold hardiness: *Rosmarinus officinalis* 'Albus', 'Bendenen Blue', 'Goodwin Creek', 'Herb Cottage', 'Logee's Light Blue', 'Miss Jessup's Upright', 'Russian River', and 'Salem'.

SAGE
Salvia officinalis

Why It's Special—The sage that we use in cooking is called "garden sage," and all varieties are within *Salvia officinalis*. This tough perennial is extremely hardy, but needs well-drained soil in order to grow. If you enjoy cooking and grilling, definitely grow your own sage. You'll save money in the long run.

How to Plant & Grow—Plant in full sun in well-drained soil when all danger of frost has passed, for best establishment. It's best to buy transplants or root cuttings from a friend. Sage is difficult to grow from seed.

Care & Problems—Once sage is established, only water if your area is experiencing extreme drought. Sage does not usually need extra fertilizer, but a once-a-year feeding in spring with a slow-release balanced fertilizer won't hurt. Slugs can attack sage when conditions are wetter than usual, and spider mites can be a problem during times of extreme drought. Both problems will resolve on their own, eventually.

Harvest & Best Selections—Beyond the straight species of garden sage, there are many varieties with interesting leaf colors, increased cold hardiness, and other desirable characteristics. 'Berggarten' is a hardier, more compact variety than the straight species. Purple sage is also a garden sage that has deep purple leaves. 'Tricolor' has leaves that are purple, green, and white; it is decorative and useful. 'Woodcote' sage has variegated green-and-white leaves. Cut stems or individual leaves to use when cooking.

SPINACH
Spinacia oleracea

Why It's Special—Why should you grow your own spinach? Because it's easy to grow and much more sanitary to pick and eat your own. Field-grown commercial crops are some of the most easily contaminated vegetables. Grow spring and fall crops.

How to Plant & Grow—Plant seeds or transplants outside in April and May in Zones 5 to 6, and in March and April in Zones 7 to 8. Sow seeds again outside in August for fall harvests in all areas. Start seeds indoors a month before you want to transplant outdoors. Soak seeds overnight before direct-planting outside. Space seeds 2 inches apart and thin to 6 inches apart after plants have three sets of leaves. Harden off transplants and space 6 inches apart.

Care & Problems—Keep the soil evenly moist during the growing season. Side-dress with a balanced fertilizer every two weeks. Prevent fungal problems by keeping water off the leaves. Use floating row covers to prevent damage from leafminers.

Harvest & Best Selections—Wait until plants have at least eight to ten decent-sized leaves before harvesting. Cut outer leaves first, always leaving six leaves on the plant to produce sugars to help the plant keep growing. Use scissors or pinch off the leaves at the base of the leaf stalk. Once spinach sends up a flower stalk, pull up the plant and compost it. Plant different varieties in spring and fall.

Fall: Space, Tyee

Spring: 'Melody', 'UniPack 151', 'Nordic IV', 'Olympia'

SQUASH, SUMMER
Cucurbita pepo

Why It's Special—Summer squash is a versatile vegetable. You can eat the fruits (botanically, they're fruits), raw on vegetable trays, or chopped up for cold salads. Hollow them out, fill with stuffing, and bake them. Sauté them to add to tomato sauce or for ratatouille.

How to Plant & Grow—Plant three seeds per hill when soil temperatures are at least 65 degrees Fahrenheit. This can range from early May to early June. When seedlings are 3 inches tall, use scissors to thin to two plants per 12 inches. As plants grow, reduce to one plant every 18 or 24 inches. (Overplanting slightly gives you more plants if you have problems with pests.)

Care & Problems—Mulch after planting and keep soil evenly moist throughout the growing season. Side-dress with a balanced fertilizer every three weeks. Squash bugs, squash vine borers, cucumber beetles, and squash beetles plague squash plants. Use row covers over young plants. Raise the covers for two hours in the early morning a few days a week to permit pollination.

Harvest & Best Selections—Purchase varieties resistant to cucumber mosaic virus, powdery mildew, and downy mildew. Read seed packets to see what the plant should look like when mature for harvest. Harvest when the flower has barely wilted at the end of a fruit. Try these:

Yellow straightneck: 'Saffron', 'Seneca Butterbar'

Yellow crookneck: 'Dixie', 'Multipik'

Zucchini: 'Costata Romanesco', 'Spineless Beauty', 'Eight Ball'

Pattypan: 'Sunburst', 'Peter Pan'

SQUASH, WINTER
Cucurbita spp.

Why It's Special—Winter squash grows in much the same way as summer squash, but its fruits take longer to mature. Popular winter squash varieties include pumpkins, acorn squash, and butternut squash. The common name "winter squash" comes from the plants' good winter storage qualities.

How to Plant & Grow—Sow seeds outside when soil temperatures are at least 65 degrees Fahrenheit. Plant two to three seeds per hole, 1 inch deep. As plants grow, thin to one plant per 24 or 48 inches.

Care & Problems—Keep squash evenly moist. Side-dress with a balanced fertilizer every three weeks. Apply calcium nitrate at a rate of 2 pounds per 100 feet of row to the soil around the base of each plant when it starts flowering. Squash bugs, squash vine borers, cucumber beetles, and Mexican bean beetles plague squash plants. Use row covers when plants are young, raising covers in early morning a few days a week to allow insects to pollinate flowers.

Harvest & Best Selections—Winter squashes are ready to harvest when the skin has thickened and is dull, not shiny. Cut squashes from the vine, leaving 1 inch of stem.

Winter squash: 'Table King', 'Bush Acorn', 'Early Butternut', 'Vegetable Spaghetti', Hubbard Types, 'Celebration', 'Delicata'

Pumpkins: Pumpkins are divided into different categories including carving (large), and pie (small and sweet). Try these varieties for **carving**: 'Autumn Gold', 'Ghost Rider', 'Jack o'Lantern', 'Howden', 'Magic Lantern', 'Merlin', 'Spirit'; try these for **pie**: 'Amish Pie', 'Small Sugar'

SWISS CHARD
Beta vulgaris ssp. cicla

Why It's Special—Swiss chard is a biennial related to beets. Both its leaves and its colorful stalks are edible. It will grow through summer if planted during cool weather, making it one of those hard-to-define vegetables in terms of seasons. If you're short on space, grow this beautiful vegetable in the perennial flower garden. It will look right at home. It's also a good container plant.

How to Plant & Grow—Plant in full sun to part shade in May in Zones 5 to 6. Plant outside in March and April and again in September or October in Zones 7 to 8. Swiss chard is not a picky plant and will grow in almost any soil.

Care & Problems—Keep chard evenly moist. Fertilize with a balanced fertilizer every two to four weeks during the growing season. Use insecticidal soap to take care of any aphids or leafminers that might attack.

Harvest & Best Selections—'Bright Lights' is a multicolored mixture of plants with stalks ranging from yellow to white to red to green. 'Rainbow' is another multicolored mix. 'Fordhook Giant' produces large green leaves with white stems. You can start harvesting Swiss chard leaves as soon as the plant has at least four or five leaves. Take the outermost leaves first, and allow the inner leaves to grow and provide sugars for the pant. Use a sharp knife, scissors, or hand pruners to cut the leaf stalks at the soil level.

THYME
Thymus vulgaris

Why It's Special—Thyme is a perennial herb that is hardy in Zones 5 to 9. There are over one hundred varieties, so try growing some unusual ones. Thyme is indispensible for cooking savory dishes. You can use it in everything from roast chicken to vegetable soup to shortbread cookies (really).

How to Plant & Grow—It is much easier to grow thyme from cuttings than it is to grow it from seed. Get transplants from the garden center or home-improvement store for best results. Plant outside after all danger of frost has passed. Thyme needs well-drained soil to grow. It will rot if kept consistently wet.

Care & Problems—Thyme does not need extra water once established. Fertilize once a year in spring with a balanced fertilizer. Aphids and spider mites will attack the plant if it is stressed—usually from too much water. Fungal diseases and root rot are also problems if the soil is too wet. Thyme leaves are most fragrant if they are cut before the plant flowers. Keep cutting back the top 4 to 6 inches of growth to stimulate fresh, new growth, which is best for cooking.

Harvest & Best Selections—There are many varieties including lemon and lime thyme! Try different varieties to see what does well in your garden. There's no need to search out specific types of thyme— just browse the garden center and see what's available.

TOMATO
Solanum lycopersicum

Why It's Special—Nothing beats the taste of a fresh-picked tomato from your garden. Grocery store tomatoes have been picked when still green and gassed with ethylene to turn them red. Skip that— grow your own!

How to Plant & Grow—Start seeds indoors six weeks before planting outdoors. Use a heat mat and grow lights elevated 2 inches above plants to grow strong transplants. Harden off and plant outside when the soil temperature is at least 65 degrees Fahrenheit and nighttime temperatures are regularly at least 65 to 70 degrees Fahrenheit. This is usually mid- to late May in Zones 7 to 8, and in early June Zones 5 to 6. Soil pH should be 6.0 to 7.0; if pH is lower, add lime before planting. Mix in slow-release organic fertilizer before planting, as well. Spacing varies.

Care & Problems—Tomatoes need steady, consistent moisture to avoid blossom-end rot. Use soaker hoses to make deep watering easier. Fertilize with a 8-32-16 fertilizer when plants start flowering. Growing resistant varieties helps avoid many pest problems. Keep an eye out for tomato hornworms, big green worms as large as your thumb. Pick and squash.

Harvest & Best Selections—Tomatoes are ripe when you need little effort to pull them off. High-performing tomatoes include 'Better Boy', 'Early Girl', 'First Lady', 'Delicious', and 'Big Beef'. Cherry tomatoes including 'Sugar Snack' and 'Sweet Million' grow well in the Mid-Atlantic. 'Yellow Pear' are indeterminate tomatoes that produce tons of yellow, lightbulb-shaped grape tomatoes.

TURNIP
Brassica napus

Why It's Special—Turnips are double-duty plants: you can eat the tops and the roots. They're a cool-weather vegetable that grows well in early spring in the Mid-Atlantic. If you time it right, you can get a fall crop out of the garden too.

How to Plant & Grow—Sow seeds in full sun August 1 to October 1 and again in March and April in Zones 7 to 8. Sow outside in late April and early May in Zones 5 to 6. Sow successively for a staggered harvest. Thin to 4-inch spacing when the plants are 4 inches tall. Thin every other plant when the roots are 1 inch in diameter.

Care & Problems—Keep the soil evenly moist, but not soggy. Add compost to the bed before planting and you won't have to add additional fertilizer. Control aphids with insecticidal soap and flea beetles by using row covers.

Harvest & Best Selections—Popular varieties include 'Purple Top', 'White Globe', and 'White Lady'. 'All Top' is grown specifically for greens. 'Hakurei' is a small, white salad turnip that tastes good when shredded raw into salads. Harvest depends on which part of the plant you want to eat. Pick young, tender greens for salads when they are 2 to 4 inches tall. Pull up small roots when they are 2 inches in diameter and use them raw in salads. When the larger roots grow to 3 or 4 inches in diameter, pull them up for roasting and mashing.

VEGETABLES & HERBS MONTH-BY-MONTH

JANUARY

- Order seeds or visit your local garden center to pick out new varieties. The seed racks should be full of new selections.

- Plan the garden so that you end up with a manageable harvest of things you actually want to eat. Do you plan to put up any produce through canning, freezing, or drying? Double or triple the space you allocate to those plants.

FEBRUARY

- Draw up a planting calendar to help you organize your seeds and seed-starting areas. This will also help you make sure you plant at the right time. Juggling 20 different varieties of vegetables and their needs can be confusing without a plan.

- Get the soil tested so that you have time to make adjustments before planting and add amendments as indicated by the soil test results. Changing the pH can take time, so do it now if necessary.

MARCH

- Plant peas early in the month as soon as the ground can be worked. In Zones 5 to 6, plant peas later in the month.

- Later in the month, sow seeds indoors for warm-season vegetables and herbs such as tomatoes, basil, peppers, and eggplants. Use grow lights if you have the room to keep transplants healthy and avoid stretching.

- In warmer areas, sow seeds of radishes, carrots, lettuce, and dill.

- Sharpen and clean gardening tools such as pruners, spades, and loppers so they're all ready to go when the weather breaks.

APRIL

- Harden off and plant transplants of broccoli, cabbage, spinach, cilantro, mustard greens, and arugula.

- In cooler areas, sow seeds of radishes, carrots, lettuce, dill, and beets.

- Cut back perennial herbs when new growth appears and clean out any other lingering plants and debris from the winter. Add to the compost pile.

- Harvest three-year-old asparagus and fertilize younger asparagus plants.

MAY

- Plant warm-weather vegetables and herbs such as tomatoes, peppers, and basil as soon as soil temperatures are at least 65 degrees Fahrenheit and nighttime temperatures are consistently above 60 degrees. Gardeners in warmer areas will be able to plant earlier in the month. Gardeners in cool areas will have to wait until Memorial Day.

- Thin cool-season vegetables. Toss the young shoots into spring salads.

JUNE

- Harvest summer squash daily. Fruits are most tender when the flower bud has just barely dried up and fallen off. Do not let the fruits linger on the vine. Baseball bat-sized zucchini aren't good for much beyond compost.

- Scout for pests frequently. Small problems can become large problems overnight. Catching problems early can allow you to use minimally invasive remedies and avoid scorched-earth solutions. For example: use water to blast away aphid populations instead of a broader spectrum insecticide. Trap slugs with beer poured into jar lids and sunk into the soil near plant stems. You can also sprinkle diatomaceous earth around plants to prevent slug damage.

- Pinch tomato suckers to keep one central stem growing and the plant channeling energy into fewer, larger fruits.

- Side-dress vegetables with organic slow-release fertilizer. Plants are really starting to take off now and can use the extra nutrient boost.

- Cut lavender to dry. Harvest flower stalks just before the flowers open. Tie them tightly in bundles and hang them upside-down to dry. These little "wands" make great holiday gifts or additions to packages.

JULY

- Water, water, water! If you plan to go out of town, arrange for someone to water your plants and show them how. Make them count to five on each plant. When you're home you might have to water twice a day. Soaker hoses and drip irrigation become invaluable during the long, hot days of summer. If you see blossom end rot in tomato and pepper plants, double down on watering efforts and mulch around the plants to keep the soil moist. Blossom end rot can be caused by calcium deficiencies, but the more common cause is a wet/dry/wet/dry cycle in the soil.

- Keep herbs groomed by cutting off flowers as they appear. You want to encourage the plants to channel energy into producing fragrant leaves, not flowers. By this time, cilantro plants will have bolted, and you can pull them up and compost. Dill is likely flowering, but leave those plants to provide nectar sources for pollinators. If you want to save the seeds for pickles, let the seeds begin to dry on the plant. Then pick the entire plant and hang it upside-down to dry over a clean sheet. The seeds will fall off, and you can collect them.

- Enjoy infused water made with fresh herbs, fruits, and vegetables from the garden. Favorite combinations include watermelon/basil, pineapple/jalepeno, strawberry/basil, cucumber/mint, and more. Experiment! Let the fresh ingredients steep in the ice water for a few hours before drinking.

AUGUST

- Sow seeds of carrots, broccoli, parsnips, cabbage, kale, spinach, arugula, and other cool-season vegetables directly into the garden. Make sure the soil stays moist as they are germinating. This will be your fall and early winter vegetable harvest.

SEPTEMBER

- Spread the compost that's been cooking all summer into the vegetable garden and work it into the soil. This will prep the beds for fall gardening.

- Take cuttings from herbs to grow indoors during the winter. Basil, mint, and sage are good candidates for windowsill gardens. You can dig up a little clump of chives to keep growing indoors. Parsley is easy to grow from seed indoors.

- Harvest the last of the tomatoes before the first frost and bring them in to ripen on the windowsill.

OCTOBER

- Harvest cool-season vegetables such as lettuce, radishes, beets, broccoli, kale, and cabbage. Leave some carrots, kale, and Brussels sprouts in the garden to harvest throughout the fall.

- Plant garlic.

- Sow seeds for cover crops in empty areas of the garden. Even in raised beds, cover crops can prevent soil erosion and add nutrients to the soil once they're mowed and turned under. Peas, fava beans, cereal rye, and annual ryegrass are good choices.

- Rebuild the compost pile with the last of the clippings from the lawn and all of the leaves that have started fall. If you can, run over the leaves with the mower once to chop them up. Layer green materials (vegetables pulled up from the garden, grass clippings) with brown materials (leaves, shredded newspaper).

NOVEMBER

- Continue harvesting vegetables left in "cold storage."

- Mulch vegetables with leaves, pine straw, or another lightweight material. (Do not cover with plastic.)

DECEMBER

- Use herbs from your windowsill garden and stored onions and winter squashes in holiday recipes.

- Browse seed catalogs and make notes for next year.

- Did you can any pickles, salsa, spaghetti sauce, peaches, or other edibles this summer? Make some personalized labels and give them out as gifts for the holidays.

VINES
for the Mid-Atlantic

There's an undeniable image of romance connected with vining plants. Arbors covered with roses and pergolas dripping with honeysuckle or jasmine vines conjure confessions of love and longing. As a practical matter, integrating vines into the landscape leads the eye up from ground level to eye level and above, with less mass and space than a shrub or small tree would.

There are annual, edible, and perennial/woody vines that all add interest in the landscape and serve different purposes. Many tropical vines have spectacular flowers and even though you can only enjoy them for a season (unless you want to overwinter them), they're worth the effort if you want something unique in the garden.

SELECTING VINES

Are you looking for vines to cover something unsightly in the yard? What about vertical interest in a container garden? Want to add height to the perennial garden or some color near the front porch? Do you need an especially vigorous groundcover? There are vines that will cover (pun intended) each of these needs. Because vines grow fast and take over, make sure you choose the right one for the place you're growing it. Here are some ideas for using the vines described in this book.

ANNUAL VINES FOR QUICK COLOR & CONTAINER GARDENS
- Allamanda
- Hummingbird vine
- Hyacinth bean
- Mandevilla
- Moon vine
- Morning glory

GROUNDCOVER VINES
- Boston ivy
- False hydrangea vine
- Hops
- Virginia creeper

SPECIMEN VINES
- Allamanda (annual)
- American wisteria
- Clematis
- Climbing rose
- False hydrangea vine
- Maypop
- Moon vine
- Sweet autumn clematis
- Hydrangea vine

LARGE VINES FOR SCREENING
- Boston ivy
- Coral vine
- Dutchman's pipe
- Five-leaf akebia
- Hardy kiwi
- Honeysuckle
- Hops
- Trumpet vine
- Virginia creeper

EDIBLES
- Grape
- Hardy kiwi
- Maypop

VINES WITH FALL COLOR
- Grape
- Hops
- Virginia creeper

PLANTING

Plant annual vines in the spring after the last frost. Hyacinth beans, morning glory vines, and hummingbird vines are easy to grow from seed. Mandevilla and allamanda vines are tropicals, available only as transplants from the garden center. Plant those after nights have warmed up to consistently be above 60 degrees Fahrenheit.

Plant perennial and woody vines in the fall, when possible. They'll roar out of the gate in the spring, raring to grow.

FERTILIZING

Fertilizer needs vary quite a bit by individual plants. Most vines will benefit from the application of a balanced (10-10-10) multipurpose fertilizer in the spring. Any other nutrient requirements are listed on individual plant profiles.

WATERING

Annual vines require more frequent watering than established perennial or woody vines. Water annual vines on the same schedule you'd use for bedding plants. Water woody vines on a similar schedule to what you'd use for shrubs. Perennial, primarily non-woody vines (such as clematis) can be watered on the same schedule you'd use for perennial plants. (Individual water needs are listed on the plant profiles.)

PRUNING

Pruning is potentially the most confusing, but most important part of caring for vines. Prune at the wrong time and you won't get any flowers. Luckily, vines are, by their very nature, vigorous, so if you overprune, they'll grow back. You might just sacrifice a season of interest.

Reasons for pruning:
- Stimulate new growth
- Remove old or diseased growth
- Control size and spread
- Guide the shape of the vine. Woody vines such as roses can require pruning to train along a wall or trellis.

Vines grown for foliage only (such as Virginia creeper, Boston ivy, or hops) can be pruned nearly anytime—winter, spring, or summer. Avoid pruning in the fall. You don't want to stimulate growth that will cause the plant to push new, frost-tender growth in the fall.

Flowering vines should be pruned after flowering to be on the safe side. Individual timing for pruning is listed in plant profiles.

TRAINING

Unless you're growing a vine as a groundcover, you'll have to do a little bit of training to get it to grow in the direction you want. The way you train the vine or secure it to the support structure depends on how the vine grows. Some vines naturally twine around a structure, but they don't have tendrils that will grab onto the structure. Other vines twine, but have tendrils that will cling to cracks or wrap around small twigs or the boards in a lattice. "Clinging" vines have aerial roots that grip the support structure. Ivy and climbing hydrangeas are clinging vines. Sprawling vines, such as climbing roses, just grow without any sort of natural inclination to attach. Those need the most intervention in order to grow in the desired direction.

CLEMATIS PRUNING GROUPS

Clematis vines are potentially the most confusing to prune. You really do need to prune these at the proper time or you'll never see them bloom. Clematis are generally labeled in pruning groups 1/A, 2/B, or 3/C. (Labeling via number or letter depends on where you're sourcing the plants.)

Pruning Group 1/A: Blooms in the spring on last year's growth.

Vigorous cultivars in this group can be pruned after flowering. Slow-growing plants should be pruned as little as possible. Remove dead or diseased growth in the spring after flowering.

Pruning Group 2/B: Blooms in late spring or early summer on last year's group, and periodically throughout the year on new growth.

This is the most confusing group. Regardless of when you prune, you'll probably sacrifice some flowers. The easiest way to deal with these plants is to cut back half of the plant stems after the spring flower every other year, alternating years.

Pruning Group 3/C: Blooms in late summer or fall on new growth.

These are the easiest to prune! Cut back in the spring after new growth emerges. Autumn clematis is in this group, and it benefits from a hard chop in the spring. Cut back to 12 inches above the ground.

HOW VINES ATTACH

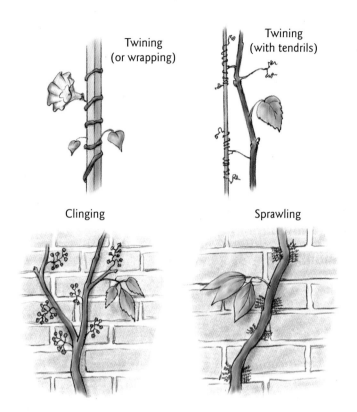

Twining (or wrapping)

Twining (with tendrils)

Clinging

Sprawling

Annual vines will grow over an arbor or can be trained and encouraged to grow up a trellis or lattice in a container. Larger, perennial and woody vines are better off trained over a fence, up a wall, or also on an arbor. You can get a climbing rose to cover a wall by making a wire lattice onto which you can anchor the stems.

Keep a pair of pruners and a row of rubber-coated wire in your toolbox so that you can anchor the vines to the trellis or support system.

PEST CONTROL

Most vines have few pest problems. Powdery mildew can be an issue during hot, humid summers in areas with low air circulation. Japanese beetles and blackspot can plague climbing roses. Try to avoid watering the leaves of all vines, which will cut down dramatically on any bacterial or fungal problems. Because vines grow so fast, unless the problem is systemic, the easiest way to deal with it is to cut out the affected part.

ALLAMANDA
Allamanda cathartica

Why It's Special—Allamanda is one of the best vines for adding height and interest to the summer container garden. Allamanda is a tropical vine with yellow, trumpet-shaped flowers. It's a fast grower. Put a trellis or obelisk in a large pot, plant allamanda, and let it go to town. **Caution:** All parts of the plant are poisonous.

How to Plant & Grow—Plant transplants or gallon containers outside when nights are warm (over 60 degrees Fahrenheit). If you want to overwinter this as a houseplant, plant it in a large pot. You can set the pot on casters to make it easier to roll in and out of the house.

Care & Problems—Allamanda vine needs to be secured to the support structure. It does not have aerial roots or tendrils to naturally cling. Keep the soil evenly moist. You can prune to encourage branching. Feed once a month with liquid fertilizer. Bring inside when temperatures drop below 60 degrees Fahrenheit.

Bloom Color—Yellow

Growth Habit—Twining; moderately aggressive; needs to be guided to get started growing up support structure

Seasonal Interest—Summer, flowers

Hardiness—10–11 (grow as annual or overwinter)

Water Needs—Medium

AMERICAN WISTERIA
Wisteria frutescens

Why It's Special—The invasive Chinese wisteria is what most people think of when they think "wisteria," but American wisteria is just as lovely and not at all invasive. It has fragrant flowers and sweet pea-like purple flowers in clusters that look somewhat like bunches of grapes when viewed from afar. Flowers attract butterflies looking for nectar.

How to Plant & Grow—Plant in full sun in moist, well-drained soil. Protect American wisteria from north winds and late summer frosts. Plant near a sturdy fence post or trellis. This vine twines clockwise around its support system.

Care & Problems—Use heavy-duty garden twine or coated wire to tie American wisteria vine to a post or trellis and to help encourage twining. Wisteria blooms on old wood. Prune after flowering to control size and promote branching. In winter, prune branches back so there are three to five buds left per branch. This is where next year's flowers will bloom. Fertilize in spring. Do not transplant.

Bloom Color—Lavender

Growth Habit—Moderate; twining; needs help to get started on a support structure

Seasonal Interest—Summer, flowers

Hardiness—5–9

Water Needs—Medium

BOSTON IVY
Parthenocissus tricuspidata

Why It's Special—This is the vine that gives the Ivy League schools of the East Coast their well-known nickname. It is an aggressive, hardy vine that climbs with holdfasts or aerial rootlets that grab onto any surface. It's best to grow this one on brick or concrete surfaces or specially built sturdy trellises. It has great fall color!

How to Plant & Grow—Plant in full sun to partial shade. It needs to be given a sturdy building or trellis to climb (or to be trained as a groundcover). Boston ivy tolerates poor soil conditions, so it is a good groundcover for tough spots. You can also use it to establish a screen where it's difficult to get other plants to grow. Water to establish.

Care & Problems—Prune to control size as needed up until August. (Late summer pruning can result in growth that is not cold hardy.) Water during extreme drought to keep plants from becoming stressed and susceptible to disease problems. This vine does not need extra fertilizer.

Bloom Color—Not grown for flowers

Growth Habit—Aggressive; clinging aerial rootlets

Seasonal Interest—Red-burgundy fall color

Hardiness—4–8

Water Needs—Low

CLEMATIS
Clematis cultivars

Why It's Special—Clematis vines have some of the most beautiful flowers you'll see on anything in the garden. Most of these are cultivars and hybrids, some of which have been bred and selected, others of which are sprouts off other plants. Give them a place of prominence; they are true specimen plants.

How to Plant & Grow—Clematis grow best in well-drained, but evenly and consistently moist soil where the top of a plant can grow in full sun and the bottom/roots will be shaded. Mulch the roots to keep them cool. Clematis require support to grow. Provide a trellis or obelisk that the plant's tendrils can twine around.

Care & Problems—Pruning is the most difficult thing about growing clematis. When you purchase a plant, make note of which pruning group it is in and then prune according to instructions on page 181.

Bloom Color—Varies: purple, pink, white, blue, fuchsia, burgundy, red, and multicolor

Growth Habit—Twining and tendrils

Seasonal Interest—Spring and summer flowers

Hardiness—Depends on cultivar. Most hardy to Zones 4–5

Water Needs—Medium

CLEMATIS, ARMAND

Clematis armandii

Why It's Special—This evergreen clematis is hardy in Zones 7 to 10, so that's not the entire Mid-Atlantic, but enough of the range that if you can grow it, you might want to try. It has glossy evergreen leaves and fragrant, white, star-shaped flowers that bloom in early spring. It's a fast grower, so will cover up an empty trellis quickly. A bonus: it's deer resistant.

How to Plant & Grow—Plant in full sun to partial shade. This fast grower needs support or something to climb over. Mulch the roots to keep them cool and protected. Water to establish.

Care & Problems—Like all clematis, the top grows best in full sun, but the roots need to be kept cool and protected. Prune this climber after it blooms. Water regularly during times of drought. It does a good job of climbing on its own, but might have to be guided a bit. Keep the coated wire handy. It's fairly pest-free.

Bloom Color—White

Growth Habit—Climbs with tendrils

Seasonal Interest—Evergreen leaves; white flowers in early spring

Hardiness—7–10

Water Needs—Medium

CLEMATIS, SWEET AUTUMN

Clematis terniflora

Why It's Special—Sweet autumn clematis is one of the easiest types of clematis to grow. It is a vigorous deciduous vine that flowers on new growth from late summer through early fall. Cascades of white, fragrant, star-shaped flowers cover the vines, adding interest to the garden before everything goes dormant for winter. Bees, butterflies, and other pollinators love this plant. The flowers turn into plumy, feathery seedheads.

How to Plant & Grow—Plant transplants in full sun to partial shade in moist, rich, well-drained soil. Like all clematis, this one grows best with full sun on the top of the plant, but moist shade at the root zone. Mulch to keep the roots cool and to conserve moisture. Water to establish and provide a sturdy trellis or fence for climbing.

Care & Problems—You almost cannot kill this plant, even if you want to. Prune back hard to 12 inches above ground in spring when the vines start growing. Water during dry periods. It's fairly pest-free.

Bloom Color—White

Growth Habit—Twining, fast-growing, aggressive

Seasonal Interest—Late summer to fall, flowers

Hardiness—5–9

Water Needs—Medium

CLIMBING ROSE

Rosa spp. and cultivars

Why It's Special—Climbing roses are really just plants that will grow long branches that can be tied onto a frame or trellis. Most climbing roses bloom on old wood, so make sure you select one with flower buds that will be cold hardy in your area.

How to Plant & Grow—Plant bare-root or container plants outside after the last frost in full sun where the plant can be trained or tied to a vertical support—a wall, trellis, post, or arbor. Water to establish and mulch the roots. Refer to bare-root planting instructions on page 104.

Care & Problems—Let climbing roses grow the first couple of years and get some size on them before you start pruning. After two or three years, you can start pruning to control size after the plants bloom. Pruning will also stimulate branching, so you'll end up with more flowers. Watch out for typical rose pests and diseases. Periodically remove old canes back to the ground.

Bloom Color—Pink, white, red, lavender, multicolor

Growth Habit—Tall and shrubby. Must be tied to support structure.

Seasonal Interest—Summer

Hardiness—Depends on the variety

Water Needs—Medium

CORAL VINE
Antigonon leptopus

Why It's Special—Coral vine is a fast-growing vine that is perennial in warmer areas but can be grown as a flowering annual in the Mid-Atlantic. It blooms with cascades of pink flowers in the late summer to early fall. It tolerates poor growing conditions. Use it as a quick screen to hide unattractive fixtures in the garden.

How to Plant & Grow—Plant in the ground or in a container after the last frost, when soil temperatures have warmed to at least 60 degrees Fahrenheit. Provide a trellis or something sturdy for this plant to climb. Coral vine is not picky about soil type and will grow nearly anywhere.

Care & Problems—Water regularly. Once a plant is established, it is more drought tolerant. It will grow to be quite large, but you can't hack on it too much if you want it to bloom. At the end of the season, cut down and compost the plant. It's relatively pest-free.

Bloom Color—Pink

Growth Habit—Climbs via tendrils. Aggressive growth habit.

Seasonal Interest—Flowers in late summer to fall

Hardiness—8–10

Water Needs—Medium

DUTCHMAN'S PIPE
Aristolochia macrophylla

Why It's Special—The Dutchman's pipe vine has amazingly interesting flowers—they look a little like a tobacco pipe with a very large and flashy bowl. Flowers are checkered burgundy and white. The real attraction of this poisonous plant is the huge heart-shaped leaves—up to 12 inches across. The vine is a vigorous grower that can cover an entire trellis in a summer.

How to Plant & Grow—You can grow this vine from seed (planted in fall) or from transplants. Plant transplants outside in full sun to partial shade after the last frost. Water to establish. Provide a large, sturdy structure for Dutchman's pipe to cover.

Care & Problems—This is a fairly problem-free vine. The main issue is that it gets to be huge. Chop it back if it outgrows its allocated space. It's a main food source for the pipevine swallowtail butterfly, so if you see caterpillars munching, leave them alone. Prune in late winter.

Bloom Color—Burgundy spotted

Growth Habit—Twining with an aggressive nature

Seasonal Interest—Summer, leaves and flowers

Hardiness—4–8

Water Needs—Medium to low

FALSE HYDRANGEA VINE
Schizophragma hydrangeoides

Why It's Special—Sometimes called the Japanese hydrangea vine, false hydrangea vine *is* part of the hydrangea family, but it is not the climbing hydrangea species. It is a large woody vine that can grow up to 50 feet tall and 30 feet across. It blooms in midsummer with white lacecap-type flowers. 'Roseum' is a cultivar with pink flowers.

How to Plant & Grow—Plant transplants or gallon containers in partial to full shade in moist, well-drained soil. False hydrangea vines can grow to be quite large, but you can prune them to maintain size. These vines cling with aerial rootlets, so allow them to grow up trees and brick or concrete structures only, not wood, unless you've built a trellis or arbor specifically for the purpose of supporting this plant.

Care & Problems—Hydrangea vine blooms on new wood, so prune during late winter or early spring. Water during droughts. It's fairly pest-free.

Bloom Color—White or pink (depending on cultivar)

Growth Habit—Woody vine with adhesive rootlets. Moderate grower.

Seasonal Interest—Summer, flowers; fall, yellow leaf color (not always showy)

Hardiness—5–8

Water Needs—Medium

HARDY KIWI
Actinidia arguta

Why It's Special—This vigorous deciduous vine has attractive, medium green leaves; creamy white flowers in early summer; and delicious, grape-sized edible fruits in fall. If you have the space and a sturdy trellis to grow it, it's well worth the effort. It's a great vine if you need to cover a wall or fence, or use as a screen.

How to Plant & Grow—Plant transplants in full sun to partial shade after the last frost. Hardy kiwi needs deep, fertile soil. Work the soil and add compost prior to planting. You need at least one male plant with one or more female plants in order to get fruit.

Care & Problems—Hardy kiwi is mostly pest-free plant. At planting, prune back to three to four buds. Let them grow to midsummer and select one as the central vine growing up the support, removing the others. Allow the main shoot to grow up the trellis. At the beginning of its second year, prune back the tip to encourage branching. At the beginning of its third year, train as a cordon (the way you'd prune grape vines).

Bloom Color—White

Growth Habit—Aggressive, twining, fast-growing

Seasonal Interest—Summer, flowers; fall, fruits

Hardiness—3–8

Water Needs—Medium

HONEYSUCKLE, TRUMPET
Lonicera sempervirens

Why It's Special—Trumpet honeysuckle is a native, easy-care vine that adds lots of color to the early summer garden. Its flowers are salmon-pink on the outside with yellow inside. Birds, hummingbirds, and butterflies are attracted to its blooms. Not only is it pretty, it's an important wildlife food source in the garden. However, even though it is an important plant for wildlife, it is deer resistant. It's also one of a few plants that will grow well under a black walnut tree, should you require that.

How to Plant & Grow—Plant transplants in full sun in moist, well-drained soil after the last frost. This vine is adaptable to a wide range of growing conditions, but flowers best in full sun. Water to establish and provide something for it to climb.

Care & Problems—After planting, help trumpet honeysuckle climb by threading the stems through its supports. It will catch on quickly. This plant blooms on old growth, so prune after flowering. Keep the soil moist.

Bloom Color—Salmon-pink and yellow

Growth Habit—Semi-woody twining stems; moderately aggressive

Seasonal Interest—Flowers, early spring

Hardiness—4–9

Water Needs—Medium

HOPS
Humulus lupulus

Why It's Special—Hops is a perennial, deciduous, fast-growing vine with papery, showy, cone-like flowers that cover the female plants in fall. You can train it over arbors, up walls, and onto fences. Because the foliage dies back in winter, it never gets too aggressive. 'Aureus' has chartreuse leaves in spring. Flowers have a piney scent and are attractive to butterflies.

How to Plant & Grow—Plant seeds in full sun in deep, moist, well-drained soils after the threat of frost has passed. You can also start from purchased transplants. Female plants are the ones that produce showy flowers, so purchase those (as seeds or transplants) if you can. This vine is a fast grower, so provide a large trellis or fence for it to scramble over.

Care & Problems—Hops vine is fairly pest-free and easy to grow. Plant it and let it go. Just keep it watered during droughty times. Cut back to the ground in winter after the plant is fully dormant.

Bloom Color—Green and papery

Growth Habit—Aggressive; twining with tendrils

Seasonal Interest—Summer, leaves; fall, flowers

Hardiness—3–8

Water Needs—Medium

HUMMINGBIRD VINE
Ipomoea quamoclit

Why It's Special—My grandma always grew hummingbird vine over the arbor leading to her flower garden, so I have fond memories of it. Hummingbird vine is also sometimes called "cypress vine" because the leaves resemble those of bald cypress trees. This is a fast-growing annual vine native to the tropics. It has tubular-shaped, bright red flowers borne on delicate, wiry stems with ferny leaves. There are white-flowered varieties also.

How to Plant & Grow—It's easy to grow from seed. Soak seeds overnight before planting out in full sun in moist, well-drained soil. Hummingbird vines needs something to climb—best make it something you want covered—otherwise, it will climb anything and everything available, as well as scrambling over nearby grass, flowers—*anything*.

Care & Problems—This plant has few problems. It is vigorous so feel free to chop as needed to keep it inbounds. Water during dry periods. It can go to seed and pop back up all over the garden in subsequent years.

Bloom Color—Red (species), white

Growth Habit—Highly prolific and aggressive during the summer; twining.

Seasonal Interest—Summer, flowers

Hardiness—Annual

Water Needs—Medium

HYACINTH BEAN
Dolichos lablab

Why It's Special—Purple hyacinth beans are annual vines in the legume family. The seeds (beans) are edible only if boiled twice (discarding the water each time). Otherwise, all parts of the plant are poisonous. It is a fast grower with attractive dark green leaves, dark purple stems, purple flowers, and burgundy seedpods. Grow this for its ornamental, not its edible, value. Hyacinth bean is equally at home in the landscape or in containers, provided that you give it a support structure to climb.

How to Plant & Grow—Plant seeds in full sun for the best growth and color. Hyacinth bean needs moderately moist, well-drained soil. It makes a nice accent plant in perennial gardens if it's trained up wire obelisks. Because it's an annual, you don't have to commit.

Care & Problems—It's an easy-care vine but it may need help finding the supports as it first emerges from the ground. Water during dry periods. Tear out and compost plants after the first fall frost.

Bloom Color—Purple

Growth Habit—Fast growing, twining habit

Seasonal Interest—Summer, purple flowers and dark purple "pea" pods

Hardiness—Annual

Water Needs—Medium

HYDRANGEA VINE
Hydrangea anomala ssp. *petiolaris*

Why It's Special—Climbing hydrangeas are such unusual plants. You don't expect to see the ubiquitous flowers of a hydrangea shrub high up in a tree. They're plants that you think should be much harder to grow, based on how pretty they are. These plants can grow to be quite long—growing up to 40 feet in trees. Because they cling with aerial rootlets, they should not be trained to grow on wood houses. Provide an arbor or trellis or allow hydrangea vine to grow up trees, on brick walls, or on concrete structures.

How to Plant & Grow—Plant container-grown plants outside in moist, well-drained soil in full to partial shade. It requires sturdy support. Water to establish.

Care & Problems—This vine has few pest problems. It grows slowly at first, but is vigorous once established. Water during dry periods. You can prune it to encourage branching.

Bloom Color—White

Growth Habit—Woody vines that twine and cling to structures with aerial rootlets

Seasonal Interest—White flowers during summer; fruits in fall

Hardiness—4–8

Water Needs—Medium

MANDEVILLA
Mandevilla × amabilis

Why It's Special—Mandevillas are tropical vines that provide big splashes of color in the summer garden. You can grow them as annuals and compost them at the end of the season or overwinter them inside in a bright, sunny location. *Mandevilla × amabilis* was one of the first, most common mandevilla hybrids available commercially. It has pink, trumpet-shaped flowers and glossy dark green leaves. There are some newer, improved options, including the gorgeous red Sun Parasol® collection.

How to Plant & Grow—Plant container-grown plants in full sun in moist, well-drained soil. Mandevilla plants also grow well in containers. Provide a trellis for the plant to climb. Plant these to dress up the mailbox, a lamp post, or porch railing.

Care & Problems—Keep the soil evenly moist throughout its growing season. Bring inside to overwinter before the last frost. Watch for whiteflies, spider mites, and mealybugs on overwintered plants. Harden off plants and cut back to 12 inches when moving them back outside for summer.

Bloom Color—Pink, white, red

Growth Habit—Twining; moderate

Seasonal Interest—Summer, pink flowers

Hardiness—Annual/tropical

Water Needs—Medium to high

MAYPOP
Passiflora incarnata

Why It's Special—Maypops, also called passionflowers, are fast-growing perennial vines with gorgeous, frilly, purple flowers. They look like they should be growing in a tropical forest, not in the temperate gardens of the Mid-Atlantic. In addition to their beautiful blooms; maypops produce edible fruits (that make a "pop" noise when crushed, lending the plants their common name). These are natives that meander around the forests and fields of the southern United States, but are hardy to Zone 5.

How to Plant & Grow—Plant seeds or transplants in full sun to partial shade after the last frost. Provide an arbor or fence for support. Maypops appreciate help initially finding their support structure. Plant it where you can admire it. Some place these vines close to the front door.

Care & Problems—The maypop is fairly carefree. This is the larval host for the orange Gulf fritillary butterfly, so if you see caterpillars eating the vines, leave them alone.

Bloom Color—Purple

Growth Habit—Climbs via tendrils; fast-growing

Seasonal Interest—Summer, flowers and edible fruit

Hardiness—5–9

Water Needs—Medium

MOON VINE
Ipomoea alba

Why It's Special—Moon vines have white, fragrant, trumpet-shaped flowers that open at dusk, making this the perfect vine to plant around a patio or porch where you enjoy evening cocktails. It's a non-aggressive tender perennial (grown as an annual in the Mid-Atlantic area), so experiment with it. Because it blooms at night, plant it somewhere you'll notice it during its peak hours. It will bloom continuously throughout summer.

How to Plant & Grow—Moon vine is easy to grow from seed; just soak the seeds overnight before planting. Plant in full sun in moist, well-drained soil. Provide a trellis or support for this plant to climb. Because it is tropical, it really takes off once the soil warms up. You can start seeds indoors to get a jump on the season.

Care & Problems—It's fairly easy-care and pest-free. Water during dry periods. If moon vine starts to look messy, pick off the dead flowers.

Bloom Color—White

Growth Habit—Twining vine; fast growth during the summer.

Seasonal Interest—Summer, white flowers

Hardiness—10–12 (grow as an annual)

Water Needs—Medium

MORNING GLORY
Ipomoea tricolor

Why It's Special—I know plenty of people who will not plant morning glories because they can reseed and be obnoxious in the garden. I love the flowers so much, though, that I find a good spot in the corner of the garden and let them go wild. They will bloom from midsummer through the first frost, so you get a lot for your effort and hospitality.

How to Plant & Grow—Plant seeds outside after the last frost. Soak seeds overnight before planting for best results. They need something to climb, and if you don't provide a trellis they will climb whatever is available, including other plants.

Care & Problems—Water during dry periods. This is a fairly pest-free plant, but it can turn into a pest by self-seeding all over the place. If this happens, be vigilant about pulling out seedlings when they sprout the following year—before they take over the garden.

Bloom Color—Shades of white, blue, deep purple, lavender, red, fuchsia, and multicolor

Growth Habit—Aggressive twining during the summer

Seasonal Interest—Summer, flowers open in the morning

Hardiness—Annual

Water Needs—Medium to low

TRUMPET VINE
Campsis radicans

Why It's Special—Trumpet vine is a deciduous woody flowering vine that is native to the eastern United States. It is the larval host for the sphinx moth, and butterflies are drawn to its scarlet-red, trumpet-shaped flowers that cover the plant in midsummer. It is aggressive, so it's easy to grow, but can take over if allowed to grow out-of-bounds. Use it to cover the fence line in your backyard. Keep it out of the perennial gardens unless you're growing a cultivar that's better behaved than the species.

How to Plant & Grow—Plant outside after the last frost in moist, well-drained soil in full sun. This vine needs sturdy support and will cover fences, trellises, and trees if allowed.

Care & Problems—Trumpet vine is drought tolerant once established and does not need extra water. Prune back in spring. It blooms on new growth, so you don't have to worry about cutting off the flowers. It tolerates poor soil.

Bloom Color—Scarlet-red, orange, apricot (depends on cultivar)

Growth Habit—Aggressive; climbs with aerial rootlets

Seasonal Interest—Summer, flowers

Hardiness—4–9

Water Needs—Medium

VIRGINIA CREEPER
Parthenocissus quinquefolia

Why It's Special—Many people think of Virginia creeper as a weed or wild plant, but it is actually quite utilitarian in the landscape. It's easy to grow and tolerant of a wide variety of growing conditions. It has reliably good fall color. Two newer cultivars, Red Wall® and Yellow Wall®, offer even better fall color than the species. It's not poison ivy, and it's not a weed.

How to Plant & Grow—Plant after the last frost in full sun to partial shade. It can be grown as a climbing vine or a groundcover. To get the plants that exhibit the best fall color, you'll need to purchase plants from a garden center or home-improvement store. Water to establish and provide good support.

Care & Problems—This plant is ridiculously easy to grow. Water during droughty periods and trim back as needed to keep it in its place.

Bloom Color—Grow for foliage and fall foliage color

Growth Habit—Aggressive; climbs with tendrils and adhesive disks

Seasonal Interest—Fall color

Hardiness—3–9

Water Needs—Medium

VINES MONTH-BY-MONTH

JANUARY

- Water evergreen vines if you're experiencing lots of sunny, windy days with the temperature below freezing. These conditions can cause drying and winter burn.

- Check on tropical annual vines that you are overwintering indoors such as allamanda vines and mandevilla vines. Pick off dead leaves and check the soil to make sure plants are staying barely moist. If whiteflies are a problem, put the pots in the shower and give them a cold soaking.

FEBRUARY

- Apply repellents to vines growing outdoors that show signs of damage from deer.

- Prune clematis vines in Group 3/C (late summer and fall bloomers). Cut vigorous bloomers and growers to 12 inches above ground. (See page 181 for more on pruning clematis types.)

- Continue to water evergreen vines if they are showing signs of winter stress.

MARCH

- Construct new trellises, arbors, and other vining support systems to introduce new vines and climbers into the garden. Match the structure to the plant you intend to grow on it. Climbing hydrangeas are quite large, woody, aggressive vines and require sturdy structures. You can get away with a much thinner arbor for an annual such as hummingbird vine.

- Prune Boston ivy, Virginia creeper, honeysuckle, trumpet creeper, and hardy kiwi to control size.

APRIL

- Start annual vines from seed indoors. Soak morning glory seeds overnight before planting or nick the seed coat with nail clippers. Most vines do not like to be disturbed, so start them in containers that are large enough to hold the plants until you move them into the garden.

- Reapply repellents on vines that show signs of animal damage.

MAY

- Move tropical vines that you've overwintered indoors outside this month. Harden them off the same way you would transplants that you started indoors. Keep them in a sheltered location for a week or two and then move to their seasonal home in the garden. (Only place outside when the forecast shows no frost in the long-range predictions.)

- Train new growth of vines using plastic-coated wire. Anchor the vine stems to the supports. Vines are starting to grow fast this month, so this is a twice-weekly activity, if not more frequent. Remember—climbing roses are not natural climbers, they're more like really tall woody plants. They will need to be tied to and woven through support structures.

- Shop for container-grown perennial and tropical vines. Garden centers and home-improvement stores will be packed with new selections right now.

- Plant new vines in the garden, including new tropical vines. Move annual vines that you started indoors outside. Plant seeds of scarlet runner bean, hyacinth bean, and other annual vines directly into the garden if you did not start the seeds indoors.

JUNE

- Mulch around clematis plants to keep the roots cool. Clematis are an interesting group of plants that need cool, shaded roots but must have full sun on the leaves in order to bloom.

- Prune early-blooming clematis (Group 1/A) after they finish flowering.

- Apply repellents to any vines that show signs of being eaten by deer or mammals.

- Thin annual vines. Morning glory and hummingbird vines have a high germination rate, and sometimes you end up with more plants than you bargained for. Thin to 6- to 12-inch spacing so that the plants don't take over the garden.

JULY

- Water vines if you're experiencing hot, dry weather.

- Deadhead climbing roses as they finish blooming. This is also a good time to renewal prune climbing roses so that they have a chance to grow new wood and let it harden before winter. Remove the oldest canes back to the ground. Trim back growth on newer canes, leaving stems that are larger than your pinky finger.

- Prune back annual vines that are out of control in the garden. Morning glory vines and hummingbird vines can be quite aggressive. They can handle being chopped. They'll grow back out.

- Fertilize vines growing in containers with liquid organic fertilizer. By this point in the summer, their root systems are getting quite large and taking up most of the pot. Frequent watering will have leached any available nutrients from the soil.

AUGUST

- Prune perennial vines to maintain size, shape, and to keep them from escaping your preferred location.

- Continue watering if you are experiencing a droughty summer. Soak the soil around the plants deeply at least twice per week. Watering deeply but infrequently will help plants establish deeper root systems.

- Lightly prune clematis in Group 2/B after the second season bloom. This group should be pruned mostly for shape. Remove any dead or diseased sections from other clematis plants.

SEPTEMBER

- Bring tender tropical vines inside for the winter. Re-pot them and set them inside the garage next to a sunny window or in the greenhouse.

- Plant new vines in the garden. Place the support structure at the time you plant the vine, even if major growth won't happen until next season. It's better not to disturb the plants after they're well-rooted. Water to establish before the ground freezes.

OCTOBER

- Apply repellents to any evergreen vines to keep deer from feasting. Make sure to change the repellent every few months, as the deer will get used to it and it will stop being as effective.

- Pull up and compost annual vines that have been killed back by a frost.

- Continue watering newly planted vines.

- Do not prune this month. Pruning will stimulate tender growth that doesn't have time to harden off before freezing weather.

NOVEMBER

- Mulch around the roots of vining plants to protect them throughout the winter.

- Use a shrub rake to remove leaves that might have become trapped in and amongst plant stems. Leaves can hold moisture, which leads to fungal and bacterial problems in plant stems.

DECEMBER

- Take a walk around the garden and determine where you could plant evergreen vines for more winter interest next year.

- Snip pieces of evergreen vines for use in winter and holiday decorations and flower arrangements.

GLOSSARY

Acidic soil: On a soil pH scale of 0 to 14, acidic soil has a pH lower than 7.0. Most garden plants prefer a soil a bit on the acidic side.

Afternoon sun: A garden receiving afternoon sun typically has full sun from 1 to 5 p.m. daily, with more shade during the morning hours.

Alkaline soil: On a soil pH scale of 0 to 14, alkaline soil has a pH higher than 7.0. Many desert plants thrive in slightly alkaline soils.

Annual: A plant that germinates (sprouts), flowers, and dies within one year or season (spring, summer, winter, or fall).

Bacillus thuringiensis **(Bt):** An organic pest control based on naturally occurring soil bacteria, often used to control harmful insects like cutworms, leaf rollers, and webworms.

Balled and burlapped (B&B): Describes plants that have been grown in field nursery rows, dug up with their soil intact, wrapped with burlap, and tied with twine. Most of the plants sold balled and burlapped are large evergreen plants and deciduous trees.

Bare root: Bare-root plants are those that are shipped dormant with the soil around their roots removed beforehand. Roses are often shipped bare root.

Beneficial insect: An insect that performs valuable services such as pollination and pest control. Ladybugs, soldier beetles, and some bees are examples.

Biennial: A plant that blooms during its second year and then dies.

Bolting: When a plant switches from leaf growth to producing flowers and seeds. Bolting often occurs quite suddenly and is usually undesirable, because the plant usually dies shortly after bolting.

Brown materials: A part of a well-balanced compost pile, brown materials include high-carbon materials such as brown leaves and grass, woody plant stems, dryer lint, and sawdust.

Bud: An undeveloped shoot nestled between the leaf and the stem that will eventually produce a flower or plant branch.

Bulb: A plant with a large, rounded underground storage organ formed by the plant stem and leaves. Examples are tulips, daffodils, and hyacinths. Bulbs that flower in spring are typically planted in fall.

Cane: A stem on a fruit shrub. Usually blackberry or raspberry stems are called canes, but blueberry stems can also be referred to as canes.

Central leader: The center trunk of a fruit tree.

Chilling hours: Hours when the air temperature is below 45 degrees Fahrenheit . Chilling hours are related to fruit production.

Common name: A name that is generally used to identify a plant in a particular regions, as opposed to its scientific or botanical name, which is standard throughout the world. For example, the common name for *Echinacea purpurea* is "purple coneflower."

Contact herbicide: An herbicide that kills only the part of the plant that it touches, such as the leaves or the stems.

Container: Any pot or vessel that is used for planting. Containers can be ceramic, clay, steel, or plastic—or a teacup, bucket, or barrel.

Container garden: A garden that is created primarily by growing plants in containers instead of in the ground.

Container grown: Describes a plant that is grown, sold, and shipped while in a pot.

Cool-season annual: A flowering plant that thrives during cooler months, such as snapdragon and pansy.

Cool-season vegetable: A vegetable that thrives during cooler months, such as spinach, broccoli, and peas.

Cover crop: A plant that is grown specifically to enrich the soil, prevent erosion, suppress weeds, and control pests and diseases.

Cross-pollinate: To transfer pollen from one plant to another plant.

Dappled shade: Bright shade created by high tree branches or tree foliage, where patches of sunlight and shade intermingle.

Day-neutral plant: A plant that flowers when it reaches a certain size, regardless of the day length.

Deadhead: To remove dead flowers in order to encourage further bloom and to prevent the plant from going to seed.

Deciduous plant: A plants that loses its leaves seasonally, typically in fall or early winter.

Diatomaceous earth: A natural control for snails, slugs, flea beetles, and other garden pests. It consists of ground-up fossilized remains of sea creatures.

Dormancy: The period when plants stop growing in order to conserve energy. This happens naturally and seasonally, usually in winter.

Drip line: The ground area under the outer circumference of tree branches. This is where most roots draw water up into the tree.

Dwarf: In the context of fruit gardening, a dwarf fruit tree is a tree that grows no taller than 10 feet tall, and is usually a dwarf as a result of the rootstock of the tree.

Evergreen: A plant that keeps its leaves year-round, rather than dropping them seasonally.

Floricane: A second-year cane on a blackberry or raspberry shrub. Floricanes are fruit bearing.

Flower stalk: The stem that supports the flower and elevates it so that insects can reach the flower and pollinate it.

Four-tine claw: Also called a cultivator, this hand tool typically has three to four curved tines and is used to break up soil clods or lumps before planting and to rake soil amendments into garden beds.

Frost: Ice crystals that form when the temperature falls below freezing (32 degrees Fahrenheit).

Full sun: Describes areas of the garden that receive direct sunlight for six to eight hours a day or more, with no shade.

Fungicide: A chemical compound used to destroy or control fungi or fungal spores.

Gallon container: A standard nursery-sized container for plants, roughly equivalent to a gallon container of milk.

Garden fork: A garden implement with a long handle and short tines used for loosening and turning soil.

Garden lime: A soil amendment that lowers soil acidity and raises the pH.

Garden soil: The existing soil in a garden bed; it is generally evaluated by its nutrient content and texture. Garden soil is also sold as a bagged item at garden centers and home-improvement stores.

Germination: The process by which a plant emerges from a seed or a spore.

Grafted tree: A tree composed of two parts: the top, or scion, which bears fruit, and the bottom, or rootstock.

Graft union: The place on a fruit tree trunk where the rootstock and the scion have been joined.

Granular fertilizer: Fertilizer that comes in a dry pellet-like form, rather than a liquid or powder.

Grass clippings: The parts of grass that are removed when mowing. Clippings are a valuable source of nitrogen for the lawn or the compost pile.

Green materials: An essential element in composting that includes grass clippings, kitchen scraps, and manure and provides valuable nitrogen in the pile. Green materials are high in nitrogen.

Hand pruners: An important hand tool that consists of two sharp blades that perform a scissoring motion. Used for light pruning, clipping, and cutting.

Hardening off: The process of slowly acclimating seedlings and young plants grown in an indoor environment to the outdoors.

Hardiness zone map: A map listing average annual minimum temperature ranges of a particular area. This information is helpful in determining appropriate plants for the garden. North America is divided into 11 separate hardiness zones.

Hard rake: A tool with a long handle and rigid tines at the bottom. It is great for moving a variety of garden debris such as soil, mulch, leaves, and pebbles.

Hedging: The practice of trimming a line of plants to create a solid mass for privacy or garden definition.

Heirloom: A plant that was more commonly grown during earlier periods of human history, but is not widely used in modern commercial agriculture.

Hoe: A long-handled garden tool with a short, narrow, flat steel blade. It is used for breaking up hard soil and removing weeds.

Hose breaker: A device that screws onto the end of a garden hose to disperse the flow of water pressure from the hose.

Host plant: A plant grown to feed caterpillars that will eventually morph into butterflies.

Hybrid: A plant that is produced by crossing two genetically different plants. Hybrids often have desirable characteristics such as disease resistance.

Irrigation: A system of watering the landscape. Irrigation can be an in-ground automatic system, soaker or drip hoses, or hand-held hoses with nozzles.

Jute twine: A natural-fiber twine used for gently staking plants or tying them to plant supports.

Larva: The immature stage of an insect. Caterpillars are butterfly or moth larvae.

Larvae: Plural of larva.

Leaf rake: A long-handled rake with flexible tines on the head, used for easily and efficiently raking leaves into piles.

Liquid fertilizer: Plant fertilizer in a liquid form. Some types need to be mixed with water, and some types are ready to use from the bottle.

Long-day plant: A plant that flowers when the days are longer than its critical photoperiod. Long-day plants typically flower in early summer, when the days are still getting longer.

Loppers: One of the largest manual gardening tools, used for pruning branches of 1 to 3 inches in diameter with a scissoring motion.

Morning sun: Describes areas of the garden that have an eastern exposure and receive direct sun in the morning hours.

Mulch: Any type of material that is spread over the soil surface around the base of plants to suppress weeds and retain soil moisture.

Nematode: A microscopic wormlike organism that lives in the soil. Some nematodes are beneficial, while others are harmful.

New wood (new growth): The new growth on plants that is characterized by a greener, more tender form than older, woodier growth from the previous growing season.

Nozzle: A device that attaches to the end of a hose and disperses water through a number of small holes. The resulting spray covers a wider area.

Old wood: Growth that is more than one year old. Some fruit plants produce on old wood. If you prune these plants in spring before they flower and fruit, you will cut off the wood that will produce fruit.

Organic: Describes products derived from naturally occurring materials instead of materials synthesized in a lab.

Part shade: Describes areas of the garden that receive three to six hours of sun a day. Plants requiring part shade will often require protection from the more intense afternoon sun, either from tree leaves or from a building.

Part sun: Describes areas of the garden that receive three to six hours of sun a day. Although the term is often used interchangeably with "part shade," a "part sun" designation places greater emphasis on the minimal sun requirements.

Perennial: A plant that lives for more than two years. Examples include trees, shrubs, and some flowering plants.

Pesticide: A substance used for destroying or controlling insects that are harmful to plants. Pesticides are available in organic and synthetic forms.

pH: A figure designating the acidity or the alkalinity of garden soil. Soil pH is measured on a scale of 1 to 14, with 7.0 being neutral.

Pinch: To remove unwanted plant growth with your fingers, promoting bushier growth and increased blooming.

Pitchfork: A hand tool with a long handle and sharp metal prongs, typically used for moving loose material such as mulch or hay.

Plant label: The label or sticker on a plant container that provides a description of the plant and information on its care and growth habits.

Pollination: The transfer of pollen for fertilization from one plant to another, usually by wind, bees, butterflies, moths, or hummingbirds. This process is required for fruit production.

Potting soil: A mixture used to grow flowers, herbs, and vegetables in containers, providing proper drainage and extra nutrients for healthy growth.

Powdery mildew: A fungal disease characterized by white powdery spots on plant leaves and stems, typically caused by water stress and poor air circulation.

Power edger: An electric or gasoline-powered edger that removes grass along flower beds and walkways for a neat appearance.

Pre-emergent herbicide: A weedkiller that works by preventing weed seeds from sprouting.

Primocane: A first-year cane on a blackberry shrub.

Pruning: A garden task in which a variety of hand tools are used to remove dead or overgrown branches to increase plant fullness and health.

Pruning saw: A hand tool for pruning smaller branches and limbs, featuring a long, serrated blade with an elongated handle.

Rhizome: An underground horizontal stem that grows side shoots.

Rootball: The network of roots and soil clinging to a plant when it is lifted out of the ground or a pot.

Rootstock: The bottom part of a grafted fruit tree. Rootstocks are often used to create dwarf fruit trees, impart pest or disease resistance, or make a plant more cold hardy.

Runner: A stem sprouting from the center of a strawberry plant. Runners produce fruit in their second year.

Scaffold branch: A horizontal branch that emerges almost perpendicular to the trunk.

Scientific name: A two-word identification system consisting of the genus and species of a plant, such as *Ilex opaca*.

Scion: The top, fruit-bearing part of a grafted fruit tree.

Scissors: A two-bladed hand tool great for cutting cloth, paper, twine, and other lightweight materials.

Seed packet: The package in which vegetable and flower seeds are sold. It typically includes growing instructions, a planting chart, and harvesting information.

Seed-starting mix: Typically a soilless blend of perlite, vermiculite, peat moss, and other ingredients specifically for growing plants from seed.

Self-fertile: Describes a plant that does not require cross-pollination from another plant in order to produce fruit.

Semidwarf: A fruit tree grafted onto a rootstock that restricts growth of the tree to one-half to two-thirds of its natural size.

Shade: Garden shade is the absence of any direct sunlight in a given area, usually due to tree foliage or building shadows.

Short-day plant: A plant that flowers when the length of day is shorter than its critical photoperiod. Short-day plants typically bloom during fall, winter, or early spring.

Shovel: A handled tool with a broad, flat blade, and slightly upturned sides, used for moving soil and other garden materials.

Shredded hardwood mulch: A mulch consisting of shredded wood that interlocks, resisting washout and suppressing weeds.

Shrub: A woody plant that is distinguished from a tree by its multiple trunks and branches and its shorter height of less than 15 feet tall. Also called a bush.

Shrub rake: A long-handled rake with a narrow head that fits easily into tight spaces between plants.

Side-dress: Adding granular fertilizer or Plant-Tone along the top of the soil to the side of the plant.

Slow-release fertilizer: A form of fertilizer that releases nutrients at a slower rate throughout the season, requiring less frequent applications.

Snips: A hand tool used for snipping small plants and flowers, perfect for harvesting fruits, vegetables, and flowers.

Soaker hose: An efficient watering system in which a porous hose, usually made from recycled rubber, allows water to seep out around plant roots.

Soil knife: A garden knife with a sharp, serrated edge, used for cutting twine, plant roots, turf, and other garden materials.

Soil test: An analysis of a soil sample that determines the level of nutrients (to identify deficiencies) and detects any existing contaminants.

Spade: A short-handled tool with a sharp, rectangular metal blade, used for cutting and digging soil or turf.

Spur: A small, compressed, fruit-bearing branch on a fruit tree.

Standard: Describes a fruit tree grown on its own rootstock or a nondwarfing rootstock. The largest of the three sizes of fruit trees.

Sucker: The odd growth from the base of a tree or a woody plant, often caused by stress. Also refers to sprouts from below the graft of a rose or fruit tree. Suckers divert energy away from the desirable tree growth and should be removed.

Systemic herbicide: A weedkiller that is absorbed by the plant's roots or foliage and destroys all parts of the plant.

Taproot: An enlarged, tapered plant root that grows vertically downward.

Thinning: Removing excess seedlings to leave more room for the remaining plants to grow. Also refers to the practice of removing fruits when still small from fruit trees so that the remaining fruits can grow larger.

Top-dress: To spread fertilizer on top of the soil (usually around fruit trees or vegetables).

Transplants: Plants that are grown in one location and then moved to and replanted in another. Seeds started indoors and nursery plants are two examples.

Tree: A woody perennial plant that typically consists of a single trunk with multiple lateral branches.

Tree canopy: The upper layer of growth consisting of the tree's branches and leaves.

Tropical plant: A plant that is native to a tropical region of the world, and thus acclimated to a warm, humid climate.

Trowel: A shovel-like hand tool that is used for digging or moving small amounts of soil.

Warm-season vegetable: A vegetable that thrives during the warmer months. Examples are tomatoes, okra, and peppers.

Watering wand: A hose attachment that features a longer handle for watering plants beyond reach.

Water sprout: A vertical shoot emerging from a scaffold branch. It is usually nonfruiting and undesirable.

Wheat straw: The dry stalks of wheat that are used for mulch. They retain soil moisture and suppress weeds.

Wood chips: Small pieces of wood made by cutting or chipping and used as mulch in the garden.

INDEX

Botanical Name Index

GARDENING NOTES

PHOTO CREDITS

Bill Adams: 115 (right), 151 (right), 152 (right), 153 (right)

Liz Ball: 132 (left), 133 (left, middle)

Heather Claus: 16, 127

Tom Eltzroth: 28 (right), 30 (left, middle), 31 (left), 32 (middle), 33 (all), 34 (middle, right), 35 (middle, right), 37 (left), 38 (left), 39 (left), 40 (right), 41 (left), 48 (both), 50 (left), 51 (left), 52 (left, right), 55 (middle, right), 56 (middle, right), 67 (left, middle), 69 (left), 70 (left, right), 71 (left, middle), 72 (left, middle), 73 (left), 74 (left), 75 (middle), 76 (middle, right), 78 (left), 79 (left, middle), 84 (left), 85 (middle, right), 87 (both), 94 (left), 95 (right), 96 (middle), 97 (left), 98 (middle), 99 (left), 107 (left), 110 (middle), 111 (left), 113 (left), 114 (middle), 116 (middle, right), 118 (left), 119 (middle), 120 (middle), 123 (middle), 126, 132 (right), 134 (left, middle), 136 (right), 138 (left, middle), 139 (middle), 141 (left, middle), 143 (left), 147 (top), 151 (left), 152 (left, middle), 153 (left), 162 (left, middle), 163 (left, right), 164 (left, right), 165 (right), 167 (left, right), 168 (all), 169 (right), 170 (left), 171 (left, right), 173 (right), 174 (all), 175 (right), 182 (left), 183 (left), 184 (middle, right), 186 (middle, right), 187 (left), 188 (left), 189 (right)

Katie Elzer-Peters: 18 (bottom), 19 (both), 20 (bottom), 21 (all), 23, 27, 28 (left), 29 (middle), 32 (left, right), 37 (right), 45, 46 (both), 50 (right), 61, 62 (all), 63, 64, 65, 80 (middle), 81 (right), 82 (right), 86 (right), 93, 94 (right), 121 (middle), 130 (all), 147 (bottom—all), 148, 149 (both), 150 (both), 158 (all), 159 (both), 165 (left), 169 (left), 175 (left)

JC Raulston Arboretum at NC State University: 66 (right), 74 (right), 78 (right), 84 (right), 110 (right), 133 (right), 135 (middle, right), 143 (middle)

Bill Kersey: 8, 9, 15, 18 (top), 104, 105 (all), 106 (top), 128

Dave MacKenzie: 81 (left)

Troy Marden: 112 (middle), 186 (left)

Jerry Pavia: 29 (right), 41 (right), 49 (left), 54 (left, middle), 57 (right), 66 (left, middle), 67 (right), 68 (left), 72 (right), 73 (right), 74 (middle), 77 (right), 80 (left), 82 (middle), 85 (left), 97 (middle, right), 99 (right), 108 (middle, right), 109 (left), 110 (left), 111 (middle), 113 (middle), 114 (right), 115 (middle), 118 (middle), 119 (left, right), 120 (right), 122 (right), 123 (left, right), 134 (right), 137 (middle), 140 (left), 182 (right), 185 (right), 187 (middle)

Proven Winners®: 107 (right), 108 (left), 121 (left)

Derek Ramsey: 115 (left)

Shutterstock: 10, 17, 20 (top), 22, 26, 28 (bottom), 29 (left), 20 (right), 31 (middle, right), 34 (left), 35 (left), 36 (all), 37 (middle), 38 (middle, right), 39 (middle, right), 40 (left), 44, 47, 49 (middle, right), 50 (middle), 51 (middle, right), 52 (middle), 53 (all), 54 (right), 55 (left), 56 (left), 57 (left, middle), 60, 68 (middle, right), 69 (middle, right), 70 (middle), 71 (right), 73 (middle), 75 (left, right), 76 (left), 77 (left, middle), 78 (middle), 81 (middle), 82 (left), 83 (all), 86 (left), 90, 95 (right), 96 (left, right), 98 (left, right), 102, 106 (bottom), 109 (middle, right), 111 (right), 112 (left, right), 113 (right), 114 (left), 116 (left), 117 (all), 118 (right), 120 (left), 121 (right), 122 (middle), 131, 132 (middle), 135 (left), 136 (left, middle), 137 (left, right), 138 (right), 139 (left, right), 140 (middle, right), 141 (right), 142 (all), 143 (right), 146, 151 (middle), 156, 161, 162 (right), 163 (middle), 164 (middle), 165 (middle), 166 (all), 167 (middle), 169 (middle), 170 (middle, right), 171 (middle), 172 (all), 173 (left, middle), 175 (middle), 178, 180, 183 (right), 184 (left), 185 (left, middle), 187 (right), 188 (middle, right), 189 (left, middle)

Ralph Snodsmith: 122 (left)

Jessie Walker: 181

Doreen Wynja for Monrovia: 79 (right), 80 (right)

RESOURCES

The Mid-Atlantic is an area rich with horticultural resources. From great garden centers to stunning botanical gardens, vibrant land-grant colleges with Cooperative Extension programs, and huge home-improvement centers, you have everything you need to grow a beautiful garden right at your fingertips.

COOPERATIVE EXTENSION SERVICE

Cooperative Extension is going to be helpful to you particularly in diagnosing any pest problems. If you're having severe problems, start by contacting your local Extension agency.

Pennsylvania: www.extension.psu.edu/plants/gardening

New York: www.gardening.cce.cornell.edu

Delaware: www.extension.udel.edu/lawngarden

Virginia: www.ext.vt.edu/topics/lawn-garden/index.html

West Virginia: www.anr.ext.wvu.edu/lawn_garden

Maryland: www.extension.umd.edu/hgic

New Jersey: www.njaes.rutgers.edu/garden

BOTANICAL GARDENS

Public gardens can be a great source of inspiration and information. The Mid-Atlantic region is a hot spot for gorgeous gardens. Here are some to visit:

Pennsylvania: Longwood Gardens, Phipp's Conservatory, Chanticleer Foundations, Hershey Gardens, Morris Arboretum, Bartram's Garden

New York: New York Botanical Garden, Brooklyn Botanical Garden, Cornell Plantations, Wave Hill, The High Line, The King's Garden at Fort Ticonderoga, Planting Fields Arboretum

Delaware: Winterthur, The Brandywine Museum, Hagley Museum

Virginia: Lewis Ginter Botanical Garden, Greenspring Gardens Park, Norfolk Botanical Garden, Mount Vernon Estate and Gardens, River Farm Gardens, Monticello

West Virginia: Core Arboretum

Maryland: Brookside Gardens, Ladew Topiary Garden

New Jersey: Reeves-Reed Arboretum, Duke Gardens

Washington, D.C.: United States Botanical Garden, Smithsonian Gardens, Dumbarton Oaks, Hillwood, US National Arboretum, National Cathedral Gardens

MAIL-ORDER NURSERIES

It's always good to check out your local garden centers, nurseries, and home-improvement stores to find what you need. You can chat with the knowledgeable staff and get started on your project right away. Sometimes, however, you need plants that you can't find locally. Here are a few mail-order nurseries with which I've had great success.

Stark Bro's: www.starkbros.com
This company has been in business for centuries and grows all of its own fruit trees and plants onsite at nurseries in several locations around the US. Some are shipped in containers and others bare root.

Garden Crossings: www.gardencrossings.com
Garden Crossings is located in Michigan, but ships some of the nicest plants I've ever received, mailorder. It doesn't overdo it with the growth regulators. Plants are all shipped container grown and landscape-ready.

Plant Delights: www.plantdelights.com
Shop here when you're looking for unusual and new varieties.

MEET KATIE ELZER-PETERS

Katie Elzer-Peters has been gardening since she could walk. It's a hobby-turned-career, nurtured by her parents and grandparents. After receiving a bachelor's of science in public horticulture from Purdue University, Katie completed the Longwood Graduate Program at Longwood Gardens and the University of Delaware, receiving a master's of science in public garden management.

Katie has served as a horticulturist, head of gardens, educational programs director, development officer, and manager of botanical gardens around the United States, including the Washington Park Arboretum in Seattle, Washington; the Indianapolis Zoo in Indianapolis, Indiana; the Marie Selby Botanical Garden in Sarasota, Florida; the Smithsonian Institution in Washington, DC; Longwood Gardens in Kennett Square, Pennsylvania; Winterthur Museum, Garden, and Library in Greenville, Delaware; the King's Garden at Fort Ticonderoga in Ticonderoga, New York; and Airlie Gardens in Wilmington, North Carolina.

Whether at a botanical garden, or for a garden center, garden club, or school group, Katie has shared her love of gardening by teaching classes and workshops, and writing brochures, articles, gardening website information, and columns. While serving as curator of landscape at Fort Ticonderoga, Katie planned and led garden bus tours along the east coast of the United States and Canada.

Today, Katie lives and gardens with her husband, Joe, and dogs Jack and Lucy, in the coastal city of Wilmington, North Carolina (zone 8a). She loves the year-round weather for gardening, but is in constant battle with the sandy soil. Katie owns GreatGardenSpeakers.com, an online speaker directory of garden, design, ecology, and horticultural speakers. She also owns the Garden of Words, LLC, a marketing and PR firm specializing in garden-industry clients.

Katie is the author of *Beginner's Illustrated Guide to Gardening: Techniques to Help You Get Started*; *Miniature Gardens: Design and create miniature fairy gardens, dish gardens, terrariums and more—indoors and out*; *Mid-Atlantic Fruit & Vegetable Gardening: Plant, Grow, and Harvest the Best Edibles*, and four other books about vegetable gardening, all published by Cool Springs Press.

The smooth leaves of the hosta (top) contrast with finely cut, dissected leaves of the fern (bottom).

The Tennis Court garden at Chanticleer Gardens in Wayne, Pennsylvania.

If you look closely at this picture, you'll notice something else: repetition. Colors, forms, and textures are repeated throughout the garden. The color chartreuse is a motif in this garden. It winds through the beds like a river. To repeat something like color, you don't have to use the same plants everywhere. You can see that they've used at least three different plants with chartreuse leaves to keep the color going throughout the garden. Silver is another color that's repeated, though in different plants with differing heights, textures, or growth forms.

CHOOSE PLANTS THAT "TALK" TO EACH OTHER

Plants that talk to one another means plants that have a similar color or colors running through each of the plants. Here's an example of that in a container garden (right).

You could also achieve this effect with texture by using a large plant and a small plant or plants, each with grassy-type leaves. Remember, repetition doesn't have to mean using the same plant over and over. You can repeat plant characteristics—the colors, forms, and textures—as well.

These are the very basics of gardening in the Mid-Atlantic. Anything plant specific will be described in the individual plant profiles. Now, let's get gardening!

Burgundy or chartreuse colors appear in each of the plants in this large container planting. The repetition between plants unifies the look.

21

ANNUALS
for the Mid-Atlantic